Using Evidence to Inform Practice for
Community and Organizational Change

Using Evidence to Inform Practice for Community and Organizational Change

Editors

Maria Roberts-DeGennaro
San Diego State University

Sondra J. Fogel
University of South Florida

BOOKS, INC.

Chicago, Illinois

© 2011 by Lyceum Books, Inc.

Published by
LYCEUM BOOKS, INC.
5758 S. Blackstone Avenue
Chicago, Illinois 60637
773–643–1903 fax
773–643–1902 phone
lyceum@lyceumbooks.com
www.lyceumbooks.com

6   5   4   3   2   1   10   11   12   13   14

ISBN 978–1-933478–25–8

Printed in the United States of America.

Library of Congress Cataloging-in-Publication Data

Using evidence to inform practice for community and organizational change / editors, Maria Roberts-DeGennaro, Sondra J. Fogel.
    p.   cm.
  Includes bibliographical references and index.
  ISBN 978-1-933478-25-8 (pbk.)
  1. Community development.   2. Organizational change.   3. Social work education.
I. Roberts-DeGennaro, Maria.   II. Fogel, Sondra J.
HN49.C6.U85   2010
361.3—dc22

                                                                    2010001557

To Paul and Matthew,
who have supported my professional career,
and to my students over the past thirty years
of teaching. Thank you.—Maria

To Dwayne,
Thank you for all your love and support.—Always, Sondra

Contents

About the Editors

Maria Roberts-DeGennaro, Ph.D., is an emeritus professor in the School of Social Work at San Diego State University (SDSU), where she taught macro-practice-related courses for almost thirty years. Her other practice experiences include working as a case manager, program director, community development specialist, and director of an interdisciplinary center. She completed the doctoral program in the School of Social Work at the University of Texas at Austin in 1980 with an emphasis on planning, administration, organization, and research. From 1989 to 1992, Dr. Roberts-DeGennaro was the first nationally elected chair and president of the board of directors of the Association for Community Organization and Social Administration. She was a recipient of a 1999 Lois and Samuel Silberman Fund Award from the New York Community Trust for her research study on welfare reform. In 2003, she received the SDSU Alumni Association's Monty Award for Outstanding Faculty Contributions in the College of Health and Human Services. Her most recent publication was the compilation and editing of the double special issue "Paradigm of Evidence-Based (Informed) Macro Practice" for the *Journal of Evidence-Based Social Work.*

Sondra J. Fogel, Ph.D., is an associate professor in the School of Social Work at the University of South Florida (USF). She completed the doctoral program in the School of Social Work at the University of Illinois at Urbana-Champaign in 1994 with an emphasis on policy issues related to homeless families and poverty. Her research interests include identifying and evaluating interventions to eradicate issues related to poverty and homelessness that occur over the life span, community-building strategies in low-income areas, housing policy, and mitigation evidence and its influence in capital punishment decisions. She is the associate editor of *Families in Society*: *The Journal of Contemporary Social Services*. Recent publications have appeared in *Journal of Sociology and Social Welfare*, *Journal of Poverty*, and *Journal of Community Practice*. She was elected in 2009 as chair of the Association of Community Organization and Social Administration beginning in fall 2010.

Acknowledgments

The editors would like to thank Dr. Christopher J. Sullivan and Dr. Shayne Jones, who are experts in research methodology and statistical procedures. They provided additional peer reviews to the research-based chapters. Their feedback to many of the authors strengthened the quality of those chapters.

Dr. Sullivan is an assistant professor at the University of Cincinnati in the Department of Criminology. He completed his doctorate at Rutgers University in 2005. Recent publications have appeared in *Criminology, Youth Violence and Juvenile Justice,* and *Journal of Research in Crime and Delinquency.*

Dr. Jones is an assistant professor in the University of South Florida's Department of Criminology. He completed his doctorate at the University of Kentucky in 2003. He also served as a postdoctoral research associate for two years in the Psychiatry and Law Program at the Western Psychiatric Institute and Clinic, University of Pittsburg Medical Center, Pennsylvania. Recent publications have appeared in *Journal of Criminal Law and Criminology, Behavioral Sciences and the Law,* and *Journal of Personality Assessment.* Finally, we would like to thank our reviewer who offered many suggestions that are incorporated throughout this edited work.

Foreword

Lorraine Gutierrez

Since the turn of the twenty-first century, the press for the development and implementation of empirically supported interventions and use of evidence-based practice in health care and human services have grown in momentum. This movement has been fueled by our desire to use the tools of science, rather than tradition or opinion, to identify policies and practices that are effective. The movement has most strongly affected the health and mental health fields, in part because of rising health-care costs. However, the evidence-based practice movement is now influencing social work practice, policy, research, and education in a wide variety of settings.

Research and education on empirically supported and evidence-based interventions have traditionally focused on the provision of direct services. Less attention has been paid to social work on the organizational and community levels. This clinical focus is shortsighted, as the context of the organization or community setting can significantly influence the implementation of evidence-based methods. This volume, *Using Evidence to Inform Practice for Community and Organizational Change*, has the potential to move our field forward in significant ways by identifying how these larger contexts can be used to support the adoption of new treatment and practice methods.

Although the language of evidence-based or empirically supported interventions is relatively recent, the desire to use social science research and methods to influence policy and practice is not. Since the inception of social work, practitioners and researchers have used data to inform policy and practice (Kirk & Reid, 2002; Thyer, 2008). For example, more than thirty years ago, Rothman (1974) applied the research and development (R&D) model used in engineering, toward the identification of intervention strategies and programs in social planning, community work, and social action based on social science research. During the same era, social work leaders proposed the need for practitioner-scholars who could evaluate the impact of their practice through single-subject and other simple research designs (Kirk & Reid, 2002). Our more recent evidence-based movement builds on this tradition while paying closer attention to the client's values and preferences, the human service organization's mission or mandate, and the environmental strengths or barriers that exist beyond the individual (Regehr, Stern, Shlonsky, 2007). This closer attention to evidence, context, and values has the potential to develop more ethical methods for social work policy and practice with different of populations and contexts (Gambrill, 2007).

Using the evidence-informed framework to inform organizational or community practice requires some changes in perspective from the more clinical approach. For example, a randomized trial is more difficult to achieve when studying organizations and communities. However, what may be lost in internal validity may be gained in external validity when research is conducted in natural settings and with the input and collaboration of managers, organizers, practitioners, and clients. This more collaborative and process-oriented approach to evidence is consonant with emerging approaches to evidence-based practice (Regehr, Stern, Shlonsky, 2007).

The chapters in this book represent the most current and best thinking in the development of evidence-based macro-practice methods in the human services. Each chapter in section 1 illustrates how the use of evidence-based practice can be adapted to investigate macro-practice methods. These chapters provide examples of how this approach can be translated for use in macro settings. Section 2 presents a different perspective by demonstrating how community and organizational practice methods can enhance the translation of evidence-based methods to real-world settings. The science of translational methods is a significant contribution that macro practice can make to current and emerging practice methods.

Although the theme of this book is the use of evidence-based practice in macro settings, it also raises the question of what a focus on macro methods brings to the evidence-based movement. It is clear that a macro focus can build our knowledge of translational processes for adopting evidence-based practices. This field of research can and should be expanded. In addition, the research in this book is highly interdisciplinary and makes use of mixed and multiple methods. The research demonstrates the value of different forms of evidence and how they should reflect the problem, population, and context that is being studied. This book opens up the focus of evidence-based practice methods and how they can inform future policy and research.

References

Gambrill, E. (2007). Views of evidence-based practice: Social workers' Code of Ethics and accreditation standards as guides for choice. *Journal of Social Work Education, 43*(3), 447–455.

Kirk. S., & Reid, W. (2002). *Science and social work: A critical appraisal.* New York: Columbia University Press.

Regehr, C., Stern, S., & Shlonsky. A. (2007). Operationalizing evidence-based practice: The development of an institute for evidence-based social work. *Research on Social Work Practice, 17*(3), 408–419.

Rothman, J. (1974). *Planning and organizing for social change: Action principles from social science research.* New York: Columbia University Press.

Thyer, B. (2008). The quest for evidence-based practice? We are all positivists! *Research on Social Work Practice, 18*(4), 339.

Introduction

Sondra J. Fogel and Maria Roberts-DeGennaro

Human service professionals are filled with questions—questions they ask to assist clients in clarifying their concerns, questions they form to specify problem areas, and questions they raise to determine whether interventions are creating the desired change in the target systems. Answers to these inquiries are typically based on the collection of data, some type of evidence, which propels the practitioner to take action, whether that is to continue with the planned change process as initially determined, adjust the contract, or redesign the intervention of choice. This professional process is an essential component of good practice for any setting and with any client system.

Questions regarding the effectiveness and efficiency of social work practice interventions in diverse situations have been stimulated by discussions on the use of evidenced-based medicine as a model for decision making in social work practice (Johnson & Austin, 2006). Evidence-based medicine is defined as "the conscientious, explicit and judicious use of current best evidence in making decisions about the care of individual patients, based on skills which allow the doctor to evaluate both personal experiences and external evidence in a systematic and objective manner" (Sackett, Richardson, Rosenberg, & Hayes, 1997, p. 71).

The practice of medicine, like social work, takes place in the context of interrelated larger systems, including the academic context, where research findings, teaching orientations, academic policies, and local and national trends at a minimum influence the preparation of future professionals. However, evidence-based medicine deliberations are primarily directed at the delivery of medical care services and health-care practices.

In its conversion to social work, the fundamentals of evidence-based medicine are commonly referred to as evidence-based practice in the literature. O'Hare (2005) provides this definition of evidence-based practice for social work "as the planned use of empirically supported assessment and intervention methods combined with the judicious use of monitoring and evaluation strategies for the purpose of improving the psychosocial well-being of clients" (p. 6). Yet the transference of the concept of evidence-based medicine to social work practice has ignited forceful debates surrounding the use of evidenced-based practice, generating questions such as, What is evidence? What are the roles of the professional and client in the selection and delivery of evidenced-based service? How is evidence disseminated to practitioners? and How has the use of evidence enhanced the growth capacity of those who are served by social work practices? (Bhattacharyya, Reeves, & Zwarenstein, 2009; Smith, 2004). This is reminiscent of past debates in the profession by social work scholars who have asked questions regarding the effectiveness and efficiency of casework social work practices (Briar, 1973; Fischer, 1978, 1981), as well as administrative and organization social work practices (Hasenfeld, 1984; Rothman, 1974). Although Fischer (1981) suggested that a "quiet revolution in the way social workers view knowledge and practice and in the ways they use knowledge to conduct practice" (p. 199) was under way, it is clear that the loud call for evidence-based practice is not going away.

Administration and Community Practice

Professional social work practice activities include the collaborative identification and assessment of the problem(s) to be addressed with the client, followed by planning and intervention activities in multiple systems on behalf of the client and other constituents. In these practice arenas, the uses of evidence to inform the daily activities of the social work agency administrator or community worker are no less important. However, until very recently, there has been less attention paid to the use and dissemination of evidence-based intervention protocols applied to these settings. A reason for this may be that the terminology used to suggest evidence-based practice is most often associated with clinical activities, and this may be misleading to those social workers with a macro orientation who emphasize the "sociopolitical, historical, economic and environmental forces that influence the human condition" (Barker, 1999, p. 285).

According to Barker (1999), macro practice is "aimed at bringing about improvements in the general society" (p. 285). Both community-based and administration practice activities are connected to the goal of macro practice. This suggests that the activities of a community-based or administrative social worker most likely involve various activities, such as working directly with multiple partners in various settings;

engaging in consistent but flexible planning activities; creating and implementing strategic and other management decisions; and planning action at target systems that are geared to create change in knowledge, action, and/or participation in services. Implied in this is that administrative and community-based social work practitioners must be experienced with and use direct practice skills to promote the goal of macro practice. Therefore, a social worker can have a macro orientation in his or her individual field of practice and work in a community or administrative capacity with the overarching purpose of improving society, which is the goal of macro practice. Clarification of these terms is important because it helps to identify the limits of the definition of evidence-based practice for administrative and community workers.

Many of the chapters in this book reference the evidence-based medicine definition that Sackett et al. (1997) provided as a starting point for how social work has embraced this concept. Yet what clearly emerges throughout the chapters is that the evidence-based process must include professional judgment regarding the client and situation; client and system input, values, and preferences; and professionals' use of the best available research evidence throughout the process.

To address this, we use the term *evidenced-informed practice* to suggest that the administrative or community practitioner uses the best available research and practice knowledge to guide the decision-making processes in planning, developing, and implementing planned change efforts while considering the values and expectation of the clients or consumers (Roberts-DeGennaro, 2008).

The practitioner who uses this approach, like others, uses multiple sources of knowledge obtained from core educational classes, such as research; human behavior and the social environment; practice theory with individuals, families, and communities; management; and policy analysis—as well as the reflection of his or her art and gained wisdom of social work practice in daily decisions. In fact, the use of evidence to inform practice for community and organizational change has substantially increased as practitioners in these fields demonstrate their growing sophistication with developing and asking questions regarding system needs, use and implementation of diverse research methods, and their ability to translate findings into action steps that consider the uniqueness of the setting and the consumer in that context.

Yet questions of how evidence is used in community and administrative practice settings remain (Adams, Matto, & LaCroy, 2009; Briggs, & McBeath, 2009; Ohmer & Korr, 2006; Simpson, 2009). As more evidence is used to inform practice decisions in these settings, further questions arise about how to create planned change when the implementation of the intervention most likely will involve consideration of all the forces that drive the system to remain intact. Rogers (1995) identifies this interactive and transactional process as a major issue in the use of innovations gleaned from emerging practice evidence. And this key element makes the implementation and diffusion of protocols, as suggested by evidence-based practice, difficult in many broad contexts. Therefore, the political and iterative aspects of community and organization systems must be acknowledged and anticipated by administrators and workers in evidence-informed planned change models. In fact, numerous scholars have suggested that organizational leadership and the work context have a significant impact on practitioners' adoption and use of evidence (Aarons, 2006; Aarons & Sawitzky, 2006; Glisson et al., 2008).

The Purpose of This Book

The overall purpose of this book is to contribute to the knowledge base related to designing, planning, implementing, evaluating, and managing evidence-informed practices in a community or organizational setting.

This edited text demonstrates how social work professionals implement and use evidence-informed practice to address presenting issues that are nested in agencies and communities. This decision-making model is critically important, as questions regarding how social work is practiced are mounting as a result of political pressures for effective, efficient, and measurable outcomes of our work in our diverse settings. Furthermore, the curricula of social work education programs are also changing as a result of the 2008 Educational Policy and Accreditation Standards that insist on the inclusion of evidence-based practice in the preparation of students and an emphasis on students learning practice competencies rather than on traditional courses of knowledge. Given these new emphases, this text is an excellent resource for community, administration, research, and policy courses that teach students how to use evidenced-informed competencies for planned change.

The chapters in this book have been divided into two sections. The first section examines how principles of evidence-informed practice are used to understand and address issues related to planned change efforts in organizations and communities. These chapters elucidate how evidence-informed principles are integrated into professional decision-making processes to improve program and client outcomes. The second section demonstrates how to use and apply various research strategies to engage clients and practitioners in planned change efforts. The chapters in this latter section illustrate how to take the knowledge gained through the application of evidence-informed principles and translate these into effective community and organization practice interventions.

We selected these chapters because of their relevance to actual work in diverse settings, as demonstrated in the conceptualization and resolution of the problem, the quality of the research methods used, and the application of the evidence to address the practice situation. In addition, each chapter describes a unique practice problem and how evidence-informed practice skills and knowledge were used to address the situation.

In the beginning of each section, an overview of the chapters is provided to introduce the reader to the issue presented. Each chapter begins with a statement of the problem, the question to be answered. What follows from this is the critical thinking and research processes that the authors used to collect evidence to inform the decision to make change in their organization or community setting. Implications and guidelines for practice are also offered. However, this text is just a beginning, as more educators, students, scholars, and practitioners must continue to develop a common language, tools, and outcomes to demonstrate how community and organizational settings use evidence to initiate change in these settings.

Discussion Questions

Using the principles of inquiry-based scholarship, the following discussion questions can be used to facilitate dialogue around the use of the evidence that is presented in the chapters to identify practice competencies and inform practice in community and organizational settings:

- Do the assertions, conclusions, and/or practice guidelines reasonably and realistically match the evidence presented in the chapters, or are these extreme and unrealistic?
- Do the authors acknowledge their own preferences, biases, expectations, and potential conflicts of interest in the chapters?
- Can you identify the practice competencies that are demonstrated throughout the intervention plan?
- Do the authors acknowledge the contribution of others' work through proper and complete citations and references, and are these limited to those that support the authors' own findings and views?
- How could you replicate the research methodology in the chapters to address a question related to a similar problem in a different practice setting?

- How should the characteristics (e.g., culture, age, gender) of the target client population be integrated into the design of a research study?
- What other methods could have been used in the chapters to address the research problem for the target client population?
- When is a mixture of qualitative and quantitative research methods useful in designing a study?
- What other interventions, besides those addressed in these chapters, could be used to prevent or improve a practice situation for a target client population?
- What knowledge from these chapters could be used to strengthen the skills of a practice-informed researcher or a research-informed practitioner?
- What sources of information, other than research findings, should be used in making decisions toward planned change efforts with a target client population?

References

Aarons, G. A. (2006). Transformational and transactional leadership: Association with attitudes toward evidence-based principles. *Psychiatric Services, 57*(8), 1162–1169.

Aarons, G. A., & Sawitzky, A. C. (2006). Organizational culture and climate and mental health provider attitudes toward evidence-based practice. *Psychological Services, 3*(1), 61–72.

Adams, K. B., Matto, H. C., & LeCroy, C. W. (2009). Limitation of evidence-based practice for social work education: Unpacking the complexity. *Journal of Social Work Education, 45*(2), 165–186.

Barker, R. L. (1999). *The social work dictionary* (4th ed.). Washington, DC: NASW Press.

Bhattacharyya, O., Reeves, S., & Zwarenstein, M. (2009). What is implementation research? Rationale, concepts, and practices. *Research on Social Work Practice, 19*(5), 491–502.

Briar, S. (1973). The age of accountability. *Social Work, 18*(1), 2, 11.

Briggs, H. E., & McBeath, B. (2009). Evidence-based management: Origins, challenges, and implications for social service administration. *Administration in Social Work, 33*, 242–261.

Fischer, J. (1978). Does anything work? *Journal of Social Service Research, 1*(3), 215–243.

Fischer, J. (1981). The social work revolution. *Social Work, 26*(3), 199–207.

Glisson, C., Landsverk, J., Schoenwald, S., Kelleher, K., Hoagwood, K. E., Mayberg, S., et al. (2008). Assessing the organizational social context (OSC) of mental health services: Implications for research and practice. *Administration and Policy in Mental Health, 35*(1–2), 98–113.

Hasenfeld, Y. (1984). The changing context of human services administration. *Social Work, 29*(6), 522–529.

Johnson, M., & Austin, M. J. (2006). Evidence-based practice in the social services. *Administration in Social Work, 30*(3), 75–104.

O'Hare, T. (2005). *Evidence-based practices for social workers: An interdisciplinary approach.* Chicago: Lyceum Books.

Ohmer, M., & Korr, W. (2006). The effectiveness of community practice interventions: A review of the literature. *Research on Social Work Practice, 16*(2), 132–145.

Roberts-DeGennaro, M. (2008). Evidence-based (informed) macro practice paradigm: Integration of practice expertise and research. *Journal of Evidence-Based Social Work, 5*(3–4), 407–421.

Rogers, E. (1995). *The diffusion of innovations* (4th ed.). New York: Free Press.

Rothman, J. (1974). *Planning and organizing for social change: Action principles from social science research.* New York: Columbia University Press.

Sackett, D. L., Richardson, S., Rosenberg, W., & Hayes, R. B., (1997). *Evidence-based medicine: How to practice and teach EMB.* Edinburgh: Churchill Livingstone.

Simpson, D. D. (2009). Organizational readiness for stage-based dynamics of innovation implementation. *Research on Social Work Practice, 19*(5), 541–551.

Smith, D. (2004). Introduction: Some versions of evidence-based practice. In D. Smith (Ed.), *Social work and evidence-based practice* (pp. 7–28). London: Kingsley.

Application of Principles for Evidence-Based Practice in Organizations and Communities

The collection of chapters in this section provides the reader with methods of scientific inquiry that can easily be transported into a practice setting. The chapters communicate to the practitioner the importance of using diverse critical thinking skills to define and understand a problem, of considering ethics in the decision making processes, and of engaging in collaborative efforts with multiple partners on behalf of vulnerable communities.

Chapter 1, by Maria Roberts-DeGennaro, provides a rationale for using research to inform planned change efforts in organizations and communities. This work provides an overview of evidence-informed practice and articulates common challenges and barriers to its use. She defines and discusses the importance of using evidence-informed macro practice that integrates the best available research and practice knowledge to guide the decision-making processes in planning for change while considering the preferences, concerns, and expectations of the client population. This chapter demonstrates that it is critical for the successful implementation of any planned change effort to include participation by key stakeholders, including the client, consumer, or constituent.

Chapter 2, by John Poertner, examines some of the evidence regarding management practices and their impact on consumer outcomes, a relatively unexplored area in the literature. In this chapter, the author presents a classification system that can be used to assess research

1

studies that examine empirically supported management and supervision skills to improve staff effectiveness and client outcomes. This work highlights the important role that management practice contributes to the effective operation of organizations and to the achievement of desired outcomes.

In chapter 3, Cheryl A. Hyde investigates how management practitioners make decisions to resolve ethical dilemmas in service delivery regarding client issues. Using a qualitative methodology, she identifies important systemic issues in organizations and personal strategies of human service managers that influence decision-making processes. The chapter highlights the need for more scientific investigation of ethical challenges in administrative practice. Interestingly, she notes that evidence-based guidelines are lacking in this area despite the importance of ethical values. This chapter emphasizes the professional skill of being able to tolerate multifaceted situations and the need to develop evidence informed reasoning skills to administer ethical decisions.

Chapter 4, by Charles Auerbach and Susan E. Mason, demonstrates how evidence can be gathered to support professional roles and responsibilities in a host organization, such as a hospital. On the basis of emerging trends that suggest a reduction of social workers in hospital emergency departments, the authors engaged hospital-based social workers to collect discharge data in an effort to assess their effectiveness related to client outcomes at the time of discharge. Using readily available information, the evidence supported the use of social workers in emergency departments not only in terms of cost savings to the hospital but also, more important, in terms of achieving desired client outcomes. Through this chapter, the reader learns the importance of documenting client outcomes and relating these to organizational exigencies.

Chapter 5, by F. Ellen Netting, Kevin Borders, H. Wayne Nelson, and Ruth Huber, demonstrates how government databases that collect information on performance outcomes of social service programs can be used to assess best evidence for practice and advocacy efforts for vulnerable populations. The focus was on the Long-Term-Care Ombudsman Program, which is available in every state and connected to a national reporting system. By accessing publicly available data, the authors deduced the usefulness of empirically supported interventions for providing services in ombudsman programs. This chapter emphasizes how macro practice and policy issues are intricately linked and enhanced through a circular feedback process, which includes the analysis of evidence on program outcomes to generate best-practice initiatives for ombudsman programs.

Chapter 6, by Deborah K. Padgett, Victoria Stanhope, and Benjamin F. Henwood, discusses the empirically supported evidence of the Housing First model for homeless individuals with co-occurring disorders of mental health and substance abuse. Beginning with an innovative intervention to address this complex problem, the chapter highlights the importance of beginning where the client is, a fundamental principle in which services are negotiated to meet the needs of a client. Drawing on results from two large-scale studies that used qualitative and quantitative methods, the authors discuss how cumulative findings can influence local and national policies affecting homeless mentally ill adults.

Sondra J. Fogel and Kathleen A. Moore in chapter 7 describe the challenges of importing evidence-informed practices into a new program established by a diverse set of organizations. The chapter provides a case example of a collaboration involving faith-based, secular, and government organizations formed to develop an innovative service for homeless adults living on the streets in a downtown area in Pinellas County, Florida. Evidence was collected on how to implement this innovation in the community. The chapter concludes with some guidelines for identifying and using evidence to inform practice in the area of supporting diverse collaborations.

Combined, the seven chapters demonstrate the use of essential principles of evidence-informed practice by professionals engaged in macro-practice activities. From demonstrating the value of reviewing the literature and using available data sources to showcasing how to implement research activities to capture empirically supported evidence for advocating on behalf of vulnerable populations, these chapters provide examples of how to integrate the principles of evidence-informed practice into daily organizational and administrative practice competencies.

CHAPTER ONE

Planned Change Efforts in Organizations and Communities

Evidence-Informed Practice

Maria Roberts-DeGennaro

In an ideal world, practitioners would include the findings from research in building their knowledge base, would use systematic decision-making processes in the pursuit of efficient practice, and would become competent in the delivery of known effective service interventions. Increasingly, practitioners in diverse professional fields are supporting the use of research to inform practice, particularly evidence based on valid, relevant, and reliable findings. Initial interest in evidence-based practice (EBP) focused on the use of evidence to make clinical practice decisions, with scant attention directed toward the process of making decisions related to planned change efforts in community or organizational settings (Drake, Hovmand, Jonson-Reid, & Zayas, 2007; Howard, McMillen, & Pollio, 2003).

The empirical practice movement is reshaping public social policy, as well as fiscal policy, in the distribution of grants and contracts for health and human services (Roberts-DeGennaro, 2006, 2008b, 2010). Forces such as regulatory agencies, third-party payers, and licensing boards are exerting influence on organizations to measure effectiveness on the basis of evidence. Even accreditation, government, and other monitoring bodies have been handing down directives to use EBPs, sometimes without consideration of real-world practice issues or support for implementing the practice with fidelity (Bellamy, Bledsoe, Mullen, Fang, & Manuel, 2008).

In the evolving movement to use the process of EBPs for making decisions, there is a caveat when searching and selecting a "best" practice; that is, was the "best" methodology used in the research to support the finding of evidence? For example, Ohmer and Korr's (2006) review of some of the literature on community practice suggests the need for more sophisticated research methodologies to establish empirical support for a best practice. Nevertheless, the use of research evidence to guide practice and develop policies is becoming increasingly important given the limited resources and the pressures to document service outcomes (Johnson & Austin, 2006). Fortunately, there is a growing demand for transparency in the transfer and uptake of research into policy and practice (Ross, Lavis, Rodriguez, Woodside, & Denis, 2003).

Using Evidence to Guide Practice

Gambrill (2007, 2008) describes EBP as a philosophy and evolving process designed to forward the effective use of professional judgment in integrating information regarding the client's unique characteristics, preferences, and actions with external research findings. The decision-making processes related to adopting an EBP model require the evidence to be based on a scientifically sound research methodology that supports the application of the model in different community or organizational settings. Thus, EBP encompasses practice experience, a commitment to placing the concerns of the client first, and a determination to use the best evidence to guide decision-making processes (Gibbs, 2003).

One of the most important aspects of implementing any intervention is the selection of outcome measures used to evaluate whether the intervention was effective. Likewise, critical-thinking skills are needed in the use of fidelity scales to determine whether specific programmatic standards were adhered to during the implementation of an EBP or empirically supported intervention. Examples of fidelity scales can be accessed at the Web site of the New York State Office of Mental Health (see www.omh.state.ny.us/omhweb/ebp/fidelityscales.htm).

Although the expectation is that the best available evidence will be used to inform decision-making processes, the rhetoric continues to exceed the reality of implementing an EBP with fidelity. Empirical testing of implementation or dissemination strategies is lacking. Improving the appropriate use of research evidence in decision making is a challenge. In a systematic review of twenty-four studies investigating the use of research evidence by policy makers, personal contact between the policy makers and researchers, the timely relevance of the research, and the inclusion of summaries with policy recommendations were the most commonly reported factors to facilitate the use of research evidence (Innvaer, Vist, Trommald, & Oxman, 2002).

Decision-Making Processes in Planned Change Efforts

Evidence-informed macro practice is the use of the best-available research and practice knowledge to guide decision-making processes in planning, developing, and implementing planned change efforts while also considering the values and expectations of clients (Roberts-DeGennaro, 2008b). As Figure 1.1 depicts, these processes inform and interact with one another. Each should be grounded in sound knowledge about the needs of a target population and informed by the practice expertise of professionals and by practice relevant research. Therefore, a practitioner working to achieve a planned change effort in an organization or a community setting needs to have professional

FIGURE 1.1. *Evidence-informed macro practice*

expertise in the use of the best available research in the context of the unique characteristics, culture, and preferences of the clients who represent the target population.

No theoretical or conceptual approach to practice is universally applicable to all practice situations. The development of evidence-informed macro practice is an iterative process, as evidence is progressively accumulated and different interventions are examined in community or organizational settings. However, policy makers increasingly are prescribing and, in some cases, mandating that specific best practices are implemented, when those practices probably are promising but not specifically supported for the problem context or culturally appropriate for a practice situation (see Atkinson, Bui, & Mori, 2001).

After assessing a problem in a practice situation, the practitioner should not merely consult a list of empirically supported interventions and then select an intervention with the best empirical evidence of effectiveness. The expertise of the professional practitioners involved in the planned change effort and the characteristics, values, and preferences of the target population must be considered in these decision-making processes (Walker, Briggs, Koroloff, & Friesen, 2007).

In some practice situations, there is no available formal research. Consequently, decision makers rely on either the funding source or the expertise of their practitioners and other stakeholders to determine which intervention is the best for meeting the needs of a target population. Nevertheless, as Gambrill (2006) states, "EBP requires considering research findings related to important practice or policy decisions and sharing what is found (including nothing) with clients" (p. 340).

In planning for change, the bottom line for evaluating an intervention is whether the intervention improved the condition or quality of life of the target population in the organization or community setting (Netting, Kettner, & McMurtry, 2008). Measuring client outcomes is critical to the iterative process of building relevant sources of evidence on which practitioners can then base their practices in a community or an organization. For example, a report by the U.S. Department of Justice, Office of Juvenile Justice and Delinquency Prevention (n.d.) describes research that tested the effectiveness of a comprehensive gang model. Findings are reported from evaluations of several programs that demonstrated variations of the model in different community sites. On the basis of the evidence from those research activities, best practices were identified that address community gang problems.

For practitioners, a set of clearly defined specifications for implementing the intervention should accompany information related to an empirically supported intervention. Torrey et al. (2001) suggest that implementation tool kits are needed that include the following: general recommendations for promoting change in a practice setting; a brief document that lays out recommended practice processes, such as staffing, training, meeting structure, supervision, and fidelity monitoring; and administrative consultation to help organizations overcome obstacles to establishing the practice. In addition, McHugo et al.'s (2007) systematic study of the fidelity of evidence-based practice implementation concluded that one year appeared to be the average amount of time needed for successful implementation to occur.

Yegidis and Weinbach (2009) contend that becoming a practitioner who uses research findings for decision making requires support from all levels of an organization. Implementing an EBP with fidelity requires a clearly established organizational structure and administrative support system. In addition, management must store the evidence supporting the intervention in a way that allows for easy retrieval throughout the decision-making processes.

Gray (2001) describes an evidence-based organization as having "an obsession with finding, appraising, and using research-based knowledge as evidence in decision making" (p. 250). He also suggests that evidence-informed management skills are needed in providing the tools and training that staff need to offer clients the evidence-informed services. Rousseau (2006) perceives evidence-based management as a tool to help managers share power with workers (and clients) rather than as arbitrary decision making in selecting interventions for planned change efforts.

Practitioners must have access to sufficient resources to engage in the activities that use of the EBP process requires: to search for a best practice and then to implement it with fidelity (Briggs & Rzepnicki, 2004; Roberts & Yeager, 2006; Roberts-DeGennaro, 2008a; Straus, Richardson, Glasziou, & Haynes, 2005; Woody, D'Souza, & Dartman, 2006). For example, an important transportability issue is identifying who will implement the intervention and what specialized training is required to adhere to specific programmatic standards (Franklin & Hopson, 2007).

Gray, Elhai, and Schmidt (2007) suggest that although a favorable disposition toward EBPs does not necessarily connote that one actually uses such interventions in practice, it is arguably the case that unfavorable opinions about EBPs preclude their usage in practice. Likewise, Glisson, Dukes, and Green (2006) suggest that the behavioral expectation to use an empirically supported intervention might reflect the values and assumptions of the organizational leaders rather than those of the rank and file who simply comply with the expectations (without adhering to implementation fidelity).

Barriers to the Use of Evidence in Practice

Probably the single most important aspect of implementing an empirically supported intervention pivots around the thinking of planners who promote change in organizations and communities. Yeager and Saggese (2008) suggest that a common mistake is for planners to focus on the administrative system needed to implement the intervention rather than on the clients, consumers, or constituents and their desired outcomes. Developing strategies to engage the client in the decision-making processes is critical to the successful implementation of a planned change effort. Yeager and Saggese (2008) contend that if planners do not have the necessary mental maps in their thinking to match the territory they must cross to bring about the change, the plans they make will most likely not take into account all the important features of the reality they must traverse.

A second important factor to consider is that knowledge of empirically supported interventions should be accessible, particularly information on the implementation of culturally competent best practices. Research is needed that explores the cultural competence of evidence-based approaches to planned change efforts in community and organizational settings. Whaley and Davis (2007) contend that cultural adaptations might be needed to modify changes in an EBP, for example, adaptations in its approach to service delivery to accommodate the cultural beliefs, attitudes, and behaviors of the target population. The Institute for the Advancement of Social Work Research (2007) suggests that not all evidence-based services are effective across all cultural groups and that, "when adapting interventions to other groups, it is important to be cautious, to have effective cross-cultural communication skills, and to understand the nature and scope of the problem from the clients' perspectives and cultural backgrounds" (pp. 12–13). In turn, York (2009) advocates that measurement tools be scrutinized for culturally specific language and tested for validity with people of the cultures that are relevant to the specific study population.

The American Psychological Association's Presidential Task Force on Evidence-Based Practice with Children and Adolescents (2008) suggests that there are several methodological, measurement, and analytic challenges in implementing new practice models that practitioners should consider:

1. Lack of reliable or valid methods for determining the preparedness of providers, agencies, regions, or specific stakeholder groups in adopting or sustaining new EBP technologies.
2. Lack of metrics or measures for determining the efficacy and effectiveness of implementation efforts.
3. Lack of adequate measures for assessing the fidelity of implementation efforts at multiple levels (families/youth, clinicians, supervisors, administrators, policy makers) and contexts (e.g., rural vs.

urban, or Korean Americans in South Central Los Angeles vs. Ethiopian Americans in Silver Lake, MD).

4. Problems of using data collected within real-world service systems for research purposes, often compromised by missing elements due to random and/or nonrandom factors, as well as observer biases.

5. Un-ideal nature of service organization and delivery, such that rigorous control of potential confounds or even knowledge of potential sources of bias are increasingly difficult. (p. 10)

The combination of the foregoing items makes clear that the informed use of EBPs requires consideration of multiple systems in the environment and informed knowledge of the condition of the target problem and consumer condition. Evidence-based practice is not a manualized implementation of a static intervention plan.

Recommendations

Mullen (2008) suggests that the fundamental challenge to the evidence-based policy and practice initiative is to rethink how best to facilitate the rapid generation, sharing, and application of knowledge in a manner that closes the policy and practice gap. The management of knowledge, including knowledge derived from experience and research, is critical in responding to complex issues. Innovative approaches to gathering and disseminating information will be instrumental in striving for excellence in systems of care.

For example, portals need to be designed that provide online access to practice-relevant research on a given topic or social problem and that allow users to narrow the search to the unique characteristics, culture, or preferences of a target population. Cournoyer (2004) suggests that practitioners should continuously compile and organize sources of information into a portfolio as follows: information related to the special population in one folder, social problem in another folder, measurement instruments in a third folder, and materials pertinent to the nature and effectiveness of services (e.g., empirically supported interventions) for members of a target client group in a fourth folder.

Networking Web sites need to be developed on multiple topics and managed to help disseminate timely information and contribute to the translation of new knowledge into practice arenas. For example, the Substance Abuse and Mental Health Services Administration launched the Homelessness Resource Center Web site (see www.homeless.samhsa.gov), which is designed to help users communicate with other providers of homelessness services to share knowledge and their experiences. Other features include accessing literature from the library, downloading resources and practical tools, rating and commenting on content, posting helpful information, and learning about upcoming events.

Through online access to research portals and networking sites, macro practitioners have the opportunity to appraise the research-based knowledge and to critically evaluate whether to use the evidence to inform their practice. Besides applying the evidence of what works for planning a community or organizational change effort, practitioners must also remember to incorporate the ethical principles of their profession and to respect the wisdom derived from not only their practice experience but also from the experiences of other colleagues and the knowledge gained from working with clients. Most important, they must always reflect on the following question: did the intervention support the planned change effort toward achieving the client's desired outcome?

References

American Psychological Association, Presidential Task Force on Evidence-Based Practice with Children and Adolescents (2008, August). *Executive summary.* Washington, DC: Author.

Atkinson, D. R., Bui, U., & Mori, S. (2001). Multiculturally sensitive empirically supported treatments: An oxymoron? In J. G. Ponterotto, J. M. Casas, L. A. Suzuki, & C. M. Alexander (Eds.), *Handbook of multicultural counseling* (pp. 542–574). Thousand Oaks, CA: Sage.

Bellamy, J., Bledsoe, S. E., Mullen, E. J., Fang, L., & Manuel, J. I. (2008). Agency-university partnership for evidence-based practice in social work. *Journal of Social Work Education, 44*(3), 55–75.

Briggs, H. E., & Rzepnicki, T. L. (Eds.). (2004). *Using evidence in social work practice: Behavioral perspectives.* Chicago: Lyceum Books.

Cournoyer, B. R. (2004). *The evidence-based social work skills book.* Boston: Pearson/Allyn and Bacon.

Drake, B., Hovmand, P., Jonson-Reid, M., & Zayas, L. (2007). Adopting and teaching evidence-based practice in master's-level social work programs. *Journal of Social Work Education, 43*(3), 431–446.

Franklin, C., & Hopson, L. M. (2007). Facilitating the use of evidence-based practice in community organizations. *Journal of Social Work Education, 43*(3), 377–404.

Gambrill, E. (2006). Evidence-based practice and policy: Choices ahead. *Research on Social Work Practice, 16*(3), 338–357.

Gambrill, E. (2007). Transparency as the route to evidence-informed professional education. *Research on Social Work Practice, 17*(5), 553–560.

Gambrill, E. (2008). Evidence-based (informed) macro practice: Process and philosophy. *Journal of Evidence-Based Social Work, 5*(3–4), 423–452.

Gibbs, L. (2003). *Evidence-based practice for the helping professions: A practical guide with integrated multimedia*. Pacific Grove, CA: Brooks/Cole-Thomson Learning.

Glisson, C., Dukes, D., & Green, P. (2006). The effects of the ARC organizational intervention on caseworker turnover, climate, and culture in children's service systems. *Child Abuse and Neglect, 30*(8), 855–880.

Gray, J. A. M. (2001). *Evidence-based healthcare* (2nd ed.). London: Churchill Livingstone.

Gray, M., Elhai, J., & Schmidt, L. (2007). Trauma professionals' attitudes toward and utilization of evidence-based practices. *Behavior Modification, 31*(6), 732–748.

Howard, M., McMillen, C., & Pollio, D. (2003). Teaching evidence based practice: Toward a new paradigm for social work education. *Research on Social Work Practice, 13*(2), 234–259.

Innvaer, S., Vist, G., Trommald, M., & Oxman, A. (2002). Health policy-makers' perceptions of their use of evidence: A systematic review. *Journal of Health Services Research and Policy, 7*(4), 239–244.

Institute for the Advancement of Social Work Research. (2007, April). *Partnerships to integrate evidence-based mental health practices into social work education and research* (National Institute of Mental Health, Contract Order No. 263-MI-613011). Washington, DC: Author.

Johnson, M., & Austin, M. J. (2006). Evidence-based practice in the social services: Implications for organizational change. *Administration in Social Work, 30*(3), 75–104.

McHugo, G., Drake, R., Whitley, R., Bond, G., Campbell, K., Rapp, C., et al. (2007). Fidelity outcomes in the national implementing evidence-based practices project. *Psychiatric Services, 58*(10), 1279–1284.

Mullen, E. J. (2008). Evidence-based policy and social work in health and mental health. *Social Work in Mental Health, 7*(1–3), 267–283.

Netting, F. E., Kettner, P., & McMurtry, S. (2008). *Social work macro practice* (4th ed.). Boston: Allyn and Bacon.

Ohmer, M., & Korr, W. (2006). The effectiveness of community practice interventions: A review of the literature. *Research on Social Work Practice, 16*(2), 132–145.

Roberts, A., & Yeager, K. (Eds.). (2006). *Foundations of evidence-based social work practice*. New York: Oxford University Press.

Roberts-DeGennaro, M. (2006, February). *Addressing the challenges and opportunities of evidence-based macro practice*. Panel presentation at the Annual Program Meeting of the Council on Social Work Education, Chicago.

Roberts-DeGennaro, M. (2008a). Case management: Using the integrative and collaborative process of the evidence-based practice paradigm. In T. Mizrahi & L. Davis (Eds.), *Encyclopedia of social work* (20th ed., pp. 222–227). New York: Oxford University Press.

Roberts-DeGennaro, M. (2008b). Evidence-based (informed) macro practice paradigm: Integration of practice expertise and research. *Journal of Evidence-Based Social Work, 5*(3–4), 407–421.

Roberts-DeGennaro, M. (2010). Using an evidence-based program planning model in a macro practice course. *Journal of Teaching in Social Work, 30*(1), 46–63.

Ross, S., Lavis, J., Rodriguez, C., Woodside, J., & Denis J. L. (2003). Partnership experiences: Involving decision-makers in the research process. *Journal of Health Services Research and Policy, 8*(Suppl. 2), 26–34.

Rousseau, D. (2006). Keeping an open mind about evidence-based management: A reply to Learmonth's commentary. *Academy of Management Review, 31*(4), 1091–1093.

Straus, S., Richardson, W. S., Glasziou, P., & Haynes, R. B. (2005). *Evidence-based medicine: How to practice and teach EBM* (3rd ed.). London: Churchill Livingstone.

Torrey, W. C., Drake, R. E., Dixon, L., Burns, B. J., Flynn, L., Rush, A. J., et al. (2001). Implementing evidence-based practices for persons with severe mental illnesses. *Psychiatric Services, 52*(1), 45–50.

U.S. Department of Justice, Office of Juvenile Justice and Delinquency Prevention. (n.d.). *Best practices to address community gang problems: OJJDP's comprehensive gang model.* Retrieved January 6, 2009, from http://www.ncjrs.gov/pdffiles1/ojjdp/222799.pdf.

Walker, J., Briggs, H., Koroloff, N., & Friesen, B. (2007). Guest editorial—Implementing and sustaining evidence-based practice in social work. *Journal of Social Work Education, 43*(3), 361–375.

Whaley, A. L., & Davis, K. E. (2007). Cultural competence and evidence-based practice in mental health services: A complementary perspective. *American Psychologist, 62*(6), 563–574.

Woody, J., D'Souza, H., & Dartman, R. (2006). Do master's in social work programs teach empirically supported interventions? A survey of deans and directors. *Research on Social Work Practice, 16*(5), 469–479.

Yeager, J., & Saggese, M. (2008). Making your agency outcome informed: A guide to overcoming human resistance to change. *Families in Society, 89*(1), 9–18.

Yegidis, B. L., & Weinbach, R. W. (2009). *Research methods for social workers* (6th ed.). Upper Saddle River, NJ: Pearson/Allyn and Bacon.

York, R. O. (2009). *Evaluating human services: A practical approach for the human service professional.* Upper Saddle River, NJ: Pearson/Allyn and Bacon.

CHAPTER TWO

Empirically Supported Management Behavior

Review of the Research Literature on Consumer Outcomes

John Poertner

Statement of the Problem

The most important transaction in the human service organization is that of the consumer and service provider. It is primarily through this interaction that consumers achieve the benefits they seek. Among the many tasks of the social administrator are establishing and maintaining conditions in the organization so that consumers achieve desired outcomes.

The movement toward research-informed practice suggests that it is direct service workers' ethical responsibility to critically appraise and use empirically supported interventions in their work with consumers. Similarly, it is the responsibility of social administrators to help create the conditions for the selection and faithful implementation of empirically supported interventions (i.e., adherence to the evidence-based practice model). This includes the use of management behavioral practices that have been empirically shown to make a difference to consumers.

There is an accumulating body of evidence relating to the impact of specific direct service interventions on consumer outcomes. In contrast, the research base for management behavior has lagged behind that of direct services. Yet there is research that links specific management behavioral practices to achieving desired outcomes for consumers. It is this literature that this chapter presents.

Although this body of research is growing, it is difficult to find or easily access. The journal *Administration in Social Work* is a good outlet to search for this type of research. However, much of the management research that exists is related to a field of practice. Locating research that links organizational variables to outcomes for consumers requires knowledge of a diverse range of services in the social work field, including child welfare, mental health, addictions, services for older adults, and so on. Therefore, searching the literature can be a challenge for any practitioner or researcher. To begin this task, it is important that one first be clear as to what an empirically supported intervention is.

Evidence-based practice requires the integration of the best research evidence with practice expertise and the client's unique values and circumstances (see Sackett, Rosenberg, Gray, Haynes, & Richardson, 1996; Straus, Richardson, Glasziou, & Haynes, 2005). This definition has many implications. Of key importance is the question, What is meant by "best" research evidence? Fortunately, there has been considerable discussion of this that has resulted in the development of categories for levels of evidence.

There are differences in the way that various authors or organizations identify levels of evidence. For the purpose of this chapter, the levels of evidence that Thomlison (2003) reports are useful in differentiating best evidence.

> Level 1. Well-supported, efficacious treatment with positive evidence from more than two randomized clinical trials.
>
> Level 2. Supported and probably efficacious treatment with positive evidence from two or more quasi-experimental studies, or where researchers found positive evidence from only one clinical trial.
>
> Level 3. Supported and acceptable treatment with positive evidence from comparative studies, correlation studies, and case control studies; one nonrandomized study; or any type of quasi-experimental study.
>
> Level 4. Promising and acceptable treatment with evidence from experts or clinical experience of respected authority or both. (p. 544)

Best evidence, therefore, refers to those interventions based on valid and relevant research that places them in the most rigorous level on this typology. If an intervention has a research base consisting of more than two clinical trials that found positive results, then it is a level 1 intervention and represents current best evidence. This level of evidence places emphasis on research with subjects who have been randomly assigned to a treatment group or a comparison group, followed by observation of posttreatment difference. Level 1 also emphasizes replication of the research study. It is through multiple trials producing similar outcomes that increased confidence can be gained, as this suggests that the changes observed are real and not just due to chance.

Level 1 is a very high level of evidence and is not always available. However, our professional commitment is to use interventions with the highest level of evidence. For a newly recognized social problem, it is likely that only level 4 interventions are available. Therefore, that evidence becomes the current best evidence.

In the area of social administration or management behavior, there are no level 1 interventions. Yet there are an increasing number of research studies that link organizational variables to positive outcomes for consumers. These are primarily correlation studies and thus level 3 interventions. Although this state of affairs may at first seem disappointing, this current review found twenty published reports of studies linking administrative behavior to consumer outcomes. A few short years ago, this was a smaller list (Poertner, 2006).

Literature Review

THE AGENCY CONTEXT

Littell and Tajima (2000) conducted a study that presents a useful way to think about the relative contribution of various organizational components to consumer outcomes. The researchers used parent participation in family preservation as their dependent variable. This is not a consumer outcome, but they argue that it is predictive of outcomes. They found that case variables such as characteristics of the parent or family, including presence of substance abuse, mental health problems, and teenage parent, explained 83 percent of the variance in parent participation. Worker characteristics explained 13 percent, and program characteristics explained 4 percent of the variance in parent participation.

One might be surprised that the worker and the program explained only 17 percent of the variance in the outcome. However, this is a significant contribution. There are several features of Littell and Tajima's (2000) study that we can learn from. First, the study was organized according to levels, with characteristics of consumers constituting one level; worker characteristics, a second level; and program characteristics, a third level. This is a useful way to think about the human service organization. Consumers come to the organization for assistance and bring with them their own histories, unique values, and circumstances. Caseworkers who similarly have complex backgrounds and diverse perceptions of their job and the organization engage those consumers. Consumers and workers operate within the framework of a program that is a set of activities that aims to achieve a desired consumer outcome.

Second, in Littell and Tajima's (2000) study, the program was not a level 1 intervention. From an empirically supported point of view, one would expect level 1 interventions to make more of a contribution to consumer outcomes than an intervention of levels 2–4. We also know that it is not easy to transfer a level 1 intervention from an experimental setting to the real world and achieve the same results with consumers.

Third, Littell and Tajima's (2000) study did not directly measure management behavior. Yet each of the organizational levels studied is, in some way, the responsibility of management. Managers are responsible for the selection of an intervention and the development of a program. This is a strong statement, given constraints such as funding sources, agency history, and community pressures. From a consumer-centered perspective, social administrators take on the responsibility of selecting and shaping the program to yield the best results possible for consumers. (For more discussion of this management role, see Poertner & Rapp, 2007.)

Managers are responsible for the recruitment and selection of caseworkers. To achieve maximum benefit for consumers, the caseworkers' background and experiences need to match program requirements, and it is the manager who does this matching. In the Littell and Tajima (2000) study, caseworker characteristics also included supervisory adequacy, job clarity, autonomy, and burnout. These are clearly related to the responsibility of management.

Managers are also responsible for matching consumers with the program. Social programs are designed and tested to engage and succeed with consumers who have specific characteristics. Managers are responsible for being clear on the types of consumers who can expect to be successful by engaging with a program and for then communicating this information to consumers, workers, and other key actors.

In an ideal world, social administrators operating from an empirically supported or evidence-based framework would select a program with level 1 evidence of effectiveness and then match worker and consumer characteristics to program requirements. However, the world is far more complex than that. A study by Schoenwald, Sheidow, Letourneau, and Liao (2003) demonstrates some of this complexity.

In Schoenwald et al.'s (2003) study, multisystemic therapy (MST) was implemented in thirty-nine organizations, and the researchers examined the relationships among the therapists' adherence to MST, organizational climate, and organizational structure to outcomes for youths.

Schoenwald et al. (2003) argue that MST has shown positive results for youth with serious antisocial behavior and that it is well supported by multiple clinical trials. However, others who have examined these trials do not agree with their claims (see Littell, 2005).

IMPLEMENTATION FIDELITY OF PROGRAM INTERVENTIONS

Regardless of how one evaluates the arguments on either side of the debate on the effectiveness of MST, Schoenwald et al.'s (2003) study has valuable lessons for implementing interventions in organizations. In their study, they used the MST Therapist Adherence Measure to assess therapists' fidelity to nine principles of the program model. Fidelity instruments are an important part of the implementation of an empirically supported intervention. Practice models are designed and tested on the basis of specific expectations of those involved in the service transaction. When implementing a program in another setting, it is critical to know whether people are adhering to program expectations in the model. If they are not, then the program being implemented is not the one that was tested, and the same results for consumers cannot be expected. Measures of program fidelity are important management tools when implementing empirically supported interventions.

Overall, Schoenwald et al.'s (2003) study found that the MST program demonstrated positive outcomes for youths. The researchers conducted several analyses of the data. For purposes of this chapter, I review the finding that the organizational variables had a differential effect on outcomes depending on the therapists' level of adherence to MST principles.

The organizational variables studied were climate and structure. Climate was defined to include the concepts of fairness and cooperation, energy and effectiveness, emotional demand, job satisfaction, and opportunities for advancement. When therapists' adherence to MST principles was high, the study found no significant effect of any of the climate variables on youths' behavior. When adherence to the MST principles was low, some climate variables were significant. In this case, greater job satisfaction was related to youths' more positive behavior. However, more opportunities for advancement for the therapists were related to poorer outcomes for youths. Although this is counterintuitive, it demonstrates that the relationships can be complex.

Organizational structure was defined to include participation in decision making, hierarchy of authority, and procedural and rule specification. These variables had no relationship to youth outcomes when adherence was low. However, when adherence was high, the variables were related to poorer outcomes for youths. Again, this is counterintuitive.

The most direct way to summarize these confusing results is to say that it is important to align organizational climate and structure with the demands of the intervention. For example, organizational structure variables were found to predict poorer youth outcomes when therapists followed MST principles. This suggests that the organizations had methods of decision making, hierarchy, or rules that were inconsistent with MST principles. The lesson here is that it is important to compare these organizational elements to the specifications of an intervention before implementation.

THE IMPORTANCE OF LEADERSHIP AND SUPERVISION

Supervisors are often considered the most important management level in the human service organization. They are closest to the consumer and caseworker transaction. They are charged with monitoring the quality of that transaction. They help others in the organization understand what is needed so that consumers receive the assistance they require. Fortunately, there is a growing body of research that links supervisory behavior to consumer outcomes.

Corrigan, Lickey, Campion, and Rashid (2000) examined the effect of team leadership on consumer satisfaction and quality of life. They used Bass's (1990) transformational leadership model. This model features three styles of leadership. The first type of leader is a transformational leader, that is, a leader who helps team members transform programs to meet the evolving needs of consumers. This includes the dimensions of charisma, inspiration, intellectual stimulation, and consideration of the interests of others. The second type is a transactional leader, that is, a leader who uses goal setting, feedback, self-monitoring, and reinforcement. The third type of leader uses a laissez-faire style, in which the leader is aloof, uninvolved, and disinterested in the day-to-day activities of the team.

Corrigan et al. (2000) surveyed thirty-one clinical teams in a mental health setting. They obtained ratings of leadership style from 143 leaders and 473 subordinates. Consumers of the teams ($N = 184$) rated their satisfaction with treatment and their quality of life. The researchers then analyzed the relationship between the leaders' and the subordinates' ratings of leadership to consumer satisfaction and quality of life. Only those variables that had a significant relationship to consumer satisfaction or quality of life are included in the following results.

- Consumers from teams in which leaders rated themselves higher on the transformational leadership dimension of inspiration were more satisfied with the services received.

- Consumers from teams in which leaders rated themselves higher in the transactional leadership dimension of contingent reward were more satisfied.
- Consumers from teams in which leaders rated themselves higher in laissez-faire leadership and the use of passive management by exception were less satisfied with the services received.
- Consumers from teams in which the subordinates rated their leader as using active management by exception were less satisfied.
- Consumers from teams in which leaders rated themselves higher on laissez-faire management reported a lower quality of life.
- Consumers from teams in which subordinates rated their leaders higher on charisma, inspiration, and consideration of the interests of individual staff members reported a greater quality of life.

With a focus on the outcome of quality of life, which is arguably a better outcome, the conclusion is that supervisors who use the transformational model have a positive effect on consumers. Similarly, supervisors who use the laissez-faire style of leadership have a negative effect.

Grasso (1994) also examined supervisory leadership style in a large, private child welfare agency serving troubled adolescents and their families. The study used Likert's (1967) management survey instrument to classify leadership styles as exploitive, authoritative, consultative, or participatory. Grasso studied the link between these styles and job satisfaction to service effectiveness, which included placing children in the least restrictive setting and three-month posttreatment follow-up on work and school functioning. The study found no relationship between leadership style and child outcomes.

Sosin (1986) surveyed child welfare agencies in counties in Wisconsin and examined the child welfare outcome of permanency. One preliminary finding was that in counties where supervisors reminded workers that case reviews were needed, fewer children were in care for long periods. However, this relationship was not significant in the final analysis, possibly indicating that other factors, such as the use of a review board that demanded changes in the case plan, were more influential. Sosin's intervention of having supervisors or review boards remind workers of the need for case reviews is goal-directed behavior.

Moos and Moos (1998) report the results of a study based on the outcomes of fifteen substance abuse treatment programs that included programs being goal directed. Patients of these programs ($N = 3,228$) reported on their treatment environment and their participation and satisfaction with the treatment, goal of abstinence, confidence in achieving abstinence, situational confidence, depression, perceived benefits of abstinence, substance abuse coping skills, and general coping skills. Staff of these programs ($N = 329$) rated several dimensions of the work environment, including involvement, such as the extent that staff were concerned committed to their jobs; task orientation; work pressure; clarity, such as the extent to which staff members know what to expect in their daily routine; and clarity of rules and procedures; and managerial control. They also assessed coworker cohesion, supervisory support, and treatment. Moos and Moos (1998) found that patients of programs in which staff were supportive and goal directed participated in more substance abuse, educational, social, and family treatment services. They were more involved in self-help groups, more satisfied with the program, improved more during treatment, and more likely to participate in outpatient mental health services after discharge.

Harkness and Hensley (1991) and Harkness (1997) reported on a study of client-focused supervision in a mental health agency. Client-focused supervision was defined as asking questions of therapists about the goodness of fit between the clients' presenting problems and method of intervention and the outcomes of practice. One supervisor with four therapists and 161 clients participated in the sixteen-week study. The supervisor used her usual style of supervision for the first eight weeks, followed by client-focused supervision for the remaining eight weeks. Client satisfaction, goal attainment, and generalized contentment were the outcomes assessed. Client-focused supervision had a positive effect on goal attainment and client satisfaction but had no effect on generalized contentment.

Ahearn (1999) studied the impact of supervisory behavior on permanency rates for foster children. One hundred teams participated in the study, with an average of 4.4 workers per team. The behaviors of interest were client-centered supervision from the supervisors' and workers' perspectives, supervisors' political skills as assessed by both supervisors and their workers, supervisors empowerment from their workers' perspective, supervisors' years of experience, team caseload, average age of children in caseload, average number of placements of children served by the team, and proportion of kinship to regular foster care in caseload.

Workers' assessment of client-centeredness in Ahearn's (1999) study was measured through nine items selected from the Managerial Practices Survey and six additional items reflecting client-centeredness. Yukl, Wall, and Lepsinger (1990) designed the Managerial Practices Survey to measure the supervisory behaviors of monitoring, clarifying, and problem solving. Examples of these latter items include "Your supervisor handles work-related problems and crises in a confident and decisive manner" and "Your supervisor follows up after making a request to see that it was done." Examples of client-centeredness items are "Your supervisor refers to clients in a positive manner" and "Your supervisor analyzes cases with bad outcomes, identifies mistakes, and shares these insights."

Ahearn (1999) assessed political skills using the work of Ferris et al. (1999). These skills include the ability to read, understand, and exert influence and control in social situations in a way that is not considered overt or controlling. Examples of these items are "I find it easy to envision myself in the position of others" and "I am good at getting others to respond positively to me."

Findings from Ahearn's (1999) study include the following:

- Higher supervisors' client-centeredness as rated by workers is associated with increased permanency rates.
- Higher supervisor self-ratings of political skills are associated with increased permanency rates.
- Larger team caseloads are associated with a lower permanency rate.
- A higher proportion of children in regular foster care is associated with higher permanency rates.

Using Research Evidence for Decision Making

SUPERVISORY BEHAVIOR

The seven aforementioned empirical studies linking supervisory behavior to outcomes for consumers yield the lesson that supervisors have an impact on consumers. This effect can be positive or negative. The magnitude of this effect is not clear. There are some promising practice guidelines that can be drawn from these studies.

- Supervisors who are charismatic, inspirational, and consider the interests of each staff member tend to have a positive effect on consumers.
- Supervisors who manage teams, in which staff are concerned about and committed to their jobs, there is a task orientation, work pressures are manageable, there is clarity on rules and procedures, and management uses these rules and procedures to structure the work tend to have a positive effect on consumers.
- Supervisors who ask questions of workers about the fit between consumer problems and interventions used, and the outcomes of intervention have a positive effect on consumers.
- Supervisors who monitor, clarify, and problem solve with staff; are client centered; and have political skills tend to have a positive effect on consumers.

• Supervisors who operate with a laissez-faire leadership style might have a negative effect on consumers.

ORGANIZATIONAL CLIMATE

Supervisors are part of complex organizations with many elements. One of these is organizational climate. Glisson (2000) defines organizational climate in terms of employees' perceptions of how the work environment affects them either negatively or positively. Because there are so many things that can affect workers' perceptions, there are many elements of organizational climate. Glisson identifies ten elements of climate that have been studied: (1) support, (2) conflict, (3) challenge, (4) depersonalization, (5) equity, (6) opportunity, (7) stress, (8) ambiguity, (9) task significance, and (10) emotional exhaustion.

Perhaps the most widely referenced study of organizational climate is that of Glisson and Hemmelgarn (1998), in which they examined the relationship between organizational climate and interorganizational coordination on outcomes for children. This study was conducted in twenty-four counties (twelve pilots and twelve controls) in Tennessee. Six hundred children who entered state custody and the caseworkers in the organizations serving them were the study subjects. In the study, child behavior was the consumer outcome measured by the Child Behavioral Checklist and the Teacher Report Form.

Organizational variables included in Glisson and Hemmelgarn's (1998) study were service quality (i.e., comprehensiveness, continuity, responsiveness), services coordination (i.e., authorization, responsibility, monitoring), interorganizational relationships (i.e., noncooperation, dumping, red tape, blaming, unreasonable demands, withholding information, disputes), and organizational climate. The study used the Psychological Climate Questionnaire. This measurement instrument assessed workers' perceptions of fairness, role clarity, role overload, role conflict, cooperation, growth and advancement, job satisfaction, emotional exhaustion, personal accomplishment, and depersonalization.

Glisson and Hemmelgarn (1998) found that service quality and interorganizational coordination had no effect on child behavior. However, positive organizational climates were associated with improved child behavior. The reader is reminded of the findings from Schoenwald et al.'s (2003) study, which found organizational climate to have a different effect depending on the therapist's adherence to MST principles.

It seems to be intuitive in the context of social services that job satisfaction, a dimension of organizational climate, would by itself be related to outcomes for consumers. Yet the studies that focused on satisfaction show mixed results. Yoo (2002) conducted a qualitative case study (level 4 evidence) of a child welfare agency and found that case managers' job satisfaction was inversely related to client outcomes. That is, higher job satisfaction was related to poorer performance on client outcomes. Grasso's (1994) study described earlier found no relationship between job satisfaction and outcomes. Also mentioned earlier, Schoenwald et al.'s (2003) study found that job satisfaction was positively related to child outcomes when therapists' adherence to the model was low. Likewise, a study in three psychiatric institutions found that job satisfaction had a positive impact on resident improvement (Holland, Konick, Buffum, Smith, & Petchers, 1981).

Job satisfaction is frequently related to the concept of burnout. There has been much interest and research on burnout. However, this review found only one study that linked burnout to a consumer outcome. Garman, Corrigan, and Morris (2002) linked burnout to client satisfaction in a survey of thirty-one behavioral health teams. Burnout is usually examined as a condition of individuals. Garman et al.'s study investigated the interactive effect of the team level and burnout in relationship to client satisfaction. They found that a significant amount of the variance (16 percent) in client satisfaction was attributable to the team level. It was the emotional exhaustion component of burnout that had the clearest relationship to client satisfaction.

The mixed findings regarding job satisfaction suggest that, by itself, it is not very useful in explaining what is important to workers and consumers. In contrast, organizational climate includes job satisfaction and appears to be more useful. The results of organizational climate studies are mixed, probably reflecting the many elements of organizational climate and their possible interactions and relationships. Still, Garman et al.'s (2002) study suggests that managers need to attend to the importance of workers' perceptions of their work environment and the impact that this can have on achieving desired consumer outcomes.

ORGANIZATIONAL STRUCTURE

Even though organizational climate and structure are frequently studied together, they deserve separate attention. Structure refers to the ways that organizations divide up the work to be done. In the context of this review, structural variables that have been studied include the extent of bureaucracy, degree of centralization, control, and complexity.

Crook (2001) conducted a qualitative study of the relationship between the extent of bureaucracy and client satisfaction in three transitional housing programs for homeless families. She found that high levels of bureaucracy were inversely related to client satisfaction. In other words, the more bureaucratic an agency was, the poorer the outcomes were for consumers. Her definition of bureaucracy included organizational size, structure, rules, and leadership.

Martin and Segal (1977) conducted an early study of organizational structure. The outcome studied was staff expectations of residents in halfway houses. The measure asked workers to indicate whether, in their role as a staff member, they felt that residents in the halfway house were obligated to have a job, to prepare dinner for some friends, to go on errands when asked, and so on. This is not a direct consumer outcome measure, and one might ask whether it should be included in this review of the research literature. Because this is one of the few studies to attempt to link organizational structure to a reasonable outcome proxy, it is included here. A count of the number of residents who had a job or ran errands would be preferable, but staff expectations might predict the actual outcome.

Martin and Segal (1977) measured organizational structure by assessing horizontal and vertical complexity. They measured horizontal complexity by counting the number of distinct job titles of all paid staff. Vertical complexity included two dimensions. One was whether staff of the halfway house or someone outside (e.g., the board of directors) made policy decisions. The second was the number of job titles that entailed indirect functions versus direct service activities.

Neither complexity nor decentralization alone was associated with staff expectations. Martin and Segal's (1977) study did find that the number of staff had a negative relationship to staff expectations. In other words, the larger the halfway house, the lower were the staff's expectations of consumers. However, the ratio of staff to residents had a positive relationship to expectations. The more staff that were assigned per resident, the higher were the expectations of residents.

Schmid (1992) studied the relationship between decentralization of authority in community service organizations in Israel and a dimension of service effectiveness. This was defined as the ratio of the number of community residents served compared to the number targeted. Again, one might argue that this is not a direct consumer outcome. Nevertheless, the independent variables studied were decentralization, autonomy, coordination, and control.

Schmid (1992) defined decentralization as the degree of influence perceived as held by program directors with respect to policy making and operations. Autonomy was defined as the degree of freedom that directors perceived in supervising their staff, running their programs, and mobilizing financial and human resources. Coordination was defined as the degree of interdepartmental coordination in use of resources and the degree of efficiency in planning. Control was defined in terms of control of program implementation, planning, and results. Schmid (1992) found that decentralization had the strongest relationship with service effectiveness. Autonomy, coordination, and control were related only weakly to the outcome.

The study by Holland et al. (1981) was previously mentioned in regard to their findings regarding job satisfaction. They also studied the relationship between resident improvement and their participation in decision making, staff participation in treatment decisions, organizational centralization, and staff practices in organizing the daily schedule for residents. In addition to finding that job satisfaction was positively related to residents' improvement, they found that organizational centralization demonstrated a weak but positive association with the outcome. Staff involvement in decision making had a significant but negative direct association with resident improvement. However, staff decision making interacted with job satisfaction and resident management practices, which had a positive impact on residents. In other words, staff members' satisfaction with their job, involvement in decision making, and management practices with residents were all important in predicting outcomes. It is interesting that resident involvement in treatment decisions had little impact on outcomes.

The results of the research on organizational structure and consumer outcomes are disappointing. There are few studies, and the outcomes measures are not the strongest. Concepts such as complexity and decentralization do not show much relationship to consumer outcomes. On the positive side, the few variables that demonstrated positive results were the number of staff compared to the number of residents and the way that staff worked with residents. This supports the idea that the transaction between consumers and workers is the most important in producing positive outcomes.

POLICY CHOICE AND RESIDENT INPUT

There is a little-known line of research on the role of residents and how it contributes to results in treatment environments. Much of this work is linked to Rudolf Moos, who in 1974 published the book *Evaluating Treatment Environments: A Social Ecological Approach.* This line of research examines the role of program policies that are related to resident choice and how these contribute to consumer outcomes.

David, Moos, and Kahn (1981) surveyed ninety-three sheltered-care settings for older adults. The outcome was community integration. The independent variables were physical access, program policies, social climate, and characteristics of settings. They found that community integration was correlated with policies that permit resident control of facility decision making.

Timko and Moos (1989) and Moos and Lemke (1994) conducted similar studies, surveying, respectively, 244 and 262 residential facilities for older adults. The first study found that, after controlling for level of care and residents' functional ability, policy choice and resident control together made a significant contribution to community integration. Similarly, the second study found that after controlling for level of care, social resources, and resident functioning abilities, facilities with greater levels of policy choice, resident control, privacy, and policy clarity had greater resident involvement in community activities.

McCarthy and Nelson (1991) studied social support and democratic decision making by residents of a supported housing program that provided emotional and problem-solving support for former psychiatric patients. The outcomes included were empowerment (skills needed to function independently in the community) and quality of life (satisfaction with several similar domains). Findings from the McCarthy and Nelson study include the following:

- Emotional support is positively correlated with resident satisfaction with housing and privacy.
- Problem-solving support is positively correlated with resident satisfaction with the facility and empowerment.
- Staff control is inversely correlated with resident satisfaction with privacy and empowerment.
- Shared control (resident and staff) is positively correlated with resident satisfaction with the facility.
- Resident control is inversely related to satisfaction with how decisions were made but positively correlated with empowerment.
- Authoritarian management control is inversely correlated with resident satisfaction with staff and privacy.
- Democratic management control is positively correlated with resident satisfaction with staff, privacy, and the way that decisions are made.
- Permissive management is inversely correlated with resident satisfaction with staff.

McCarthy and Nelson's (1991) study demonstrates the complexity of residents' roles in residential settings and how these might contribute to outcomes. A general summary for this study is that residents were more satisfied with shared decision making and a democratic style of management. This study, as well as that of Corrigan et al. (2000), found that some management practices are harmful, such as permissive management. Permissive supervisors are those who take a hands-off approach and allow workers to do whatever they want.

Schmid and Nirel (1995) moved the line of research related to the role of the resident out of residential settings and into care services for older adults in Israel. The outcomes were adaptation (i.e., services adapted to client needs), satisfaction with the organization, assessment of performance, and rate of complaints. The organizational variables of interest were empowerment, such as the extent to which clients or workers had power to determine the care plan; control, such as the number of meetings between worker and supervisor; equity, such as how the organization exercises fairness in the delivery of services; training programs; and working conditions. They found that, for the 317 older adults whom the programs served, adaptation and satisfaction increased as a result of empowerment and equity. However, there was no relationship between control and those outcomes. None of the organizational variables was a good predictor of assessment of performance or complaints.

This line of research studying the contribution of the role of client decision making to achieving client outcomes is in its infancy. Given the importance of the ethical standard of respecting client self-determination, this is somewhat surprising. Just as self-determination is not the same across all social problems and services, knowing which consumer decision-making role is most effective varies by setting and requires more research. There is an indication that in some settings, clients value having a major role, whereas in other settings, shared decision making is more effective. However, management control over all of the decision-making processes related to planning, implementing, and evaluating services is not supported.

PERFORMANCE IMPROVEMENT TEAMS

There is a lot of management literature on quality improvement or performance improvement. However, like so much of the management literature, there is little empirical support for these ideas. Yeaman, Craine, Gorsek, and Corrigan (2000) conducted the only known study that has examined the impact of performance improvement teams on consumer outcomes.

The performance improvement team implemented in Yeaman et al.'s (2000) study involved four phases. Phase 1 was organizing for change, which involved planning the change process, developing a guiding mission, identifying leaders, and assessing needs. Phase 2 was preparing the environment, including educating staff, fostering appreciation for quality, developing a customer orientation, obtaining commitment, forming the improvement team, and empowering the team. Phase 3 was focusing the environment, including selecting the direction for change, deciding on change, delegating responsibility for change, identifying indicators of change, measuring change, and analyzing follow-up data. Phase 4 was institutionalizing performance improvement.

The performance improvement team approach took place in a hospital for serious and persistently mentally ill adults that focused on symptom stabilization, education about their illness, and psychiatric rehabilitation. The outcomes of interest were consumer satisfaction, skills acquired, and number of aggressive incidents. After implementation of the teams, consumer satisfaction increased by 42 percent. Consumers showed a 25 percent increase in knowledge about key skill areas, including medication, symptom management, and leisure time. There was also nearly a 50 percent reduction in aggressive incidents.

Performance improvement teams appear to work toward improving consumer outcomes. To be certain of this, consumer outcomes need to be part of the care or service plan from the beginning. Imagine what we might learn if all quality improvement efforts included client participation in assessing consumer outcomes as well as program outcomes.

Practice Guidelines

Empirical support for management behavior that contributes to consumer success is a developing field. There is no known management practice that meets the highest level of evidence (level 1). However, there are now several level 3 studies. Therefore, these studies represent current best evidence.

Much of the research literature reviewed here has focused on supervisory behavior with promising results. This review also suggests that some practices can be harmful. Supervisors who are aloof, uninvolved, and disinterested in the day-to-day activities of the team can actually harm consumers. The following are empirically supported management behaviors for effective supervision:

- Be charismatic and inspirational, and consider the interests of each staff member.
- Create or maintain staff who are concerned about and committed to their jobs in an environment where there is task orientation, work pressures are manageable, there is clarity of rules and procedures, and management uses those rules and procedures to structure the work to have a positive effect on consumers.
- Ask questions of workers about the fit between consumer problems and the selection of interventions, as well as the outcomes from the intervention.
- Monitor, clarify, and problem solve with staff; be client centered; read; understand; and exert influence and control in social situations in a way that is not considered overt or controlling.

It makes a lot of sense to most people who work in social services that job satisfaction be positively associated with achieving desired consumer outcomes. The research does not support this. It is not that job satisfaction is not important; rather, it is embedded in the broader concept of organizational climate that includes support, conflict, challenge, depersonalization, equity, opportunity, stress, ambiguity, task significance, and emotional exhaustion. The results of organizational climate studies are complex. Still, this research draws managers' attention to the importance of workers' perceptions of their work environment and the impact that this can have on consumers. The work of Glisson and Hemmelgarn (1998) found that climate had a positive association with achieving desired consumer outcomes. The work of Schoenwald et al. (2003) considered climate in the context of implementing an empirically tested program and found more complex relationships. Current best evidence regarding organizational climate can be summarized as follows: managers need to be aware of workers' perceptions of the work environment and align the components of climate (support, conflict, challenge, depersonalization, equity, opportunity, stress, ambiguity, task significance, and emotional exhaustion) with what is required to produce consumer outcomes.

Yeaman et al.'s (2000) study suggests that the implementation of a performance improvement plan is related to organizational climate in that part of implementing such a plan is developing a supportive climate. Although this is only one study, and not a controlled experiment, the results were very positive and suggest that current best evidence is as follows:

- Implement program improvement plans by focusing on consumer outcomes from the start and planning the change process by developing a guiding mission, identifying leaders, and assessing needs.
- Prepare the environment by educating staff, fostering appreciation for quality, developing a customer orientation, obtaining commitment, forming the improvement team, and empowering the team.
- Focus the environment on the tasks and desired outcomes.

Organizational structure is certainly important to how the work gets done and consumer benefits. However, the current research does not support this idea. That is likely because of the relative lack of research attention that the idea has received. The few positive results indicate that current best evidence in this area suggests that managers need to pay attention to the consumer-to-staff ratio and that managers need to monitor consumer and worker interactions.

Decision making in organizations is even less well understood. Although we value client self-determination, operationalizing this concept is a bit complex. There is the indication, noted earlier, that, in some settings, clients value having a major role, whereas in others, shared decision making is more effective. The evidence does suggest that management control of all decisions regarding the planning, implementing, and evaluating of services for consumers does not lead to better outcomes.

We know more about empirically supported management behavior than we did twenty years ago. Still, we do not know very much. There are no randomized controlled experiments focusing on management behavior and consumer outcomes, yet there are many promising practices. Readers are reminded that this review of the research literature was conducted at a specific point in time; future studies will certainly contribute to the knowledge of what works in management practice. Managers need to have a way to keep up to date on new research developments and the evidence for improving practice. Gray (2001) suggests that every evidence-based organization establish an evidence center to address the challenge of disseminating the current research. Management, in turn, will have to meet the challenge of storing and sharing this knowledge to inform practice.

References

Ahearn, K. K. (1999). *The impact of supervisory behavior on permanency rates for foster children in a child welfare context.* Unpublished doctoral dissertation, University of Illinois at Urbana-Champaign.

Bass, B. M. (1990). *Bass and Stogdill's handbook of leadership: Theory, research, and managerial applications* (3rd ed.). New York: Free Press.

Corrigan, P. W., Lickey, S. E., Campion, J., & Rashid, F. (2000). Mental health team leadership and consumer satisfaction and quality of life. *Psychiatric Services, 51*(6), 781–785.

Crook, W. P. (2001). Trickle-down bureaucracy: Does the organization affect client responses to programs? *Administration in Social Work, 26*(1), 37–59.

David, T. G., Moos, R. H., & Kahn, J. R. (1981). Community integration among elderly residents of sheltered care settings. *American Journal of Community Psychology, 9*(5), 513–526.

Ferris, G. R., Berkson, H. M., Kaplan, D. M., Gilmore, D. C., Buckley, M. R., Hochwarter, W. A., et al. (1999, August). *Development and initial validation of the political skill inventory.* Paper presented at the Academy of Management, 59th Annual National Meeting, Chicago.

Garman, A. N., Corrigan, P. W., & Morris, S. (2002). Staff burnout and patient satisfaction: Evidence of relationships at the care unit level. *Journal of Occupational Health Psychology, 7*(3), 235–241.

Glisson, C. (2000). Organizational climate and culture. In R. J. Patti (Ed.), *The handbook of social welfare management* (pp. 195–218). Thousand Oaks, CA: Sage.

Glisson, C., & Hemmelgarn, A. (1998). The effects of organizational climate and interorganizational coordination on the quality and outcomes of children's service systems. *Child Abuse and Neglect, 22*(5), 401–421.

Grasso, A. J. (1994). Management style, job satisfaction, and service effectiveness. *Administration in Social Work, 18*(4), 89–105.

Gray, J. A. M. (2001) *Evidence-based healthcare* (2nd ed.). London: Churchill Livingstone.

Harkness, D. (1997). Testing interactional social work theory: A panel analysis of supervised practice and outcomes. *Clinical Supervisor, 15*(1), 33–50.

Harkness, D., & Hensley, H. (1991). Changing the focus of social work supervision: Effects on client satisfaction and generalized contentment. *Social Work, 36*(6), 506–512.

Holland, T. P., Konick, A., Buffum, W., Smith, M. K., & Petchers, M. (1981). Institutional structure and resident outcomes. *Journal of Health and Social Behavior, 22*(4), 433–444.

Likert, R. (1967). *The human organization.* New York: McGraw-Hill.

Littell, J. H. (2005). Lessons from a systematic review of effects of multisystemic therapy. *Children and Youth Services Review, 27*(4), 445–463.

Littell, J. H., & Tajima, E. A. (2000). A multilevel model of client participation in intensive family preservation services. *Social Service Review, 74*(3), 405–435.

Martin, P. Y., & Segal, S. (1977). Bureaucracy, size, and staff expectations for client independence in halfway houses. *Journal of Health and Social Behavior, 18*(4), 376–390.

McCarthy, J., & Nelson, G. (1991). An evaluation of supportive housing for current and former psychiatric patients. *Hospital and Community Psychiatry, 42*(12), 1254–1256.

Moos, R. H. (1974). *Evaluating treatment environments: A social ecological approach.* New York: Wiley.

Moos, R. H., & Moos, B. S. (1998). The staff workplace and the quality and outcome of substance abuse treatment. *Journal of Studies on Alcohol, 59*(1), 43–51.

Moos, R. H., & Lemke, S. (1994). *Group residences for older adults.* New York: Oxford University Press.

Poertner, J. (2006). Social administration and outcomes for consumers: What do we know? *Administration in Social Work, 30*(2), 11–24.

Poertner, J., & Rapp, C. (2007). *Textbook of social administration: The consumer-centered approach.* New York: Haworth Press.

Sackett, D. L., Rosenberg, W. M. C., Gray, J. A. M., Haynes, R. B., & Richardson, W. S. (1996). Evidence based medicine: What it is and what it isn't. *British Medical Journal, 312*(7023), 71–72.

Schmid, H. (1992). Relationship between decentralized authority and other structural properties in human service organizations: Implications for service effectiveness. *Administration in Social Work, 16*(1), 25–39.

Schmid, H., & Nirel, R. (1995). Relationships between organizational properties and service effectiveness in home care organizations. *Journal of Social Service Research, 20*(3–4), 71–92.

Schoenwald, S. K., Sheidow, A. J., Letourneau, E. J., & Liao, J. G., (2003). Transportability of multisystemic therapy: Evidence for multilevel influences. *Mental Health Services Research, 5*(4), 223–239.

Sosin, M. R. (1986). Administrative issues in substitute care. *Social Service Review, 60*(3), 360–377.

Straus, S. E., Richardson, W. S., Glasziou, P., & Haynes, R. B. (2005). *Evidence-based medicine: How to practice and teach EBM*. New York: Elsevier Churchill Livingstone.

Thomlison, B. (2003). Characteristics of evidence-based child maltreatment interventions. *Child Welfare, 82*(5), 541–569.

Timko, C., & Moos, R. H. (1989). Choice, control, and adaptation among elderly residents of sheltered care settings. *Journal of Applied Social Psychology, 19*(8), 636–655.

Yeaman, C., Craine, W. H., Gorsek, J., & Corrigan, P. W. (2000). Performance improvement teams for better psychiatric rehabilitation. *Administration and Policy in Mental Health, 27*(3), 113–127.

Yoo, J. (2002). The relationship between organizational variables and client outcomes: A case study in child welfare. *Administration in Social Work, 26*(2), 39–61.

Yukl, G., Wall, S., & Lepsinger, R. (1990). Preliminary report on validation of the managerial practices survey. In K. E. Clark & M. B. Clark (Eds.), *Measures of leadership* (pp. 223–238). West Orange, NJ: Leadership Library of America.

CHAPTER THREE

What's Ethics Got to Do with It?

Using Evidence to Inform Management Practice

Cheryl A. Hyde

Statement of the Problem

Social work is considered a value-based profession, with a code of ethics delineating standards of ethical practice (National Association of Social Workers [NASW], 1996). Despite the centrality of ethics to the practice of social work, relatively little attention has been paid to this topic in the movement toward empirical practice. Although the NASW Code of Ethics supports the philosophy and principles of evidence-based practice (EBP), most of the literature focuses on why empirical evidence is important to practice and how it should inform practice. In addition, there is a gap between the understanding of emerging knowledge relevant to social work and the need to avail oneself to research and evaluation evidence (Gibbs, 2003; O'Hare, 2005; Roberts & Yeager, 2004). Yet as Gambrill (2006) cautions, "Ethical and evidentiary concerns are closely intertwined," and ethical codes are meaningful only if professionals "draw on practice-related research" (p. 351).

As if to underscore this concern, much of the literature on ethics and ethical decision making is prescriptive rather than empirical. Most

The author thanks Professor Bernie Newman for her insights and feedback.

often, decision-making frameworks are offered as guides for addressing ethical concerns or dilemmas, and case studies are used to illustrate difficult or ambiguous situations (Carey, 2007; Harrington & Dolgoff, 2008; Landau & Osmo, 2003; Loewenberg, Dolgoff, & Harrington, 2000; Peters, 2008; Reamer, 1990, 2001; Rhodes, 1991).

Research studies on ethics, which tend to be small scale, exploratory, and descriptive, have addressed the perception of ethical dilemmas and decision-making processes (Csikai, 2004; Gummer, 1990; Healy, 2003; Landau, 1999, 2000; Lonne, McDonald, & Fox, 2004), challenges to program accessibility (Egan & Kadushin, 2002; Ezell, 1994; Jansson & Dodd, 2002; Jones, 2006; Millstein, 2000), and ethical code deviations and violations (DiFranks, 2008; Strom-Gottfried, 2003). Essentially, evidence in support of sound ethical practices, per se, has not been developed.

This chapter explores ethics, or more specifically ethical dilemmas and their resolution, which managers contend with in organizational settings. The analysis, derived from interviews with managerial practitioners in human and social service agencies, empirically illuminates aspects of ethical practice at the organizational level. This focus also assists in understanding the relationship between ethics and the use of evidence to inform practice.

Literature Review

Much of the ethics literature, by default or design, focuses on clinically oriented social work practice (Hardina, Middleton, Montana, & Simpson, 2007; Healy & Pine, 2007; Lohmann & Lohmann, 2002), a bias reinforced through the use of case examples that overwhelmingly focus on ethical dilemmas regarding client values, confidentiality, and relationship boundaries (see Brody, 2004; Reamer, 2003).

Unfortunately, the macro-practice literature does little to correct this bias. Most macro–social work texts emphasize relevant ethical principles and values such as social justice and empowerment, but they do not examine in depth any unique ethical responsibilities and concerns of macro practitioners or more suitable ethical resolution processes (see Hardcastle & Powers, 2004; Homan, 2007; Kettner, Moroney, & Martin, 2007; Netting, Kettner, & McMurtry, 1993). However, some recent social administration texts include a chapter on ethics (see Aldgate et al., 2007; Hardina et al., 2007; Lohmann & Lohmann, 2002; Patti, 2000).

The NASW (1996) Code of Ethics includes specific standards that hold social work administrators responsible for ensuring adequate resources, supervision, and a working environment that upholds ethical practice. The National Network for Social Work Managers (2005) has delineated sixteen competency areas, one of which is ethics, which includes the following: "Commitment to meeting the needs of clients within the purview of the services offered by the organization. Commitment to the work and the organization that transcends personal desires. Loyalty to the mission of the organization. Commitment to the social work values of social justice, equity, and fairness" (n.p.).

There is not, however, an extensive managerial (or macro) code of ethics comparable to that of the Clinical Social Work Federation (Loewenberg et al., 2000). The small body of social work literature on ethical organizational practice focuses on three related themes: supervision, risk management, and quality assurance of staff and programs. In particular, Reamer (2000a, 2000b, 2004, 2005a, 2005b, 2008) has drawn attention to the critical import of organizational protocols and standards as strategies to minimize risk and error (see also Kirkpatrick, Reamer, & Sykulski, 2006; Lynch & Versen, 2003; McAuliffe, 2005). Yet these writings are primarily prescriptive; there is scant empirical evidence that the strategies and recommendations are implemented with fidelity or are effective.

Some small-scale studies have examined aspects of ethical dilemmas such as barriers to services (Egan & Kadushin, 2002; Walden, Wolock, & Demone, 1990), impact of privatization and program contracting (Anderson, 2004; Lonne et al., 2004), responses to the effects of policy mandates on agency functioning (Yang & Kombarakaran, 2006), and conflicts between management and direct line staff (Landau, 2000; Millstein, 2000). In contrast, other disciplines, such as business and counseling psychology, have begun to develop more analytic and empirical bodies of literature on ethics and mentoring, communication, supervisee behaviors, decision making, and peer consultation (see Gottlieb, 2006; Moberg, 2006, 2007; Moberg & Velasquez, 2006; Reinsch, 1996; Schwepker, 2001; Worthington, Tan, & Poulin, 2002).

Methodology

This exploratory study addressed two broad questions:

1. What do management practitioners identify as ethical dilemmas or concerns?
2. What strategies do management practitioners employ to address or resolve ethical dilemmas or concerns?

The findings presented in this chapter are from a larger exploratory, qualitative study on facets of human service management. Organizational researchers increasingly have employed qualitative methods because such approaches capture the naturalistic dimensions of organizational life (Cassell & Symon, 1994; Lee, 1999; Locke, 2001). Specifically, the constant comparative method (Charmaz, 1983, 2006; Chenitz, 1986; Locke, 2001; Strauss & Corbin, 1990) guided the gathering and analysis of the data. This is a qualitative approach in which the researcher engages in the iterative process of moving between collection and analysis, and between inductive and deductive stances with respect to the data.

STUDY POPULATION AND SAMPLING PROCEDURES

Data for the present study are from in-depth interviews with forty individuals who were in management or supervisory positions in human service or social change organizations. All interview respondents are from a large mid-Atlantic urban area; pseudonyms for individuals and organizations are used here for confidentiality purposes.

The author constructed the sample from a list of seventy-five individuals who served as macro field or task instructors for the area's schools of social work. In addition to convenience, these individuals were chosen because they had familiarity with social work education, including the importance of ethics and the components of macro social work practice. All of these individuals were in management positions (broadly defined as, for example, executive director, program director, or coordinator), supervised staff, and had planning responsibilities. Initially, twenty individuals were randomly selected from the sample. However, the total number of people interviewed expanded to forty, as an additional twenty individuals were randomly selected from the remaining fifty-five original participants to achieve theme saturation related to ethics and the resolution of ethical dilemmas.

Table 3.1 summarizes some of the characteristics of the forty respondents. The sample comprises sixteen men and twenty-four women; twenty-five whites, eleven African Americans, and four Latinos or Latinas; thirty people who hold MSWs (field instructors); and eight individuals (task instructors) with graduate degrees in related fields, such as public policy, divinity, nursing, and education. The age range is from thirty-seven to sixty-six, though most were in their late forties or early fifties. Their areas of practice reflect a wide array of interests, including child welfare, mental health, community development, homelessness, juvenile justice, and the environment. Seven respondents (Anna, Beth, Evelyn, Jay, Mike, Ruth, and Valerie) worked in the public sector, and the others were in nonprofit organizations; seven other individuals (Celeste, Jessica, Nancy, Richard, Sara, Ted, and Tom) characterized their organizations as faith based.

TABLE 3.1.   Characteristics of respondents (N = 40)

Name	Race	Degree	Position	Practice area/issue
Allen	White	MSW	Director	Community development
Andrew	Af. Am.	MPH	Director	Health/addictions
Anna	White	MSW	Affirmative action officer	City hospital/health
Barbara	White	MSW	Program director	Housing
Beth	Af. Am.	MSW	Unit supervisor	Child welfare
Celeste	Latina	MSW	Director	Poverty
Cynthia	White	MSW	Director	Community mediation
Darnell	Af. Am.	Urb. Pl MA	Executive director	Youth mentoring
Deanna	White	MSW	Coordinator	Women's issues
Don	White	MSW	Director	Veterans services
Emily	White	MSW	Education director	Women's issues
Emma	White	MSW	Outreach coordinator	Peace issues
Evan	White	MPA	Associate director	Environmental impact
Evelyn	Af. Am.	MSW	Assistant manager	Juvenile justice
Frank	White	MSW	Executive director	Community development
Jay	White	MBA	State representative	Politics
Jessica	White	MSW	Program director	Community center
Joe	White	MSW	Director of social services	Mental health
Jose	Latino	MSW	Program director	Mental health
Julie	Af. Am.	RN	Vice president	Health
Karen	White	M.Ed	Principal	Elementary education
Linda	White	MSW	Public policy director	Homelessness
Marcus	White	M.Div	Director	Anti-racism/social change
Marian	Latina	MSW	Program director	Workforce development
Martin	Af. Am.	M.Div	Board member	Civil rights
Maureen	White	J.D.	Community specialist	Homelessness
Mike	Af. Am.	MSW	Executive director	Juvenile justice
Nancy	White	MSW	Program director	Children recreation
Paula	White	MSW	Program director	Children and youth
Richard	White	MSW	President	Foster care
Rick	Af. Am.	Urb. Pl. MA	President	Community development
Rosemary	White	MSW	Executive director	Health/HIV-AIDS
Ruth	White	MSW	Director Employment	
Sandy	Af. Am.	MSW	Supervisor	Counseling center
Sara	White	MSW	Education supervisor	Violence against women
Tamika	Af. Am.	MSW	Transplant social worker	Health
Ted	White	MSW	Director	Poverty
Tom	White	MSW	Program director	Mental health
Tony	Latino	MSW	Consultant	Organizational development
Valerie	Af. Am.	MSW	Deputy director	City-neighborhood relationship

PROCEDURES FOR CLASSIFYING AND CODING OBSERVATIONS

Unstructured schedule interviews (Denzin, 1989), of two or more hours in length, were conducted. This type of interview covers a list of questions or items, but there is flexibility in terms of order, phrasing, follow-up, and the pursuit of tangents or unanticipated ideas. Interviews covered the following:

- Review of the respondent's education and career path
- Description of a typical agency day
- Key knowledge areas and skill sets needed
- Organizational strengths and limitations
- Ethical issues and/or dilemmas and how they were resolved
- Political environment of the agency

Because the author engaged in data coding while collecting the data, emergent themes or coding categories informed later interviews, primarily to clarify or verify findings (Charmaz, 2006). The author and three graduate students conducted the interviews, which were taped and transcribed.

Data Analysis

Per the constant comparative method, initial descriptive coding of the data followed the topics outlined in the interview protocol, though unexpected insights or ideas also were coded. This initial coding began once the first three interviews were completed so that emergent themes could be incorporated into the interview protocol; this iterative process continued as interviews were completed. Through this descriptive coding process, core themes were identified. As the core themes became more robust, more in-depth categorical and theoretical coding schemes were developed. The codes were grouped into substantive categories. The categories were compared across all interviews and with the literature to determine areas of common focus and points of divergence within the sample and between the sample and the literature, all of which were recorded in theme memos. Emergent themes and coding conflicts guided further interviewing. In this way, codes and categories were continuously examined against newly collected information (Charmaz, 2006; Chenitz & Swanson, 1986). Analytical categories and themes concerning various facets of ethical challenges and resolutions were developed.

   Two people, the interviewer and one other member of the research team, coded each interview. When disagreements arose, a third person coded the interview. For each interview, the research team met to discuss coding and emergent themes; identify and (if possible) resolve differences; and determine the need, as well as parameters, for any additional interviewing. The author composed theme memos that captured key points of the interview and linked the findings to those in other interviews. Coding and analysis ended when theme saturation occurred. Theme saturation means that any additional data for a given analytical category would not contribute any new information. A coherent, systematic, and rigorous condensation, as well as interpretation of the data, supported the integrity of the research in that all possible explanations were taken into account or eliminated (Charmaz, 2006; Chenitz & Swanson, 1986; Strauss & Corbin, 1990).

Theme saturation is the primary way in which internal validity is enhanced in the constant comparative method. Also key to this study's internal validity was the use of triangulation (Denzin, 1989), specifically through the convergence of different interpreters (coders) and explanations (emergent analysis and existing scholarship). External validity and reliability are more problematic given the exploratory nature of this study. This research has limited generalizability, as it used a relatively small, nonrandom sample located in one geographic area. It also has limited reliability (though perfect replication is difficult given the uniqueness of a qualitative study) (Cresswell, 1994; Lee, 1999).

Discussion of Findings

The study identified important themes regarding ethical challenges and their resolutions that warrant discussion. Findings are organized under two broad categories:

1. What constituted an ethical dilemma or challenge?
2. How were these dilemmas or challenges resolved?

In each category, themes were clustered and illustrated. These findings also establish a foundation for future inquiry into the relationship between ethics and evidence-based practice in organizational settings.

WHAT CONSTITUTES AN ETHICAL DILEMMA?

Financial or regulatory constraints. Respondents offered a range of situations that they considered ethical dilemmas or challenges. The most frequently mentioned ethical concern involved clients not having sufficient access to services or not receiving appropriate interventions, primarily because of financial or regulatory constraints. Examples of responses related to these constraints included the following:

> It seems as though we are always running up against wanting to promote or encourage client self-determination with the pressure to conform to the standards or rules of outside entities that monitor and fund us. (Julie)

> We really believe in client empowerment. Unfortunately one of our contractors is really, really strict with its guidelines and we couldn't pursue the level of client participation that we really had wanted to. (Linda)

> We have some older psychiatric patients, who have histories of homelessness and chronic mental illness, and the system out there really doesn't, or isn't able to meet their needs. At times we have to discharge people to shelters and we know that they just go right back out onto the street. The hospital and insurance companies will not support interventions that take time. We can't do what we really know should be done. (Joe)

> The worst part of my job is having to enforce regulations, since that can get in the way of actually helping the residents either because it takes too much of my time or a particular rule is too rigid and doesn't allow for empowerment. (Barbara)

In each of these examples, respondents underscore the difficulties of sufficiently and appropriately working with clients because of the constraints of various rules and protocols that, in turn, alter the nature of the social work intervention.

Agency missions and orientations. A related theme is represented in a second cluster of ethical situations that centered on compromised agency missions and orientations, usually because of financial mandates. The difference between this and the prior theme is that the focus is on agency values rather than specific client access. Examples of responses included the following:

> We have a mission which says that we are in the settlement house tradition and we're about social justice and empowering people through advocacy and education and so forth. So I think ethically we need to look at where we're going. There are times when a request for proposals has come out that we are going after because of the money, rather than is it really meeting the mission, and so that's a bit of a struggle. (Frank)

What we're dealing with requires long-term interventions, but I feel as though we mostly do short-term fixes. You can't solve poverty or other problems that immigrants face with a four week program. But that's all we can get funding for. So I guess we've decided its better to stay open than risk that for the sake of pursuing more long-term, deeper changes. (Celeste)

For other respondents, consistency with agency mission is challenged when partnering with another organization that may not share some or all of the agency's core values. Sara, who oversees a domestic violence program, identified the issue of providing educational trainings as part of a lead agency's program in which some principles were at odds with those of her organization:

Working with the [XYZ] agency definitely presented problems because it is a program that imparts some values that we don't necessarily agree with. So it's a question about—do we want to have sort of a purist stance and decide we are not going to associate ourselves at all with this work or are we going to say well, its better for us to at least be able to infuse some of our philosophy into the program, even if it means we can't really have a purist stance. And I think there are issues that come up like this all the time which are tricky and they don't have black or white answers and we have to talk them over and struggle. And some in our agency said that they wouldn't participate because they were so uncomfortable. That was okay; we still did the presentations but didn't mandate staff involvement.

Staff competencies. A third grouping of ethical concerns involved various aspects of staff competency and performance and underscored the challenges that human service managers encounter as supervisors. In the following example, the dilemma related to compliance with regulations or mandates is expressed:

I have a model of empowerment and engagement with staff. Everyone has a say. But then there are things that we have no choice in, we have to do them. We can bitch and moan and debate about breaking the rules, and in the end we grit our teeth and do what is required of us. But it can be exhausting to have to keep reminding, and at times, nagging staff to do what they need to do. And these stupid reports just get in the way of us doing the work we do so well. So that

> makes me, and I think everyone, feel ethically challenged. (Ruth)

With respect to practice skills, cultural competency was the primary area of concern for the respondents, with several respondents noting how difficult it was to get staff engaged in this aspect of professional development. In many respects, Beth echoed the sentiments of others: "It's hard to get staff to take diversity training seriously or at least for them to take the time to learn. But I think it is unethical for staff to be racially unaware." Problems with organizational members also extended to the actions of superiors. Evan cited the following problems with how organizational management mandated training for everyone but themselves:

> I get really frustrated because the top management along with the board mandates diversity training, but then they don't participate. This results in staff backlash and an unwill-ingness to engage in cross-cultural work because they [staff] feel forced to do it. So that's an ethical problem. And I sup-pose what I think of as the abuse of power by the executive and the board would also be unethical. In the end, it cost us our team building and undermined our diversity initiative.

Some respondents reflected on their own competencies and how that related to ethical practice. For example, Sandy noted, "I'm not sure that it's really ethical for me to be doing community engagement work. I was trained as a clinician and when I got promoted [into current supervisor position] I was asked to do outreach and I just don't know what I'm doing."

Environment. Finally, several respondents suggested that the external environments in which they operated were unethical. For example, Evelyn noted that the politics of being part of a city system was "one giant ethical headache, but you just have to deal with it." Broadening the scope, Andrew said it was "ethically bad to have a prison located right in the neighborhood, because it sends the wrong message to kids." Darnell cited the "damage that drugs do on our community, especially our children, which is a big ethical problem because it's all so wrong." On a slightly different track, Rick thought it was unethical for community residents to not be involved or participate in the life of their community.

HOW ARE ETHICAL DILEMMAS RESOLVED?

Peer consultation. Respondents primarily engaged in one of three processes to address ethical concerns. The first can be categorized as peer consultation. Jessica offered the following rationale for seeking this type of assistance: "If I made a decision [about an ethical issue] in a vacuum without consultation from either other staff members or consumers or leaders of consumer groups, then I'm not serving my population the best that I can."

Often, the decision to engage in peer consultation is situational. That is, as a result of a given set of circumstances, respondents sought out assistance and guidance from various individuals or groups. For example:

> I think [resolving ethical dilemmas] is different for different issues. I think for some issues our strategy is just sitting down and having a conversation and making an agreement as a group and I think, when possible, that's what we try to do. I think that with other issues I think it does come down to what the director feels needs to happen. I think particularly when it is a more public issue in which our name is going to be out there, that it will be a decision made by somebody who is in management. (Sara)

In another case, the decision to engage in peer consultation was quite informal: "One thing I like about this agency is that you can talk to anyone about your concerns. And I do. Whoever is available, that's who I bounce ideas around with" (Jose).

Emily provided an example of a more purposeful decision-making process to engage in peer consultation. She worked for a feminist organization that had received an invitation from the Playboy Foundation to apply for program funds, which meant having to weigh taking the money versus upholding feminist ideals. Emily and the executive director (who also held an MSW) facilitated discussions with the other staff, the board, and their political peers in the community before making a decision. They chose not to apply for the money because it would be too much of a political liability in feminist and progressive circles. Similarly, Deanna noted that she and other staff "engage in continuous group dialogue and analysis that link programs to social change goals, so we can monitor whether we are staying true to our mission." Note that, in both examples, the decision-making process was grounded in a political ideal.

Policies and regulations. In contrast, a second means of resolving ethical dilemmas is the following of orders. With this strategy, practitioners essentially deferred to agency policy or chain of command, outside regulations, or funder requirements. Examples of these ethical dilemmas include the following:

> I work at the pleasure of the mayor, so what he says to do, I do even if I might disagree. And since we're regulated, you pretty much stay within regulations and policies. (Mike)

> I do what my supervisor wants and my staff does what I want. (Nancy)

> Funder restrictions [for client access to services] always seem to take precedent. We really want some of these people, who need our services, to get them but our funding source doesn't allow them [active substance abusers] to attend the programs and get help. It's frustrating, but we need the money. (Marian)

This latter approach to resolving ethical dilemmas externalized the decision-making process. Although some practitioners expressed some regret over decisions "having" to be made in this way, they did not convey any urgency or willingness to alter the process. Rather, some seemed relieved that another person or entity had made the decision for them.

Commitment based on faith. The final process that the practitioners used is having faith, which typically (though not exclusively) involved prayer or some other form of spiritual guidance. For example, Ted, who was worried about the "displacement of poor folks through economic development," spoke of his "faith commitment" to serving the poor and often "prayed for guidance in dealing with the economic fall-out of development." Similarly, Tom tried to understand how to address concerns by invoking "the mission spirit" as noted in the following example:

> I get in touch with the mission spirit—talking about seeking the guidance of God. This is part of the [agency's] mission: seeking God's guidance and believing we are responsible to each other as members of one family. That's how I deal with problems. I see what God has to say about it, and encourage my staff to do the same.

Along secular lines, the more activist-oriented practitioners manifested deep faith in a principle, such as antiracism or social justice, and this commitment helped them disentangle ethical dilemmas. The following is an example of this latter commitment to faith:

> I always keep in mind my goal of peace and justice and what will get us there. There are not a lot of moments when working for these things that you feel a great sense of satisfaction, and so you have to, for your mental health, you have to figure out how to stay the course. For me, what I've often said is, I do this, because I can't *not* do it. Physically I think that I probably just have to do it, and I remember what Gandhi said, "You may never see the fruits of your labor." I hold that in my head. (Emma)

Interestingly, none of the practitioners indicated that they employed any of the decision-making frameworks mentioned in much of the social work ethics literature. A few practitioners, however, seemed to follow some type of value ranking, placing "best interest of the client," social change, or a principle of faith over other considerations. Only one respondent, Marian, made a specific mention to the NASW Code of Ethics as a possible tool for resolving ethical concerns.

None of the practitioners referred to existing literature or evidence to assist in their decision making, though a few referenced prior efforts as rationales for the ways decisions were made. Nor did they convey any confidence that the "right" decision had been made or the preferred outcome achieved. Overall, there was a general lack of systematic and evidence-based protocols for addressing concerns, as if goodwill and luck would suffice: "We are making guesses when we work with the really difficult clients and if we make enough correctly, mathematically we end up in the right place" (Don).

Implications for Ethical Decision Making

Findings from this exploratory study in which human service managers were asked to identify ethical challenges and how they resolved them have several implications. Few respondents identified ethical dilemmas in the truest sense of the definition—that of competing and equally compelling values in a situation that has no perfect resolution (Reamer, 1990; Rhodes, 1991). Instead, more generic problems or challenges were identified as constituting an ethical dilemma. This may indicate a relatively simple or basic approach to ethical practice.

Among the challenges identified, however, the impact of external factors looms over social work practice. Respondents consistently mentioned rules, regulations, and mandates as constraints. The recognition of outside threats is not new (Austin, 2002; Hopkins & Hyde, 2002; Lohmann & Lohmann, 2002), though identifying them as ethical dilemmas might be. With increased privatization and contracted services, these concerns are likely to deepen (Anderson, 2004; Carey, 2007; Healy & Pine, 2007; Lonne et al., 2004; Reamer, 2000a, 2008). Such developments represent a considerable threat to social work, as such external factors often supersede social work values or principles when a decision has to be made. Lonne et al. (2004) similarly noted the erosion of social work values from these environmental threats. Human service managers need to be particularly attuned to these developments because they are often the agency personnel charged with compliance tasks.

Perhaps most significant is the dearth of evidence that respondents provided to indicate that their resolution strategies were grounded in research or practice principles. Rather, a case-by-case approach seemed to be adopted in those instances in which a decision needed to be made, though in a number of instances, there was no true choice because respondents took their cues from rules and regulations. The research findings presented here parallel those of Holland and Kilpatrick (1991), who note in their qualitative study on resolving ethical issues that their respondents did not use the NASW Code of Ethics or another framework to resolve ethical dilemmas and often deferred to some form of authority. Moreover, Holland and Kilpatrick assert that the "profession suffers from a lack of systematic studies of ethics in practice" (p. 138), which suggests that there may not be much in the way of best ethical practices from which social workers can draw.

Decisions about social work practice in organizations ought to reflect, and be guided by, the ethics of the profession. To some extent, key social work standards, such as commitment to social justice and best interests of the client, informed the thinking of those who were interviewed in this research study. Yet they were expressed in a general way rather than as a clear guidepost for ethical resolution. In addition, these were superseded by other considerations, such as regulations, funders, intraorganizational power dynamics, and principles derived from other reference points (e.g., faith). Thus, decisions regarding social work practice seem to be largely informed by non–social work values and procedures. One gets the sense that, in some instances, attempts to enact social work values create more problems given various external factors and barriers.

Decisions should incorporate evidence on what works and what does not, thereby minimizing idiosyncratic or off-the-cuff responses. Overall, respondents in the present study had an almost ahistorical approach to resolving ethical dilemmas.

Summary

Recently, a Pennsylvania grand jury indicted nine individuals in the horrific starvation death of a child who was a client of the Department of Human Services (DHS) (Sullivan & McCoy, 2008; Tanfani, 2008). Among the nine individuals are DHS workers and supervisors, as well as employees of a vendor organization that DHS had contracted to monitor the child's situation. The grand jury's report provides, in graphic detail, the failure of professional human service workers (some of whom the press referred to as social workers) to protect a highly vulnerable child from her abusive and neglectful parents. From the front lines to management, the grand jury's report concluded that if one person had done his or her job, then the child might very well be alive today.

Although this is an extreme case of professional malfeasance and incompetence, it nonetheless provides a cautionary tale in the importance of ethical and evidence-based organizational practice. This is especially the case because staff training, particularly for supervisors, has been emphasized, although much of it appears to focus more on regulatory compliance and less on the analytical skills needed for ethical problem solving. Such an approach is likely to add to the findings of this study in terms of idiosyncratic (i.e., case-by-case) and rule-bound (i.e., directives or requirements) decision-making strategies and a minimization of social work values.

This study suggests that the resolution of ethical challenges and evidence-based practice have not yet been integrated, at least for human service management. Perhaps practitioners assume that when they use an evidence-based practice, they are, in effect, behaving ethically. And it may also be the case that practitioners do not deem evidence important when an ethical determination needs to be made. Regardless, both of these possibilities suggest that managerial practice ethics are not being addressed in thoughtful and substantive ways. Yet a profession's ethics is what gives it a unique identity or sense of purpose. Once that is diminished or lost, then the craft and science of social work is eroded.

References

Aldgate, J., Healy, L., Malcolm, B., Pine, B., Rose, W., & Seden, J. (Eds.). (2007). *Enhancing social work management: Theory and best practice from the U.K. and U.S.A.* Philadelphia: Jessica Kingsley.

Anderson, S. (2004). Developing contracted social service initiatives in small nonprofit agencies: Understanding management dilemmas in uncertain environments. *Families in Society, 85*(4), 454–462.

Austin, M. J. (2002). Managing out: The community practice dimensions of effective agency management. *Journal of Community Practice, 10*(4), 33–48.

Brody, R. (2004). *Effectively managing human service organizations* (3rd ed.). Thousand Oaks, CA: Sage.

Carey, M. (2007). Some ethical dilemmas for agency social workers. *Ethics and Social Welfare, 1*(3), 342–347.

Cassell, C., & Symon, G. (Eds.). (1994). *Qualitative methods in organizational research: A practical guide.* London: Sage.

Charmaz, K. (1983). The grounded theory method. In R. Emerson (Ed.), *Contemporary field research* (pp. 109–126). Boston: Little, Brown.

Charmaz, K. (2006). *Constructing grounded theory: A practical guide through qualitative analysis.* Thousand Oaks, CA: Sage.

Chenitz, W. (1986). Qualitative research using grounded theory. In W. Chenitz & J. Swanson (Eds.), *From practice to grounded theory* (pp. 3–15). Menlo Park, CA: Addison-Wesley.

Chenitz, W., & Swanson, J. (1986). *From practice to grounded theory.* Menlo Park, CA: Addison-Wesley.

Cresswell, J. (1994). *Research design: Qualitative and quantitative approaches.* Thousand Oaks, CA: Sage.

Csikai, E. (2004). Social workers' participation in the resolution of ethical dilemmas in hospice care. *Health and Social Work, 29*(1), 67–76.

Denzin, N. (1989). *The research act: A theoretical introduction to sociological methods* (3rd ed.). Englewood Cliffs, NJ: Prentice Hall.

DiFranks, N. (2008). Social workers and the NASW Code of Ethics: Belief, behavior, disjuncture. *Social Work, 53*(2), 167–176.

Egan, M., & Kadushin, G. (2002). Ethical conflicts over access to services: Patient effects and worker influence in home health. *Social Work in Health Care, 35*(3), 1–21.

Ezell, M. (1994). Advocacy practice of social workers. *Families in Society, 75*(1), 36–46.

Gambrill, E. (2006). Evidence-based practice and policy: Choices ahead. *Research on Social Work Practice, 16*(3), 338–357.

Gibbs, L. E. (2003). *Evidence-based practice for the helping professions: A practical guide with integrated multimedia.* Pacific Grove, CA: Brooks/Cole-Thomson Learning.

Gottlieb, M. (2006). A template for peer ethics consultation. *Ethics and Behavior, 16*(2), 151–162.

Gummer, B. (1990). *The politics of social administration: Managing organizational politics in social agencies.* Englewood Cliffs, NJ: Prentice Hall.

Hardcastle, D., & Powers, P. (2004). *Community practice: Theories and skills for social workers* (2nd ed.). New York: Oxford University Press.

Hardina, D., Middleton, J., Montana, S., & Simpson, R. (2007). *An empowering approach to managing social service organizations.* New York: Springer.

Harrington, D., & Dolgoff, R. (2008). Hierarchies of ethical principles for ethical decision making in social work. *Ethics and Social Welfare, 2*(2), 183–196.

Healy, L. M., & Pine, B. A. (2007). Ethical issues for social work and social care managers. In J. Aldgate, L. Healy, B. Malcolm, B. Pine, W. Rose, & J. Seden (Eds.), *Enhancing social work management: Theory and best practice from the U.K. and U.S.A.* (pp. 81–104). Philadelphia: Jessica Kingsley.

Healy, T. (2003). Ethical decision making: Pressure and uncertainty as complicating factors. *Health and Social Work, 28*(4), 293–301.

Holland, T., & Kilpatrick, A. (1991). Ethical issues in social work: Toward a grounded theory of professional ethics. *Social Work, 36*(2), 138–144.

Homan, M. (2007). *Promoting community change* (4th ed.). New York: Brooks/Cole.

Hopkins, K., & Hyde, C. (2002). The human service dilemma: New expectations, chronic challenges and old solutions. *Administration in Social Work, 26*(3), 1–15.

Jansson, B., & Dodd, S. (2002). Ethical activism: Strategies for empowering medical social workers. *Social Work in Health Care, 36*(1), 11–28.

Jones, J. M. (2006). Understanding environmental influence on human service organizations: A study of the influence of managed care on child caring institutions. *Administration in Social Work, 30*(4), 63–90.

Kettner, P., Moroney, R., & Martin, L. (2007). *Designing and managing programs: An effectiveness-based approach*. Thousand Oaks, CA: Sage.

Kirkpatrick, W., Reamer, F., & Sykulski, M. (2006). Social work ethics audits in health care settings: A case study. *Health and Social Work, 31*(3), 225–228.

Landau, R. (1999). Professional socialization, ethical judgment and decision making orientation in social work. *Journal of Social Service Research, 25*(4), 57–75.

Landau, R. (2000). Ethical dilemmas in general hospitals: Differential perceptions of direct practitioners and directors of social services. *Social Work in Health Care, 30*(4), 25–44.

Landau, R., & Osmo, R. (2003). Professional and personal hierarchies of ethical principles. *International Journal of Social Welfare, 12*(1), 42–49.

Lee, R. (1999). *Using qualitative methods in organizational research*. Thousand Oaks, CA: Sage.

Locke, K. (2001). *Grounded theory in management research*. Thousand Oaks, CA: Sage.

Loewenberg, F., Dolgoff, R., & Harrington, D. (2000). *Ethical decisions for social work practice* (6th ed.). Itasca, IL: F. E. Peacock.

Lohmann, R. A., & Lohmann, N. (2002). *Social administration*. New York: Columbia University Press.

Lonne, B., McDonald, C., & Fox, T. (2004). Ethical practice in the contemporary human services. *Journal of Social Work, 4*(3), 345–367.

Lynch, J., & Versen, G. (2003). Social work supervisor liability: Risk factors and strategies for risk reduction. *Administration in Social Work, 27*(2), 57–71.

McAuliffe, D. (2005). Putting ethics on the organisational agenda: The social work ethics audit on trial. *Australian Social Work, 58*(4), 357–369.

Millstein, K. (2000). Confidentiality in direct social work practice: Inevitable challenges and ethical dilemmas. *Families in Society, 81*(3), 270–282.

Moberg, D. (2006). Ethics blind spots in organizations: How systematic errors in person perception undermine moral agency. *Organization Studies, 27*(3), 413–428.

Moberg, D. (2007). Practical wisdom and business ethics. *Business Ethics Quarterly, 17*(3), 535–561.

Moberg, D., & Velasquez, M. (2006). Best intentions, worst results: Grounding ethics students in the realities of organizational context. *Academy of Management Learning and Education, 5*(3), 307–316.

National Association of Social Workers. (1996). *Code of ethics.* Washington, DC: Author.

National Network for Social Work Managers. (2005). *Competency areas.* Retrieved January 10, 2010, from http://www.socialworkmanager.org/standards.php?id=competencies.

Netting, F. E., Kettner, P., & McMurtry, S. (1993). *Social work macro practice.* New York: Longman.

O'Hare, T. (2005). *Evidence-based practices for social workers: An interdisciplinary approach.* Chicago: Lyceum Books.

Patti, R. (Ed.). (2000). *The handbook of social welfare management.* Thousand Oaks, CA: Sage.

Peters, H. (2008). Theory, science, ideology and ethics in social work. *Ethics and Social Welfare, 2*(2), 172–182.

Reamer, F. (1990). *Ethical dilemmas in social service* (2nd ed.). New York: Columbia University Press.

Reamer, F. (2000a). Administrative ethics. In R. Patti (Ed.), *The handbook of social welfare management* (pp. 69–85). Thousand Oaks, CA: Sage.

Reamer, F. (2000b). The social work ethics audit: A risk-management strategy. *Social Work, 45*(4), 355–366.

Reamer, F. (2001). *Tangled relationships: Managing boundary issues in the human services.* New York: Columbia University Press.

Reamer, F. (2003). Boundary issues in social work: Managing dual relationships. *Social Work, 48*(1), 121–133.

Reamer, F. (2004). Ethical decisions and risk management. In M. Austin & K. Hopkins (Eds.), *Supervision as collaboration in the human services: Building a learning culture* (pp. 97–109). Thousand Oaks, CA: Sage.

Reamer, F. (2005a). Documentation in social work: Evolving ethical and risk-management standards. *Social Work, 50*(4), 325–334.

Reamer, F. (2005b). Ethical and legal standards in social work: Consistency and conflict. *Families in Society, 86*(2), 163–169.

Reamer, F. (2008). Social workers' management of error: Ethical and risk management issues. *Families in Society, 89*(1), 61–68.

Reinsch, N. (1996). Management communication ethics research. *Management Communication Quarterly, 9*(3), 349–358.

Rhodes, M. (1991). *Ethical dilemmas in social work practice.* Milwaukee, WI: Family Service of America.

Roberts, A., & Yeager, K. (2004). Systematic reviews of evidence-based studies and practice-based research: How to search for, develop, and use them. In A. Roberts & K. Yeager (Eds.), *Evidence-based practice manual: Research and outcome measures in health and human services* (pp. 3–14). New York: Oxford University Press.

Schwepker, C. (2001). Ethical climate's relationship to job satisfaction, organizational commitment, and turnover intention in the sales force. *Journal of Business Research, 54*(1), 39–52.

Strauss, A., & Corbin, J. (1990). *Basics of qualitative research.* Newbury Park, CA: Sage.

Strom-Gottfried, K. (2003). Understanding adjudication: Origins, targets, and outcomes of ethics complaints. *Social Work, 48*(1), 85–94.

Sullivan, J., & McCoy, C. (2008, August 1). Nine charged in deadly neglect: DHS's care for an ailing girl was lacking, and she died. *Philadelphia Inquirer*, pp. 1, 14, 15.

Tanfani, J. (2008, August 1). Nine charged in deadly neglect: Documents were forged, and falsified, report says. *Philadelphia Inquirer*, pp. 1, 15.

Walden, T., Wolock, I., & Demone, H. (1990). Ethical decision making in human services: A comparative study. *Families in Society*, 71(2), 67–75.

Worthington, R., Tan, J., & Poulin, K. (2002). Ethically questionable behaviors among supervisees: An exploratory investigation. *Ethics and Behavior*, 12(4), 323–351.

Yang, J., & Kombarakaran, F. (2006). A practitioner's response to the new health privacy regulations. *Health and Social Work*, 31(2), 129–136.

CHAPTER FOUR

Importance of Social Workers in Hospital Emergency Departments

An Evidence-Based Perspective

Charles Auerbach and Susan E. Mason

Statement of the Problem

This chapter reports a study in which social workers assigned to a hospital emergency department systematically collected data to evaluate the effect of their intervention on discharge-planning outcomes. The findings suggest that social workers perform valuable services to both the consumers and the hospital. Emergency room personnel triaged patients according to clinical and environmental factors. When clinical conditions permitted, social workers found alternative levels of care, thereby saving patients the stress of unneeded medical hospitalizations and keeping hospitals from admitting patients with difficult-to-discharge profiles.

The evidence-based practice model has traditionally focused on grounding clinical practice in evidence that is identified by positing a practice question and then answering it by conducting a review of empirical studies (Roberts, Yeager, & Regehr, 2006). Through this process, the appraisal and selection of a best-practice intervention is integrated with practice expertise while considering the values and circumstances of the clients. Then this evidence is used to inform practice (O'Hare, 2005).

Strictly speaking, this study can be referred to as service systems research because the interventions, though clinical, apply to the functioning of a hospital department, not to individuals (Shern & Evans, 2005). Further, the social workers collected the evidence in a noncontrolled environment. Nevertheless, this study provides some evidence to inform the delivery of health-care services in the context of an emergency room in a hospital setting.

Literature Review

SOCIAL WORKERS IN HOSPITALS

A survey conducted under the auspices of the National Association of Social Workers (NASW) reported that 12.2 percent of licensed social workers worked in hospitals, and 72 percent of their time was devoted to direct patient contact (Whitaker, Weismiller, Clark, & Wilson, 2006). The number of social workers assigned to emergency departments is unknown, as there are no national data available. What we do know is that there has been an overall decline in the number of hospital social work departments in the United States. A recent review of hospital social work leadership concluded that cutbacks and a pervasive devaluation of social work services in the health system severely challenge social work administrators (Mizrahi & Berger, 2005). The struggle to maintain a social work identity in hospitals has also been experienced in Canada (Globerman, Davies, & Walsh, 1996; Globerman, White, Mullings, & Davies, 2003). In both the United States and Canada, there is a trend to place social workers in hospital departments and then have them report directly to nursing staff or medical doctors in the hospital.

Social workers are often assigned to hospital units such as HIV, cardiology, or pediatrics, where they become specialized providers. As members of multidisciplinary teams in specialized departments, social workers share with other disciplines the traditional social work assignments of family counseling, case management, and discharge planning. On a team, the social worker is usually the most skilled in these practice areas, and when difficult patients are identified, social workers are often assigned to manage the care plan. Their role is to counsel the most difficult patients and their families and to negotiate appropriate discharge plans (Auerbach, Mason, & Heft-LaPorte, 2007).

LINKS TO THE COMMUNITY FROM THE EMERGENCY ROOM

Knowledge about community resources is a key component to achieving an effective and efficient discharge plan for patients from emergency rooms (Bristow & Herrick, 2002; Freedman, Joubert, & Russell,

2005). This is where social workers excel. Their knowledge of the community resources coupled with their assessment skills enable them to negotiate successful discharges to levels of care that are both available and appropriate. It has been shown that social workers in emergency departments who have extensive links to community resources have reduced the rate of hospital admissions (Freedman et al., 2005). It has also been shown that social workers can reduce emergency room recidivism by linking patients to appropriate community resources (Keehn, Roglitz, & Bowden, 1994). One study that aimed to reduce pediatric emergency visits by having social workers refer families to primary-care pediatric services in the community resulted in successful outcomes (Ross, Roberts, Campbell, Solomon, & Brouhard, 2004). Data suggest that social workers have saved hospitals money by averting admissions and reducing unnecessary time spent with medical staff. This was especially true for larger emergency departments, but small departments also benefited (Gordon, 2001).

Even though there are a limited number of studies on the effectiveness of having social workers in emergency departments, it appears that social workers do make an important contribution. Positive experiences in the United Kingdom with social workers in medical emergency rooms have led researchers, such as Bywaters and McLeod (2003), to suggest that more large-scale studies are needed to strengthen the case for using social workers in emergency departments

Methodology

The aim of this study was to explore whether the referral of emergency room patients to social workers affected hospital admissions, lengths of stay, and discharges from the emergency room to home or other health-care-related facilities. Types of problems that patients presented in the emergency department and patient demographics were important factors in investigating the effect of social work services on helping patients achieve desired outcomes.

SAMPLE

Three years of discharge-planning data were collected from self-reports that social workers prepared in a medical emergency room at a large, teaching hospital in the metropolitan New York area. The sample consisted of 3,370 patients who were admitted to the emergency room and received services from a social worker between January 1, 2001, and December 31, 2004.

Demographic characteristics of the patients were obtained from data from the hospital's intake system. The mean age of the sample was 48.9 years (standard deviation [*SD*] = 28.2 years). A quarter of the sample was younger than eighteen years of age, and a third was seventy years or older. Most of the patients were female (59.7 percent, n = 2,011) and white (56.53 percent, n = 1,554). African Americans represented 33.28 percent of patients (n = 915), Hispanics represented 4.8 percent (n = 188), Asians represented 2.87 percent (n = 79), and other represented 0.5 percent (n = 13). For 621 patients, race was unknown. Most patients, 58.1 percent (n = 1,959), were single, but 21.6 percent were married (n = 727), 15.7 percent were widowed (n = 524), and 3.7 percent (n = 124) were divorced. For thirty-six patients, marital status was not known. The results of a two-tailed t-test indicted that patients referred to social work did differ in age, with a mean age of 48.9 years (n = 3,370) compared to 30.5 years (n = 215,639) for those who did not see a social worker, t = 44.3, p < .0001 (two tailed). They did not differ significantly on gender, marital status, or race.

Although we do not have detailed demographic information about the social workers, it is important to note that all social workers in the acute care and emergency departments in the hospital had earned MSW degrees. Two full-time workers and one part-time bilingual (Spanish) worker were assigned to the emergency department. All three workers at the time of this study were certified by the State of New York. It was the hospital's policy that all social workers be certified within one year of being hired by the hospital.

DATA COLLECTION

A scan sheet was completed for each patient whom a social worker saw on discharge from the emergency room. This sheet consisted of data related to prior living arrangement, discharge disposition, type of problem, and interventions. Types of problems were classified under seven major categories. Examples of items within each category included the following: (1) care and activities of daily living (ADL) (e.g., home supports, skilled professional care, placement of patient), (2) relationships (e.g., spouse/partner, family, parent-child), (3) environment (e.g., financial, insurance and medical coverage, housing), (4) behavior (e.g., substance abuse; thought, mood, and personality; self-esteem and depression); (5) suspected abuse (e.g., child physical, child neglect, adult physical), (6) patient family adjustment (e.g., adjustment to acute illness, adjustment to hospital, adjustment to placement), and (7) legal (e.g., power of attorney, health-care proxy, guardian).

Findings

Data were not collected on the dispositions of patients whom a social worker did not see in the hospital's emergency department. Of the 3,370 patients in the emergency department who were referred to a social worker, more than half (54 percent) returned home on discharge, whereas 16.2 percent were admitted to the hospital, and 8.4 percent were discharged to a nursing facility.

The study explored the differences between the two groups, those patients whom a social worker saw and those patients whom a social worker did not see in the emergency department. Two-tailed t-tests were used to test the differences between the groups on age, length of stay, and type of discharge problem. Patients whom a social worker saw and admitted to the hospital had a mean length of stay of 7.6 days (SD = 9.9) compared to 5.0 days (SD = 9.8) for those whom a social worker did not see, t = 8.7, $p < .001$ (two tailed). Patients whom a social worker saw and admitted to the hospital had a slightly higher mean age of 50.3 years compared to 48.2 years for those whom a social worker did not see, t = 1.7, $p > .05$ (two tailed). Almost 19 percent (18.8 percent) of white patients were admitted to the hospital, compared to 12.1 percent of African American patients and 18.6 percent of Hispanic patients. Therefore, Hispanic patients had a similar admission rate to that of white patients, χ^2 (2, N = 2,657) = 19.21, p = .000. Marital status and gender did not increase the likelihood of admission to the hospital.

Figure 4.1 depicts types of problems that appear to have an influence on who was admitted to the hospital. In Figure 4.1, the x-axis represents the number of problems that the patients had, and the y-axis displays the percentage of patients with those problems. For example, more than 60 percent of the patients admitted had at least one ADL problem.

For the purpose of analysis, the numbers of items within a problem were counted. For example, a patient could have between zero and nine care and/or ADL discharge-related problems. Table 4.1 displays the mean problem type by admit status (admitted or not admitted to the hospital). Four of the seven problem areas had statistically significant differences according to t-test scores, including (1) relationships, (2) environment, (3) behavior, and (4) suspected abuse. Patients who were not admitted to the hospital had higher mean scores than patients who were admitted for the following problems: relationships (.19 compared to .09) and environment (.92 compared to .75). In contrast, patients who were admitted to the hospital had higher mean scores than patients who were not admitted for the following problems: behavior (.58 compared to .30) and suspected abuse (.63 compared to .39).

A binary logistic regression analysis was conducted to find the best-fitting model for the type of disposition (admitted or not admitted).

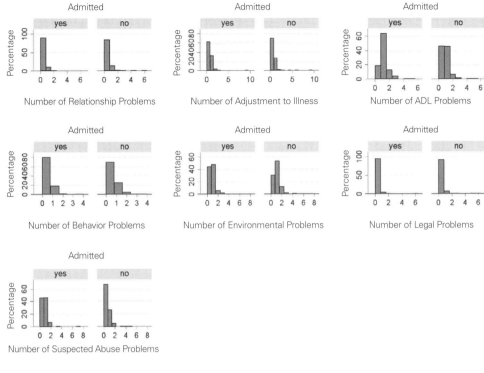

FIGURE 4.1. *Admitted by type of discharge problem*

TABLE 4.1.   **Mean problem type by admit status**

| | Patients admitted to hospital | | | | | | | |
| | No | | | Yes | | | | |
Problem type	M	SD	n	M	SD	n	t	p
Care/ADL	.67	.71	2823	.71	.72	547	1.38	.17
Relationship	.19	.45	2823	.09	.32	547	4.59	.00
Environment	.92	.84	2823	.75	.71	547	4.45	.00
Behavior	.30	.5	2823	.58	.63	547	10.34	.00
Suspected abuse	.39	.64	2823	.63	.69	547	7.75	.00
Adjustment	.35	.65	2823	.34	.74	547	.43	.69
Legal	.10	.39	2823	.07	.44	547	1.47	.14

This method provides the odds or probability of the occurrence and/or nonoccurrence of an outcome (admitted or not admitted) based on the influence of predictor variables (covariates). The rationale for using this technique is the development of a profile of patients who were most likely to be admitted to the hospital. Thus, an estimate of the probability of admission to the hospital can be projected. The odds-ratio estimates confirm the assumption that problems related to care and/or ADL, behavior, relationships, and environment are associated with the likelihood of being admitted to the hospital from an emergency room (Table 4.2).

The dependent variable, admitted to the hospital, was coded as 1 for admitted and 0 for all other dispositions. The indicators used were age in years and gender (0 = female, and 1 = male); race was dummy coded as African American, Hispanic, and white ("Asians and other" served as the reference category); and married was coded as 1 for yes and 0 for no (alone). The types of problems were entered as continuous variables. As Table 4.2 depicts, none of the background variables, age, gender, race, or marital status was statistically significant.

In contrast, the problems care and/or ADL, relationships, behavior, and environment were statistically significant. The odds ratios indicate that care and/or ADL (odds = 1.3) increases the likelihood of admission. For every ADL problem, there is a 30 percent increase in the odds of admission. For example, the odds of a patient with two ADL problems being admitted increase by 60 percent (2 × 30 percent). In fact, for every

TABLE 4.2.   Logistic regression: Dependent variable of patients admitted to hospital

Covariates	Coefficient	z	P	Odds ratio
Gender	−0.11917	−1.071	0.284	0.8877
Age	−0.00315	−1.398	0.162	0.9969
African American	−0.28554	−0.883	0.377	0.7516
Hispanic	0.21969	0.608	0.543	1.2457
White	0.19999	0.633	0.526	1.2214
Married/alone	0.10393	0.769	0.442	1.1095
Care/ADL	0.25747	3.400	0.001	1.2936
Relationship	−0.91486	−5.173	0.000	0.4006
Environment	−0.34149	−4.513	0.000	0.7107
Suspected abuse	0.12177	0.940	0.347	1.1295
Adjustment	−0.00936	−0.097	0.923	0.9907
Legal	−0.11125	−0.610	0.542	0.8947
Behavior	0.68251	4.944	0.000	1.9788

behavior problem (odds = 1.98), the odds of admission increase by 98 percent. On the contrary, when relationship problems (odds = .40) or environment problems (odds = .71) are present, the chances of admission decrease.

Implications for Practice Decisions

The data in the present study suggest that most social work dispositions were discharge plans for the patient to return home (54 percent) rather than be admitted to the hospital. What is remarkable is that only 16 percent of the patients who saw a social worker were admitted to the hospital. With an emphasis on cost containment in hospitals, these findings support the cost-effective nature of social work services in a medical emergency setting. Preventing unnecessary admissions helps alleviate growing problems of availability of beds for patients in a hospital and costs associated with hospitalization.

Furthermore, the results of the logistic regression suggest that the criteria that social workers used to assess patients are based on sound psychosocial criteria. Patients who are assessed as having problems related to the environment or with relationships are much less likely to be admitted. In contrast, patients with care and/or ADL or behavior problems have an increased chance of admission. Many of the cases assigned to social workers usually involve an array of factors beyond the scope of services that a traditional medical provider provides, which further confirms the importance of social work services in acute-care hospitals (Auerbach et al., 2007).

In addition to stressing the importance of social work services in a medical emergency department, this study confirms the value of using evidence to inform practice. In the present study, the data set was originally created to make the case for including social workers on a multidisciplinary team in a hospital emergency department. Yet beyond that, the data tell an important story. Patients with problems related to relationships or the environment who are not in need of medical emergency care are best not admitted to the hospital. This emphasizes the need for staff in hospital settings to have knowledge about and links to community resources. It also calls attention to the work that social workers do with families in guiding them to accepting community-based care rather than hospitalization.

Practice-based research can contribute to building a knowledge base that can improve the quality of care for patients in medical settings. Research projects that are expanded to include multiple sites are even more valuable because they could provide additional numbers and diversity to the study of care in emergency departments. This study affirms both the importance of social work services in hospital settings and the value of research informing practice. The evidence from the present study suggests that short-term care and discharge planning are essential social work skills. As the debate related to universal health care intensifies in the United States, the role and responsibilities of medical social workers should be promoted and supported. Well-trained social workers have the ability to effect change in hospital settings.

References

Auerbach, C., Mason, S. E., & Heft-LaPorte, H. (2007). Evidence that supports the value of social work in hospitals. *Social Work in Health Care, 44*(4), 17–32.

Bristow, D. P., & Herrick, C. A. (2002). Emergency department case management: The dyad team of nurse case manager and social worker improve discharge planning and patient and staff satisfaction while decreasing inappropriate admissions and costs: A literature review. *Lippincott's Case Management, 7*(3), 121–128.

Bywaters, P., & McLeod, E. (2003). Social care's impact on emergency medicine: A model to test. *Emergency Medicine Journal, 20*(2), 134–137.

Freedman, C., Joubert, L., & Russell, N. (2005). Practitioner evaluation of a brief intervention approach in emergency services: The Sunshine Hospital quick response team. *Journal of Social Work Research and Evaluation, 6*(2), 207–216.

Globerman, J., Davies, J. M., & Walsh, S. (1996). Social work in restructuring hospitals: Meeting the challenge. *Health and Social Work, 21*(3), 178–188.

Globerman, J., White, J. J., Mullings, D., & Davies, J. M. (2003). Thriving in program management environments: The case of social work in hospitals. *Social Work in Health Care, 38*(1), 1–18.

Gordon, J. A. (2001). Cost-benefit analysis of social work services in the emergency department. *Academic Emergency Medicine, 8*(1), 54–60.

Keehn, D. S., Roglitz, C., & Bowden, M. L. (1994). Impact of social work on recidivism and non-medical complaints in the emergency department. *Social Work in Health Care, 20*(1), 65–75.

Mizrahi, T., & Berger, C. (2005). A longitudinal look at social work leadership in hospitals: The impact of a changing health care system. *Health and Social Work, 30*(2), 155–165.

O'Hare, T. (2005). *Evidence-based practices for social workers.* Chicago: Lyceum Books.

Roberts, A. R., Yeager, K., & Regehr, C. (2006). Bridging evidence-based health care and social work. In A. R. Roberts & K. R. Yeager (Eds.), *Foundations of evidence-based social work practice* (pp. 3–20). New York: Oxford University Press.

Ross, J. W., Roberts, D., Campbell, J., Solomon, K. S., & Brouhard, B. H. (2004). Effects of social work intervention on nonemergent pediatric emergency department utilization. *Health and Social Work, 29*(4), 263–273.

Shern, D. L., & Evans, M. E. (2005). The importance of research in mental health service delivery. In R. E. Drake, M. R. Merrens, & D. L. Lynde (Eds.), *Evidence-based mental health practice* (pp. 123–139). New York: Norton.

Whitaker, T., Weismiller, T., Clark, E., & Wilson, M. (2006). *Assuring the sufficiency of a front line workforce: A national study of licensed social workers.* Washington, DC: National Association of Social Workers.

CHAPTER FIVE

Long-Term-Care Ombudsman Program

Challenges of Accessing and Comparing Secondary Databases

F. Ellen Netting, Kevin Borders, H. Wayne Nelson, and Ruth Huber

Statement of the Problem

During the 1990s, a number of converging forces pushed health and human service providers toward greater accountability to their various stakeholders. Kettner, Moroney, and Martin (1999) described how "these concerns [about accountability] became part of a national debate, and funding agencies at all levels began to require that service providers develop mechanisms to respond to these issues" (p. 3). In 1993, Congress passed the Government Performance and Results Act (GPRA) (Pub. Law No. 103–62), which required all levels of government to develop performance measures. This became a driving force for federally funded programs to develop measurable outcomes (Kautz, Netting, Huber, Borders, & Davis, 1997). One federal program blown forward in the winds of greater accountability was the Long-Term-Care Ombudsman Program (LTCOP), a national long-term-care advocacy program.

The authors acknowledge the assitance of Abigail Kauffman Wyche in locating state Web sites and in tirelessly searching for annual reports.

At first blush, the idea of being more accountable is a goal most practitioners would embrace. Developing mechanisms to carry out that accountability is a logical next step in achieving this goal. However, it is the implementation of GPRA-mandated accountability mechanisms that test a program's ability to articulate performance measures and then fully implement feasible data-collection methods. This is a hard and tedious process.

For the LTCOP, the development of a national database across all states, districts, and territories sounds ideal, but the cultures in each state ombudsman unit are based on different politics and dynamics. Complicating the situation is that most state units oversee regional (local) ombudsmen, hundreds of whom are volunteers (Huber, Borders, Netting, & Kautz, 2000). These differences across states create the potential for infidelity, and the fact that data are aggregated at each level (regional, then state, then federal) means that the capacity for analysis becomes more limited, unless access to raw data is available and analyses that are viewed as relevant to regional programs can be performed.

This chapter presents the challenge of accessing national databases and the transportability and fidelity issues related to using information from those databases. On the basis of an analysis of those databases, we present here a set of practice guidelines that can be used to support changes in advocacy efforts to improve the quality of long-term care.

BACKGROUND

Congress established the LTCOP in 1972 as a Public Health Service demonstration project designed to respond to growing concerns about nursing-home quality of care. In 1978, the LTCOP became a mandated part of the Older Americans Act (Pub. Law No. 89–73), which required each state to develop its own program (Estes, Zulman, Goldberg, & Ogawa, 2004). In the 1992 reauthorization of the act, the LTCOP was transferred from title III to title VII, Vulnerable Elder Rights Protection Activities, symbolizing congressional recognition that residents of long-term-care facilities are vulnerable to abuse, neglect, and exploitation (Harris-Wehling, Feasley, & Estes, 1995; Netting, Huber, Paton, & Kautz, 1995). Today, all fifty states; Washington, D.C.; and the territories of Guam and Puerto Rico have ombudsman programs, most of which operate out of state units on aging and most of which have regional (local) ombudsmen (both paid and volunteer).

Ombudsmen were originally mandated to identify, investigate, and resolve individual complaints, as well as attempt to identify and address the broader, underlying causes of problems that affect residents in long-term-care facilities. In some states, over the years, their scope of practice expanded to include board and care homes, as well as home- and community-based services. Ombudsmen are located in various agencies in local communities throughout the country (Huber, Netting, & Kautz, 1996).

Originally, there was no formal complaint-reporting system, although ombudsmen were encouraged to use a recommended reporting form. Thus, it was not possible to evaluate a local or state program, much less compare what was happening in other states. As more researchers chimed in, it became clear that states needed guidance and assistance in developing comprehensive reporting systems for the LTCOP (*GAO 160*, 1991; Huber, Netting, & Paton, 1993; Netting, Paton, & Huber, 1992; U.S. Department of Health and Human Services, 1991).

Concerned about the lack of a comprehensive complaint reporting system within and across states, in 1994, the Administration on Aging (AOA) awarded a grant to one of the authors to conduct a pilot study involving five states. The outcome from this study was the development of a revised complaint-reporting tool and accompanying software for national distribution to ombudsmen. This moved the program closer toward evaluating local ombudsman programs and creating a local program-focused empirical base from which data could drive future interventions. Attending to the process of developing a more sophisticated complaint-reporting system, many lessons learned in developing alliances with ombudsmen, administrators, and other practitioners were reported. Working toward developing comparable data so that state and national analyses could be conducted, paired with sensitivity to idiosyncratic needs in state and local programs, proved a complex process (Huber, Borders, Netting, & Kautz, 1997). In 1995, the Institute of Medicine (IOM) reported on a study of the LTCOP's effectiveness, reiterating that the program needed a better complaint reporting system (Harris-Wehling, Feasley, & Estes, 1995) and lending credence to database development.

By October 1996, the AOA-mandated National Ombudsman Reporting System (NORS) designed a reporting form that every state was required to use. This standardized form contained a typology of 133 complaints developed by AOA in collaboration with state and local ombudsmen. The 133 complaint categories were placed under five general headings: (1) resident rights, (2) resident care, (3) quality of life, (4) administration, and (5) problems not related to the facilities in which residents live (i.e., other agencies, systems or people) (Huber et al., 2000).

Literature Review

In the 1970s and 1980s, there was limited research on the ombudsman programs (Buford, 1984; Monk, Kaye, & Litwin, 1984). During the 1990s, before a national database had been established, researchers studied various aspects of the LTCOP, sometimes using state-level ombudsman complaint data (Cherry, 1993; Connor & Winkelpleck, 1990; Huber et al., 1993; Nathanson & Eggleton, 1993; Nelson, 1995; Nelson, Huber, & Walter, 1995), and nursing-home scandals precipitated a number of governmental studies (e.g., U.S. Department of Health and Human Services, 1993). The AOA requested that the National Long Term Care Ombudsman Resource Center, a joint venture of the National Association of State Units on Aging (NASUA) and the National Citizens Coalition on Nursing Home Reform conduct studies (see NASUA, 1993). "Until the mid-1990s, research focused primarily on single state and local program studies or historical-policy pieces" (Estes et al., 2004, p. 105).

With the development of NORS in 1995, research using state-level, program-specific complaint data became more feasible. For example, Keith (2001) analyzed correlates of reporting complaints ($n = 1,866$) by 633 volunteer ombudsmen in one Midwestern state. Keith found that "the number of complaints volunteers reported on behalf of nursing facility residents were outcomes of their work and were a more objective measure than were feelings about their experiences" (p. 44).

Huber, Borders, Netting, and Nelson (2001) examined the relationships among race, gender, and types of complaints lodged, verified, and fully resolved. They used a six-state ombudsman database ($n = 23,787$ complaints) from 1996. The results indicated that a greater percentage of verified complaints were lodged on behalf of racial minorities but a lower percentage was fully resolved. They found that physical abuse appeared in the top five most frequently reported complaints for four racial and gender groups: (1) Caucasian men, (2) Caucasian women, (3) African American men, and (4) African American women. Minority men had reported gross neglect and unresponsive staff. Minority women had reported unresponsive staff, unattended symptoms, and wandering. In contrast, these complaints were not reported as often for Caucasian men and women. Huber et al. noted that the mandated ombudsman reporting form did not require the collection of resident demographics, and argued that the collection of these data would allow ombudsmen to watch for patterns and "trends from the data to prevent further maltreatment" (p. 65). Still, despite this shortcoming, Kautz (2002) noted that Huber et al.'s study was able to make a valuable contribution about gender and racial and ethnic differences because it was able to drill down into disaggregated state data.

Huber, Borders, Badrak, Netting, and Nelson (2001) proposed national standards, as recommended by the aforementioned 1995 IOM study, and introduced the Huber-Badrak-Borders Scales to measure compliance of local programs to those standards. The best practices detailed in the latter study were placed into ten component scales:

(1) program structure, (2) qualifications of local ombudsmen, (3) legal authority, (4) financial resources, (5) management information systems, (6) legal resources, (7) human resources, (8) resident advocacy services, (9) systemic advocacy, and (10) educational services.

Acknowledging Huber and her colleagues as having developed "the most empirical effort to address the [IOM's] recommendation to develop and implement an objective method to assess compliance of state LTCOP programs," Estes et al. (2004) reported the results of a telephone survey of all fifty state programs (as well as those of Washington, D.C., and Puerto Rico) to determine effectiveness in meeting the program mandates. In that survey, three elements were key in perceived programmatic effectiveness: "sufficient resources, sufficient organizational autonomy, and a supportive political and social environment" (Estes et al., p. 104).

Research Elements

Throughout the history of the LTCOP, there have been various types of empirical evidence generated. First, ombudsmen were surveyed to gain insights into their perceptions of how their programs were functioning; for example, Estes et al. (2004) surveyed state ombudsmen. Other studies surveyed local ombudsmen (both volunteer and paid) to assess their perceptions of what makes their programs work and what makes them able to do their jobs (e.g., Huber et al., 1993; Keith, 2001; Nelson, Pratt, Carpenter, & Walter, 1995). The units of analysis in these cases have been ombudsmen. In other studies, state-level ombudsmen complaint data, using state-specific reporting systems, were compared with agency abuse complaints and regulatory survey deficiency data. These data were analyzed to assess, ostensibly, nursing home quality and to determine whether ombudsmen were complementing regulatory inspections by seeing similar problems or, alternatively, were identifying different trends and problems as a result of differences in investigatory standards, patterns of involvement, and record access (Cherry, 1993; Nelson et al., 1995).

In 1995, with the creation of NORS, for the first time there was the potential to have a national database for the LTCOP. This offered a wonderful chance to improve both long-term-care ombudsman programs and the nation's elder-care system by using the data for such diverse purposes as leveraging or justifying funding, evaluating programs, identifying system problems, training, and advocacy (Kautz, 2002).

Kautz (2002) noted progress toward these goals after the implementation of NORS, especially in the rapid expansion of data collection by ombudsmen throughout the late 1990s and into the 2000s. Kautz noted that ombudsman complaint data had been used to push needed reform legislation, but he also noted the dissatisfaction with the data software, reporting processes, and performance measures, as well as problems of "data integrity and collection of disaggregated data" (p. 1).

The unit of analysis of NORS data can be cases or complaints. Cases are those encounters that ombudsmen report as they perform their investigatory and problem resolution roles. One case may have multiple complaints. For example, a long-term-care resident may complain that his or her call light is not being answered, that the food is not good, and that staff neglect him or her. This would constitute one case but three complaints.

In a rational world, then, it would seem possible for practitioners and researchers to access NORS as a public domain secondary database. Statute mandates that all states (including Washington, D.C.; Guam; and Puerto Rico) report their data according to 133 designated (and defined) complaint categories. Data reported include, for example, source of complaint, location in which the older person resides, whether the ombudsman is a paid staff person or a volunteer, and a host of other variables. These complaint data provide information for interested stakeholders to know what types of complaints are most prevalent; to target portions of the state (even long-term-care facilities in the state) that have high numbers of complaints lodged against them; and to identify needs of long-term-care residents that require intervention, as well as other issues that could be addressed through accessing the database. In addition, because all states collect the same data, comparisons could be analyzed across states.

This, then, should all come together in an integrated, informative manner. The data would be highly accessible so that practitioners could use them to develop empirically based interventions with residents and staff in long-term-care facilities. Likewise, decision makers could use the state and national data to inform policy and advocate for change in long-term care, perhaps documenting the effect of staffing shortages on quality of care. However, there were challenges in accessing the databases.

Methodology

The overriding study question was, How accessible are NORS data? Specifically, the study focused on investigating the following questions:

- What data are available at the national level?
- What data are available at the state level?

- What are the facilitating and challenging factors in accessing these data?
- What do the findings reveal about transportability and fidelity issues?

RESEARCH METHODS

Because the reports are public domain, we approached the preceding questions as if we were practitioners, academicians, or researchers interested in accessing LTCOP data for the purpose of using this evidence to inform practice. We began by contacting the AOA and accessing its Web site to examine what data are available at the national level. Next, we systematically approached each state, beginning with the Web site addresses available through the National Long-Term-Care Ombudsman Resource Center (www.ltcombudsman.org). If the Web address was not available or incorrect, we moved directly to the state Web site by typing in the name of the state and long-term-care ombudsman program. We developed an approach based on five questions to research each Web site:

1. Is the Web site linked to the National Long-Term-Care Ombudsman Resource Center?
2. Is the Web site a stand-alone dedicated to the ombudsman program or tethered to the Web site of an umbrella agency or department?
3. Is there a report of empirical data on the Web site?
4. If so, how many steps were necessary to locate those data, and what keywords were most useful in locating the report?
5. If we located a report, what data does the report include, and how up to date is its content?

STUDY POPULATION

Although we were intent on accessing available data, it is important to recognize what the data represent. The NORS data represent the complaints that residents and their advocates (e.g., families; friends; staff; and others, including ombudsmen who directly observed a problem) have lodged about what is happening on a very intimate level in the care of older people in long-term-care facilities. Each complaint represents a place in which quality of care may be compromised and quality of life may be reduced for vulnerable adults.

DATA SOURCES

The study population consisted of fifty-three state ombudsman program Web sites (including Washington, D.C.; Puerto Rico; and Guam), which constitute the universe of state programs. The search for data collected at the state level was necessary because data are aggregated across states at the national level. Starting at the lowest possible level provides greater analytical flexibility in the investigation.

CLASSIFICATION AND CODING

Because we accessed secondary data, the data were already classified and coded according to the standardized form developed by the AOA and approved by the U.S. Government Accounting Office. The strength of this classification and coding scheme is that input from researchers and practitioners had been gathered to make several revisions over the past few years. A limitation is that the revisions did not include resident demographics to analyze changes over time related to those variables (Huber et al., 2001).

DATA ANALYSIS

The present study analyzed descriptive secondary data that were available on the ombudsmen state and national Web sites. Available reports typically included basic pie charts with the top ten complaints in each respective state, along with numbers of complaints resolved, partially resolved, not resolved, referred out, or withdrawn. Depending on the state, if a report is available online, statistical procedures vary but rarely go beyond reporting frequencies in graphical format. Because data are aggregated at the national level, there is no ability to access case or complaint level. Comparative reporting of statistics across states, however, allows one to examine descriptive differences between states or across clusters of states.

DATA DISPLAY

Data display by states obviously varied by emphasis, as well as by how and what graphical presentations were provided. At the national level, the AOA reports that aggregate state data provide the opportunity to examine trends within the LTCOP. For example, Figure 5.1 illustrates trends in abuse complaints over a five-year period (2001–2005) based on data provided in AOA annual reports to Congress.

Findings

At the national level, AOA reports provide aggregate data on an annual basis by complaint categories that are posted on its Web site. Beginning

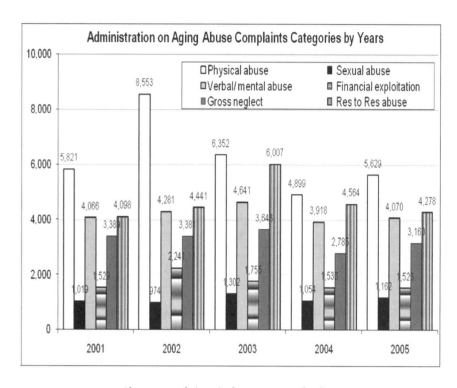

FIGURE 5.1.   *Abuse complaints in long term ombudsman programs*
as reported by the Administration on Aging

in 1996, when 144,680 complaints were reported across the nation, a gradual increase has occurred: the number reached 241,684 in 2005. Over a decade, the number-one complaint reported across the country was "call lights, requests for assistance." In every year except 1996, that was also the second-most-reported complaint. After accessing the AOA reports, the researchers examined trends across the country (as Figure 5.1 illustrates), identified the top complaints in any given year, and compared specific complaints in a given year.

In 2008, we located a list of all fifty-three state ombudsman programs (including those in Washington, D.C.; Puerto Rico; and Guam) on the Web site for the National Long-Term-Care Ombudsman Resource Center. Thirty of the programs had links to state Web sites that worked, seven programs had links that did not work, and the remaining sixteen did not contain links. All listings had contact information (including address, phone number, and fax numbers) for the state ombudsman, as well as listings for regional ombudsmen within the state.

Although twenty-three ombudsman programs were not linked to the National Long-Term-Care Ombudsman Resource Center, only three

(Guam, Rhode Island, and Puerto Rico) did not have Web sites for their ombudsman programs. In other words, forty-nine states and Washington, D.C., had some type of information available on the Internet. Web sites varied in how they were set up, with some states having a direct link to an ombudsman Web page and others requiring several steps to locate information on the ombudsman program at a state agency's Web site. For example, accessing the ombudsman program in Alabama required locating the Department of Senior Services, Arizona's program was located in the Division of Economic Security, Arkansas's program was located in the Department of Human Services, and Colorado's program was located in the Legal Center. Depending on the umbrella agency that oversees the state ombudsman program, the exact location and Web logistics varied.

Nineteen states (Colorado, Connecticut, Delaware, Florida, Hawaii, Illinois, Iowa, Kansas, Missouri, Nebraska, New Jersey, North Carolina, North Dakota, Oregon, Pennsylvania, South Carolina, Texas, Utah, and West Virginia) posted annual reports or similar documents with complaint data on the state's Web site. In addition, four other states (California, Idaho, Maryland, and Vermont) and Washington, D.C., integrated complaint data into the annual reports of their state department on aging or elder affairs. New York's site provided a link to national NORS data. Ohio provided an annual report but included no statistical complaint data. For the remaining twenty-seven state ombudsman programs (including those of Guam and Puerto Rico), the researchers were unable to electronically locate an annual report or statistical data on complaints.

Among those states that posted complaint data in some form, the nature of the data greatly varied. For example, Colorado had a 32-page comprehensive report on ombudsman data; Connecticut provided a 104-page report; and Delaware provided multiple-year reports, the most recent being 39 pages long. Similarly, Iowa reported comparable data across the past three years in a twenty-seven-page report, and Missouri provided multiple years of reports, with the last thirty-six-page report including detailed complaint data. New Jersey provided a twenty-one-page report, whereas North Carolina's seventy-six-page report was highly comprehensive with graphics. Oregon's twenty-page PDF was highly accessible and provided comparative data with other state agencies and nationally.

Posted annual reports were typically for the 2006–2007 (most recent) year, but some states posted only previous reports. For example, Arkansas's annual report was dated 2001, Hawaii and West Virginia posted their 2005 annual reports, and Pennsylvania posted an annual report dated 2005–2006. Complaint data sometimes appeared in informational brochures. For example, Illinois's four-page brochure-style report contained easy-to-read graphics, and North Dakota posted a two-page brochure titled "2007 LTCOP Fact Sheet."

Sites were uneven in terms of how many steps it took to locate the data. Some sites provided search boxes for keywords, such as "annual report," "complaint data," and "NORS." Some sites were very accessible, having the annual report posted on the home page of the ombudsman program. For example, Colorado listed "ombudsman report" with a direct link, Idaho provided an "annual report" link to the Commission on Aging's annual report that contained a one-page ombudsman report, and Texas and Utah had a link on their first page to the ombudsman annual report. Many states had a link to publications that led to a list of reports, including the ombudsman annual report.

Discussion

Netting et al. (1992) reported the results of a survey of all state ombudsmen in which they were asked to submit copies of their annual reports. At that time, there was a recommended reporting form suggested by the AOA. It was rare to find a state that had a comprehensive reporting system, and most systems were not yet computerized. Today, there is a required, standardized reporting system with accompanying software. In 1995, NORS became a reality, and since that time, refinements have been ongoing. Both quantitative and qualitative data are collected; all states contribute to the numeric database; and many states report word data that provide a richer, more intimate insight into the interpretation of the NORS-generated statistical charts. The aggregated NORS data are available online, but the qualitative data are not content analyzed. For the qualitative data, it is helpful to look at state reports. For example, on its Web site, West Virginia posted its 2005 annual report, which contained ten case-study examples.

The LTCOP is only one of thousands of programs caught in the rush toward using evidence-based practices. To generate evidence, programs need to have a built-in evaluation mechanism to determine whether the program's outcomes are achieved. Logically, if programs are designed with an evaluation plan, they could generate evidence based on a systematic collection of data that could then be helpful to others who are designing similar programs (Ohmer & Korr, 2006). There are numerous examples of program interventions reported in the literature in which the results of program evaluations provide evidence for future practice (Hoefer, 2000; Kluger, 2006; Unrau & Coleman, 2006). For example, Zimmermann and Stevens (2006) asked executive directors of 149 South Carolina nonprofits how they evaluated their programs and services and whether the results of their evaluations had an impact on operations. In the vast majority of cases, nonprofits were using evidence obtained from program evaluations to change how the programs operated, who they served, and how they were staffed. Thus, program staff members not only were collecting data that were part of an information system in those agencies but also were using that information to change their policies and practices.

Our results indicate that state ombudsman programs varied tremendously in how they made their data accessible. Once aggregated at the national level, NORS data are somewhat limited in that the ability to analyze them is greatly reduced. Thus, access to state databases enables practitioners and researchers to perform analyses that are not possible at the national level. Depending on the state, there are different levels of transparency in sharing available data.

Implications for Practice Decisions

There are multiple levels of decision makers interested in long-term care in the United States. At the national level, it is Congress that originally mandated the LTCOP and to which the AOA sends its yearly report. Ideally, having a more comprehensive, comparable-across-states database would provide more quality information to Congress, which ultimately sanctions federal programs. Realistically, the LTCOP is a small effort in a sea of thousands of federal programs. Unless a champion in Congress perceives these data as a way to advocate for a change in policy, the reports generated year after year may have little impact.

However, the fact that these reports are available as evidence of what ombudsmen are doing throughout the country offers advocates an opportunity to use the data to inform practice in long-term care. Advocates have more evidence than they did just a decade ago. Secondary databases can reveal the types of complaints being made about an industry. This information can be used to improve long-term care or reveal practices that can do great harm to an growing older population.

The published proceedings from the National Association of Long-Term Care State Ombudsman Program's (2003) retreat "Rethinking and Retooling for the Future," which examined seven key areas of ombudsman programs, including LTCOP data and information, reflected recognition of the importance of LTCOP complaint data. Retreat participants proposed moving the NORS reporting system into a new phase "that will incorporate disaggregated data that can be useful for comparisons, further study and research that supports advocacy, accountability, consumer information, and training" (National Association of State Long Term Care Ombudsman Program, 2003, p. 31). This was intended to be achieved in five years but has happened only partially, despite some progress. Other recommendations from the retreat included the following:

1. Administration on Aging will establish baseline minimum standards for state program software.
2. Administration on Aging will publish and award grants to states to purchase necessary hardware and software to meet standards and assure data integrity and security. Various aging agencies at the national level (e.g., AOA, the National Long Term Care Ombudsman Resource Center, NASUA) should identify resources that would purchase or donate state-of-the-art computer systems and software that assist them in improving services and provide ease of data entry and data analysis.
3. National Association of State Long-Term Care Ombudsman Programs should continue to develop standardized national outcome measures based on the work of the 2000–2002 Resource Center Project.
4. National Association of State Long-Term Care Ombudsman Programs should work to sensitize states to the need to analyze and improve systems advocacy to improve the quality of services in facilities serving special needs populations (e.g., Alzheimer's disease).
5. National Association of Long-Term Care State Ombudsman Programs and the National Association of Local Long-Term Care Ombudsmen should develop policies for providing complaint, inquiry, and other information to consumers and providers. (National Association of State Long Term Care Ombudsman Programs, 2003, pp. 33–34)

Although NORS data are valuable, and with these changes could be even more so, they are not the only source of data about the industry of long-term care. There are other secondary databases that can be used in triangulation with NORS to tell a broader picture of what is happening in individual states. For example, other sources of secondary data could be used to explore the relationship between ombudsman complaint counts and adult protective service abuse and neglect complaints, state survey deficiencies, and regulatory punitive actions aggregated at the facility level.

Many decisions about long-term care and its oversight occur at the state level as well. Thus, a review of multiple state Web sites reveals that evidence comes in many different forms, some more accessible than others. Thus, state-level decision makers and advocates have the potential to use what is known about the grassroots efforts of ombudsmen to inform interventions in local long-term-care facilities. For example, NORS data in Connecticut were used to examine the characteristics that might influence the reporting of complaints (Allen, Klein, & Gruman, 2003) and gender differences in patterns of resident complaints (Allen, Nelson, Gruman, & Cherry, 2006). In the latter instance, Allen et al. provided evidence for nursing home social workers to act "as agents in changing embedded stereotypes about residents and complainants" (p. 90).

PRACTICE GUIDELINES

On the basis of the previous analysis and discussion, we have developed a set of practice guidelines to support change in long-term-care ombudsman programs.

First, ombudsmen have an opportunity to get the word out about what they are finding. Posting up-to-date, accessible information on their Web sites and making deidentified data available to others for secondary analysis will contribute to long-term-care advocacy efforts.

Second, helping professionals interested in the quality of care of persons residing in long-term-care facilities need to know their local ombudsmen and the procedures to use in filing a complaint. They also need to know how to access the NORS data in their state, which will provide them with empirically based information relevant to their practices.

Third, local aging advocates may want to partner with researchers at local universities to analyze the state ombudsman database to its full extent so that they can make informed decisions about where to target their efforts. For example, if there are nursing facilities with high levels of abuse or neglect, they can target those locations for change.

Fourth, programs developed to address the needs of older persons can use ombudsman data as one source of empirical evidence. For example, when an area agency on aging develops it multiyear plan, it is important to use ombudsman data as one source of information in the prioritization process.

Fifth, professionals who work in state government and oversee various aspects of health and human service providers may find the ombudsman database especially helpful as compared to data that come from other sources, such as adult protective services, nursing-home inspection, and Medicaid. Different sources of evidence may tell a story that one database does not fully tell. Together, they may tell a more integrated story.

Last, state and national aging advocates can use ombudsman data in conjunction with other sources to propose policy changes that will affect long-term-care systems across the country. Past examples are campaigns against the use of restraints and to increase staff-to-patient ratios. Having evidence of problems can put teeth into the effort. This includes the use of eye-opening quantitative data; for example, there were 5,269 verified complaints related to physical abuse last year in U.S. nursing homes. Similarly, the use of qualitative data can provide real examples to illustrate testimony and can put a face on the problem.

Ombudsmen, both paid and volunteer, are community-based practitioners who are constantly engaged in advocacy efforts. Every action they take generates data about what is happening in long-term care, about the quality of care, and about the quality of life of older persons. The documentation of their actions can become data elements for developing state and national information systems. The power of a national database cannot be underestimated if those data are transformed into meaningful information and evidence to support the need for community and organizational change.

References

Allen, P. D., Klein, W. C., & Gruman, C. (2003). Correlates of complaints made to the Connecticut long-term care ombudsman program. *Research on Aging*, 25(6), 631–654.

Allen, P. D., Nelson, H. W., Gruman, C., & Cherry, K. E. (2006). Nursing home complaints: Who's complaining and what's gender got to do with it? *Journal of Gerontological Social Work*, 47(1–2), 89–106.

Buford, A. D. (1984). *Advocacy for the nursing home resident: An examination of the ombudsman function and its relationship to licensing and certification activities in insuring quality of care.* Washington, DC: U.S. Department of Health and Human Services.

Cherry, R. L. (1993). Community presence and nursing home quality of care: The ombudsman as a complementary role. *Journal of Health and Social Behavior*, 34(4), 336–345.

Connor, K. A., & Winkelpleck, J. (1990). Volunteer advocates: Differing role expectations of long-term care facility administrators and volunteers. *Journal of Long-Term Care Administration*, 18(2), 12–15.

Estes, C. L., Zulman, D. M., Goldberg, S. C., & Ogawa, D. D. (2004). State long term care ombudsman programs: Factors associated with perceived effectiveness. *Gerontologist*, 44(1), 104–115.

GAO 160: Access to and utilization of the ombudsman program under the Older Americans Act: Hearings before the Subcommittee on Aging, Senate Committee on Labor and Human Resources, 102nd Cong., 1 (1991) (testimony of E. Chelimsky).

Harris-Wehling, J., Feasley, J. C., & Estes, C. L. (1995). *Real people real problems: An evaluation of the long term care ombudsman programs of the Older Americans Act.* Washington, DC: Institute of Medicine, Division of Health Care Services.

Hoefer, R. (2000). Accountability in action? Program evaluation in nonprofit human service agencies. *Nonprofit Management & Leadership*, *11*(2), 167–177.

Huber, R., Borders, K., Badrak, K., Netting, F. E., & Nelson, H. W. (2001). National standards for the long-term care ombudsman program and a tool to assess compliance: The Huber Badrak Borders Scales. *Gerontologist*, *41*(2), 264–271.

Huber, R., Borders, K., Netting, F. E., & Kautz, J. R. (1997). To empower with meaningful data: Lessons learned in building an alliance between researchers and long term care ombudsman. *Journal of Community Practice*, *4*(4), 81–101.

Huber, R., Borders, K., Netting, F. E., & Kautz, J. R. (2000). Interpreting the meaning of ombudsman data across states: The critical analyst-practitioner link. *Journal of Applied Gerontology*, *19*(1), 3–22.

Huber, R., Borders, K., Netting, F. E., & Nelson, H. W. (2001). Data from the long-term care ombudsman program in six states: The implications of collecting resident demographics. *Gerontologist*, *41*(1), 61–68.

Huber, R., Netting, F. E., & Kautz, J. R. (1996). Differences in types of complaints and how they were resolved by local long-term care ombudsmen operating in/not in area agencies on aging. *Journal of Applied Gerontology*, *15*(1), 87–101.

Huber, R., Netting, F. E., & Paton, R. N. (1993). In search of the impact of staff mix in long-term care ombudsman programs. *Nonprofit and Voluntary Sector Quarterly*, *22*(1), 69–91.

Kautz, J., Netting, F. E., Huber, R., Borders, K., & Davis, T. S. (1997). The government performance results act of 1993: Implications for social work practice. *Social Work*, *42*(4), 364–373.

Kautz, J. R. (2002, January 31–February 2). *Data and information in long-term care ombudsman programs: Challenges, opportunities.* Paper presented at the National Association of Long-Term Care State Ombudsman Programs: The Long-Term Care Ombudsman Program: Rethinking and Retooling for the Future, Washington, DC.

Keith, P. M. (2001). Role orientations, attributions to nursing facility personnel, and unresolved complaints of volunteers in an ombudsman program. *Journal of Gerontological Social Work*, *24*(4), 33–46.

Kettner, P. M., Moroney, R. M., & Martin, L. L. (1999). *Designing and managing programs: An effectiveness-based approach* (2nd ed.). Thousand Oaks, CA: Sage.

Kluger, M. (2006). The program evaluation grid: A planning and assessment tool for nonprofit organizations. *Administration in Social Work*, *30*(1), 33–44.

Monk, A., Kaye, W. L., & Litwin, H. (1984). *Resolving grievances in the nursing home: A study of the ombudsman program.* New York: Columbia University Press.

Nathanson, I. L., & Eggleton, E. (1993). Motivation versus program effect on length of service: A study of four cohorts of ombudservice volunteers. *Journal of Gerontological Social Work*, *19*(3–4), 95–114.

National Association of State Long-Term Care Ombudsman Programs (2003). *The long-term-care ombudsman program: Rethinking and retooling for the future.* Retrieved from http://www.nasop.org/papers/bader.pdf.

National Association of State Units on Aging. (1993). *Placement of state and local ombudsman programs and operation of local ombudsman programs.* Washington, DC: Author.

Nelson, H. W. (1995). Long term care volunteer roles on trial: Ombudsman effectiveness revisited. *Journal of Gerontological Social Work, 23*(3–4), 25–46.

Nelson, H. W., Huber, R., & Walter, K. L. (1995). The relation of volunteer long-term care ombudsmen to regulatory nursing home actions, *Gerontologist, 35*(4), 509–514.

Nelson, H. W., Pratt, C. C., Carpenter, C. C., & Walter, K. L. (1995). Factors affecting volunteer long-term care ombudsman organizational commitment and burnout. *Nonprofit and Volunteer Sector Quarterly, 24*(3), 213–233.

Netting, F. E., Huber, R., Paton, R., & Kautz, J. R. (1995). Elder rights: The role of the long-term care ombudsman program. *Social Work, 40*(3), 351–357.

Netting, F. E., Paton, R. N., & Huber, R. (1992). The long term care ombudsman program: What does the reporting system tell us? *Gerontologist, 32*(6), 843–848.

Ohmer, M. L., & Korr, W. S. (2006). The effectiveness of community practice interventions: A review of the literature. *Research on Social Work Practice, 16*(2), 132–145.

U.S. Department of Health and Human Services. (1991). *State implementation of the ombudsman requirements of the Older Americans Act* (Office of the Inspector General Publication No. OEI-01–90–02121). Washington, DC: U.S. Government Printing Office.

U.S. Department of Health and Human Services. (1993). *State implementation of the ombudsman requirements of the Older Americans Act* (AOA and Office of the Inspector General Publication No. OEI-02–91–01516). Washington, DC: U.S. Government Printing Office.

Unrau, Y. A., & Coleman, H. (2006). Evaluating program outcomes as event histories. *Administration in Social Work, 30*(1), 45–65.

Zimmermann, J. A. M., & Stevens, B. W. (2006). The use of performance measurement in South Carolina nonprofits. *Nonprofit Management and Leadership, 16*(3), 315–327.

CHAPTER SIX

Housing-First Services for Homeless Adults with Co-occurring Disorders

An Evidence-Based Practice

Deborah K. Padgett, Victoria Stanhope, and Benjamin F. Henwood

Statement of the Problem

As the United States enters its third decade of a homelessness "crisis," programs are being reexamined and fresh solutions are being explored that are evidence based as well as consumer friendly. For the subpopulation of homeless adults with a serious mental illness (and, more often than not, substance abuse problems), this is indeed a tall order. These men and women, among the hardest to reach and engage in services, have multiple, long-standing problems that a fragmented services system cannot easily address. With regard to the latter, the overextended public mental health system, funded by state and local governments, constitutes a major source of services along with substance abuse treatment settings, homeless programs, and an array of federal entitlement programs, including Medicaid, Section 8 housing vouchers, and Supplemental Security Income (SSI).

This chapter focuses on an innovative approach known as housing first, whose origins lie in a program that began as a distinct alternative to mainstream service programs. Pathways to Housing Inc. in New York City became the focus of empirical research starting in the late 1990s that has, in turn, spurred national and international interest in housing first. The chapter describes two studies as the primary contributors to a growing body of evidence that housing first enables persons with serious mental illness to achieve a stable, independent life in the community. In addition, the chapter discusses barriers and incentives related to implementing these programs and using the evidence to inform change efforts.

Literature Review

SCOPE OF PROBLEM AND MAINSTREAM SOLUTIONS

Epidemiological studies have shown that about one-third of the homeless population has a serious mental illness, such as schizophrenia or bipolar disorder, and half or more of the population has problems with illicit drugs and/or alcohol (Kessler et al., 1994; Regier et al., 1990). Such problems may hasten the descent into homelessness, but they are neither necessary nor sufficient for it to happen. Serious mental illness typically predates homelessness, but depression and anxiety often compound psychotic symptoms, which is not surprising given the circumstances of daily life on the streets. Substance abuse may pre- or postdate homelessness, but either way, substance abuse almost always exacerbates the situation of homelessness (Drake, Osher, & Wallach, 1991; Mueser, Drake, & Wallach, 1998).

Chicken-or-egg arguments about mental illness and substance abuse as causes versus consequences of homelessness tend to overlook broader social problems and structural deficits. Indeed, the sharp downturn in affordable housing, which dates to the Reagan era of the 1980s, made homelessness virtually inevitable for many people regardless of individual problems or frailties (Lovell & Cohn, 1998). In the United States, approximately 2 million individuals are homeless per year, and such estimates are always on the low side, as thousands of individuals live doubled up with relatives or move through a series of encampments under highway overpasses, in city parks, or in abandoned buildings (Tompsett, Toro, Guzicki, Manrique, & Zatakia, 2006).

Organizations devoted to helping homeless persons with serious mental illness have proliferated since the 1980s, but their approach to outreach and engagement has remained fairly uniform and consistent with a medical-model approach favoring clinical expertise and decision making. Using trained outreach workers (along with low-threshold drop-in centers), such organizations offer treatment and case management services bundled with temporary housing. The latter, usually a congregate-style residence with on-site staff, have rules governing visitors, curfews, medication compliance, and abstinence. Residents' ability to progress toward independent housing is contingent on following the rules and demonstrating housing worthiness. In rare instances, independent housing is immediately available to those deemed worthy, but most of the time, this process takes months or years (and is often disrupted when a client prematurely departs). This revolving-door situation—in which clients traverse an institutional circuit of shelters, jails, hospitals, and rehab centers—has been criticized as inadequate at best (Carling, 1993; Hopper, Jost, Hay, Welber, & Haugland, 1997).

According to Locke, Khadduri, and O'Hara (2007), the adoption of transitional housing models for the homeless mentally ill grew out of the halfway-house model of earlier eras intended for discharged prisoners and mental patients. However, Locke et al. note that there was no strong theoretical framework for applying this concept to homelessness:

> Only recently, with transitional housing challenged by shifting federal funding priorities and by the Housing First model, have researchers begun to create a theory of transitional housing that goes beyond the simple [McKinney-Vento] programmatic rule that a transitional housing stay may not last more than two years. Much of the research on outcomes for individuals participating in transitional programs focuses on comparisons of supportive housing programs serving homeless individuals with mental illness (who often also have co-occurring substance use disorders and other disabilities) with traditional mental health treatment without a housing component. There have been few studies of transitional programs that compare them to other housing models. (p. 17)

IMPLEMENTING AN EVIDENCE-BASED PRACTICE: HOUSING-FIRST SERVICES

In 1992, Pathways to Housing was founded as a strikingly different alternative to standard care. Although the basic elements of housing first were initially proposed for persons with serious mental illness (Carling, 1993; Ridgway & Zipple, 1990), Pathways was the first program to apply these elements to the real world of homeless services.

Pathways reversed the usual continuum of services by offering immediate access to independent apartments in scattered sites around the city, along with case management, such as assertive community treatment (ACT) teams, to attend to psychiatric and other needs. Also unlike the standard approach, Pathways did not make keeping one's apartment contingent on having no previous history of violence or incarceration, maintaining abstinence from drugs and alcohol, or taking psychiatric medications. Put another way, Pathways accepted individuals that other programs screened out as too risky, and Pathways held their apartments for them if and when they were hospitalized, jailed, or entered drug or alcohol rehabilitation. The program's only requirements were that clients agree to meet with a case manager regularly and to cooperate with money management, including contributing one-third of any income (usually an SSI disability check) toward paying the rent. Table 6.1 summarizes the differences between the Pathways approach and the mainstream, or treatment-first, approach.

Skeptics argued that putting a substance-using mentally ill person in an apartment without close supervision and restrictions was risky and posed a serious danger to the client and the greater community. It was

TABLE 6.1.   Contrasts between mainstream (treatment-first) and Pathways (housing-first) for homeless adults

	Continuum-of-care housing	Pathways' housing-first model
Values	Housing to be earned and clinical expertise	Housing as a right and consumer choice
Eligibility/preconditions	Preconditions (no history of violence or incarceration; adherence to psychiatric and substance abuse treatment)	No preconditions
Housing		
Ownership	Provider/program	Private landlord
Tenure	Transitional (graduated)	Permanent
Occupancy	Congregate and individual	Individual
Location	Concentrated in building or neighborhood and scatter site	Scatter site
Services		
Staff location	On site and off site	Off site
Staff arrangement	Individual case managers	ACT teams
Program rules and expectations	Money management, curfew, no visitors, medication and treatment adherence	Money management, no curfew, visitors allowed, meet with case manager, medication and treatment voluntary
Substance use policy	Abstinence only	Harm reduction

also deemed a waste of resources because individuals' problems would sabotage efforts to keep them in the community and stably housed.

To address this skepticism, the Pathways approach became the subject of empirical research in the late 1990s that contrasted it with the mainstream treatment-first approach. This chapter presents the findings from two federally funded studies, along with reflections on their significance for policy, practice, and research. It is fair to say that all programs intended for this vulnerable population share the goal of assisting homeless mentally ill clients in achieving a stable and satisfying life in the community with minimal need for institutionalization. The key difference lies in how this goal is pursued and whether the evidence favors one of these disparate approaches.

RESEARCH ON SERVICES FOR HOMELESS ADULTS WITH SERIOUS MENTAL ILLNESS

Despite a plethora of empirical studies on homelessness, serious mental illness, and substance abuse, there is a surprising absence of research on the effectiveness of programmatic approaches for persons with all three of these problems. A small but growing number of studies on consumer preferences have consistently shown that such individuals prefer independent over supervised housing, though their case managers do not share this priority (Piat et al., 2008; Srebnik, Livingston, Gordon, & King, 1995; Tanzman, 1993). Allen (2003) has criticized the tendency of mainstream providers to leverage an offer of temporary housing and the promise of future independent housing against demands for medication adherence, abstinence, and observation of rules (violations of which can result in termination and loss of one's residence).

Perhaps not surprisingly, providers' primary emphasis is on remedying the deficiencies of clients rather than of organizations (Stanhope, Henwood, & Padgett, 2008). In this chapter, we broaden the scope of the problem (and its solutions) beyond the individual level to include the organizational level and, by implication, the larger policy sphere in which organizations operate. Study 1, the New York Housing Study, was a four-year randomized control trial (1997–2002) with quantitative outcomes that compared Pathways housing-first program with its treatment-first counterparts. Study 2, the New York Services Study, was a qualitative longitudinal study that also focused on contrasting the housing-first and treatment-first approaches using the consumer perspective.

Methodology

STUDY 1: A RANDOMIZED CONTROL TRIAL PUTTING HOUSING FIRST TO THE TEST

The New York Housing Study (NYHS) was a four-year experiment in which homeless mentally ill persons in New York City were randomly assigned to the Pathways housing-first program or to a treatment-first program. Persons with serious mental illness were recruited for the study if they fit the following inclusion criteria: (1) they spent fifteen of the previous thirty days on the street or in other public places, (2) they exhibited a history of homelessness during the previous six months, and (3) they had a *Diagnostic and Statistical Manual of Mental Disorders* (DSM) axis I diagnosis of severe mental illness (American Psychiatric Association, 2000). Although substance abuse was not a criterion for eligibility, 90 percent of the study participants had a diagnosis or history of alcohol or drug disorders according to clinical records. Psychiatric diagnoses were obtained from clinical records and interviews with referring providers.

Respondents were recruited from drop-in centers, psychiatric hospital wards, and the streets. Individuals who met the inclusion criteria were asked whether they were interested in participating in a longitudinal research study with the understanding that, on the basis of a randomized lottery system, they would be referred to different housing programs in the city. Recruitment, which lasted from November 1997 to January 1999, produced a sample of 225 people (99 in the experimental group and 126 in the control group) between the ages of eighteen and seventy years. An institutional review board at Pathways and New York University (where one member of the study team was based) approved study protocols.

Individuals assigned to the control group were referred to usual care programs that offered abstinent-contingent housing and services based on a treatment-first model. A typical program was exemplified by a group home or a single-room occupancy residence in which clients were expected to enter detox and rehab for substance abuse and attend day treatment as well as other therapeutic groups. They were also expected to follow their prescribed medication regimens as supervised by on-site staff. Sleeping, cooking, and bathing facilities were shared and house rules governed curfews, visitors, and strict prohibitions of substances. Individuals assigned to Pathways were placed in independent apartments (studio or one bedroom) and received Pathways' services (i.e., ACT teams).

Data collection consisted of a structured interview administered at six-month intervals for forty-eight months. To reduce attrition and maintain contacts, monthly five-minute call-in interviews were conducted (for which each participant was paid $5). Participants were paid $25 for nine in-person interviews and $5 for the monthly calls. The repeated contacts are one of the reasons for the study's high retention rate of 87 percent (Stefancic, Schaefer-McDaniel, Davis, & Tsemberis, 2004).

Standardized measures were used to assess key variables. These measures were validated for use with the study population and had moderate to high reliability. Table 6.2 displays the outcome measures that have been reported in the literature, including housing stability, alcohol and drug use, participation in treatment, psychiatric symptoms, and consumer choice.

The following measurements were used in the NYHS, as noted in Table 6.2:

- Residential follow-back calendar (Dartmouth Psychiatric Research Center, 1995)

TABLE 6.2.   Results of the New York Housing Study: Housing first versus treatment first

Outcome variable	Measure	Reliability	Results
Housing retention rate	Residential follow-back calendar	Test-retest .84–.92	HF more time stably housed*
Proportion of time homeless	Residential follow-back calendar	Test-retest .84–.92	HF less time homeless*
Use of alcohol and drugs	Six-month follow-back calendar	Test-retest .78–.98	No significant difference
Participation in SA treatment	Modified treatment review	Test-retest .84–.94	TF higher use*
Participation in MH treatment	Modified treatment review	Test-retest .84–.94	TF higher use*
Psychiatric symptoms	Colorado symptom index	Internal consistency .90	No significant difference
Consumer choice	Consumer choice	Internal consistency .92	HF more perceived choice**

*$p < .005$ (Bonferroni corrected value), **$p < .0005$.
Notes: HF = housing first; TF = treatment first. Results reported for six, twelve, eighteen, twenty-four, thirty-six, or forty-eight months.

- Six-month follow-back calendar (Sobell, Sobell, & Leo, 1988)
- Modified treatment review (McLellan, Alterman, & Woody, 1992)
- Colorado Symptom Index (Ciarolo, Edwards, Kiresuk, Newman, & Brown, 1981)
- Consumer choice (Srebnik, Livingston, Gordon, & King, 1995)

STUDY 2: QUALITATIVE STUDY OF HOUSING-FIRST AND TREATMENT-FIRST CONSUMERS

Funded by the National Institute of Mental Health from 2004 to 2008, the New York Services Study (NYSS) drew on the findings from the NYHS in formulating its questions and methods. As a qualitative study, it was designed to elicit consumer perspectives regarding their service use and other dimensions of their lives after enrolling in Pathways or one of three treatment-first programs in New York City. The ostensible goal of the study was to understand factors affecting engagement and retention in care for this population. However, its flexible design ensured that the scope of interest would extend beyond the service system when life circumstances (e.g., birth of a child, new partner, spiritual growth) had an impact on the participant, whether positive or negative.

Inclusion criteria for the NYSS included having a DSM axis I psychiatric diagnosis (American Psychiatric Association, 2000) and histories of substance abuse and homelessness. Phase 1 of the NYSS entailed recruiting a purposive subsample ($n = 39$) from the earlier NYHS based on positive or negative status at the end of the study (according to mental health, substance use, and housing outcomes) as well as belonging to housing-first or treatment-first group membership. The thirty-nine individuals were administered open-ended life history interviews comprising questions about their personal trajectories from birth to the present. The focus of the interviews, especially the second follow-up interview, was to learn about the sequencing of key life events (e.g., childhood abuse, onset of substance use, first psychiatric hospitalization, episodes of homelessness) and their contexts.

Phase 2 of the NYSS was a prospective study of newly enrolled housing-first and treatment-first clients who were interviewed in-depth at zero, six, and twelve months along with monthly tracking interviews (with a $30 incentive for in-depth interviews and $10 incentive for the monthly tracking interviews). With their permission, study participants' case managers were interviewed twice, once soon after baseline and again six months later (or sooner if the client departed prematurely from the program). In-depth interviews covered key domains (e.g., substance use, social support, housing, use of other services, mental health status) but also left considerable discretion for the trained interviewers to probe, especially if the participant had experienced a major life event, such as death of a loved one, incarceration, hospitalization, or relapse. A total of eighty-three clients were interviewed across the four programs (twenty-seven in the housing-first program and fifty-six in the treatment-first programs).

ANALYSIS AND STRATEGIES FOR RIGOR IN THE TWO STUDIES

Data analyses in Study 1 (NYHS) relied on multivariate predictive models (regression, logistic, survival) appropriate for repeated-measures multivariate analysis of variance (MANOVA) using SAS Proc Mixed program software. Change over time was analyzed graphically and via a growth-curve model with group-by-time interactions to assess group differences (known as hierarchical linear modeling) (Bryk & Raudenbush, 1992). When repeated-measures MANOVA showed significance, t-tests were performed at each six-month time point to detect group differences. Strategies for rigor in the NYHS built on the strength of the experimental design. Because of multiple group comparisons, a more conservative significance level was applied using Bonferroni-corrected alpha levels. The effectiveness of random assignment, strengthened by the study's high retention rate, was further checked by comparing those who left the study with those who remained; satisfactory equivalence was found (Padgett, Gulcur, & Tsemberis, 2006). Given the near inevitability of missing data in the forty-eight-month repeated-measures design (i.e., some individuals missed their six-month interviews), a maximum-likelihood approach was used in growth-curve analyses to permit individuals' inclusion even when missing some data points (Greenwood, Shaefer-McDaniel, Winkel, & Tsemberis, 2005).

Data analysis in the NYSS used two types of qualitative methodologies: (1) grounded theory to inductively derive codes and themes across cases (Charmaz, 2006) and (2) case studies to capture individual life trajectories over time (Patton, 2002). Thematic analysis involved independent co-coding by two members of the study team followed by meetings for consensus development and further iterative coding. Case study analyses drew on individual case summaries compiled for each participant that consisted of interview transcripts, interviewer notes and observations, and referring agency psychosocial records (if available). Case-study analytic meetings were held in which all members of the study team discussed each case according to key study questions (e.g., mental health status, substance use, social support) and relevant life-trajectory changes as noted in the case (e.g., recovery from substance abuse, death of close family member, incarceration).

Strategies for rigor (Padgett, 2008) included multiple interviews for prolonged engagement, triangulation using multiple sources of data, peer debriefing, support (weekly study team meetings), and keeping an audit trail (by documenting study procedures and decisions). Member checking of findings with participants was used to a limited extent (because of difficulties in scheduling).

Findings

STUDY 1: EXPERIMENTAL OUTCOMES FROM THE NYHS

As shown in Table 6.2, housing-first participants manifested significantly greater housing stability and perceived choice at twenty-four months (Tsemberis, Gulcur, & Nakae, 2004) and at thirty-six months (Greenwood et al., 2005). Group differences for alcohol and drug use were not statistically significant. The treatment-first group showed higher rates of substance abuse treatment at every time point (although statistical significance was achieved only at thirty-six months given the Bonferroni correction) (Padgett et al., 2006). Similarly, the treatment-first group was more likely to use mental health treatment, but this was statistically significant only at forty-eight months (see Table 6.2). Further details can be found in the NYHS publications listed at the end of this chapter.

In the larger context of services for the mentally ill homeless, the NYHS produced the first empirical evidence that, in contrast to treatment first, housing first is associated with positive results. The experimental design of the study, along with its strong retention rate, lent the findings greater credibility than would otherwise have been possible. The no-difference findings were noteworthy as well, as skeptics had predicted that housing-first clients would increase substance use under harm-reduction policies and would become more symptomatic if not monitored and required to take their medications. At the same time, the no-difference findings ran counter to the study interviewers' informal observations in which housing-first participants appeared to lead stabler, less troubled daily lives. This raised legitimate questions about whether the measures were accurately and/or adequately capturing what was happening in participants' lives.

STUDY 2: QUALITATIVE FINDINGS FROM THE NYSS

With its qualitative methodology, the NYSS intended to gain a deeper and more nuanced understanding of what participants experienced both within and outside of the service system. Maintaining an 81 percent retention rate (sixty-seven of the eighty-three participants) for the full twelve months of follow-up and 90 percent retention for two of the three interviews, the study produced a voluminous amount of data from in-depth and monthly tracking interviews.

One of the most striking findings was a simple group comparison related to program stability in which 54 percent of the treatment-first participants prematurely left their programs compared to 11 percent of housing-first participants. Those in treatment first who left their programs did so as a result of substance use relapse and/or a rejection of the restrictions associated with congregate living. The three individuals who left Pathways' housing-first program moved to rejoin their family outside of the city. Substance abuse was not reported to be a contributing factor.

Publications based on the research from the NYSS are listed at the end of this chapter. Some of the publications report qualitative findings from the NYSS that focus not only on the goals of the study (e.g., engagement and retention in care) but also on inductively derived and often-serendipitous themes, such as the prominence of trauma in women's life histories and the severe depletion of social networks arising from poverty-stricken lives. Another publication challenged the prevailing theory that substance abuse is a way to self-medicate the symptoms of mental illness (Henwood & Padgett, 2007). Another publication adapted Giddens's theory of ontological security to examine the significance of obtaining a home after being homeless (Padgett, 2007). Thematic findings related to engagement and retention in care included positive influences (e.g., acts of kindness by providers, pleasant institutional surroundings, access to independent housing) and negative influences (e.g., substance abuse, lack of one-on-one treatment, rules and restrictions in treatment) (Padgett, Henwood, Abrams, & Davis, 2008).

Research on housing first suggests that the high dropout rates associated with mainstream care (treatment first) are a known problem, but their juxtaposition with Pathways' retention rate provides new information and a basis for direct comparison. Moreover, the in-depth interviews in the research helped shed light on consumers' reasons for dropping out (which included programmatic restrictiveness and admitted problems with substances).

Participants who had obtained their own apartment were grateful for the autonomy in their independent living arrangement. Similarly, most of those who lived in congregate and/or institutional settings expressed frustration over their living circumstances and a longing for independence. They readily acknowledged that institutionalization was necessary during crises of mental illness or addiction, and they were grateful to have that attention and care when it was made available to them. But they also resisted the notion that these episodes, as well as the diagnoses associated with them, should define their existence and determine their ability to live independently.

In other qualitative findings, participants expressed a sense of regret over lost or missed opportunities and worried about an uncertain future marred by poor health and/or the cumulative effects of disability (Shibusawa & Padgett, 2009). Having one's own apartment, however valued, could not eliminate the effects of these concerns (Padgett, 2007).

Implications for Practice Decisions

The potent mix of serious mental illness and substance abuse, when interwoven with homelessness, presents a standing challenge that existing services struggle to meet. The studies described in this chapter have added considerably to the scarce literature on alternative housing arrangements and services for members of this vulnerable population. Indeed, the cumulative weight of evidence has tilted strongly toward housing first as appropriate for the majority of individuals who are homeless and mentally ill. Although a small subset of more psychiatrically disabled and/or addicted persons might not be able to benefit from this approach (at least while in crisis), the conclusion seems warranted that the public mental health system should be reversing its priorities (making congregate or institutional care the last rather than the first resort).

As noted in the earlier quote by Locke et al. (2007), shifting federal funding priorities and increasing attention to housing first in the popular press (Gladwell, 2006) have given a new impetus for change to housing and services for the homeless mentally ill population. Perhaps not surprisingly, unpacking and clarifying what housing first means has become necessary, as it has been promoted and adopted with varying degrees of fidelity to the original Pathways model. For example, a 2007 study of housing first sponsored by the Department of Housing and Urban Development (HUD) included the Pathways program alongside programs in Seattle, Denver, and San Diego that used supervised, congregate, and clean-and-sober requirements in their housing programs (Pearson, Locke, Montgomery, & Buron, 2007). These programs are considered housing first because they place consumers directly into housing without preconditions and do not put an arbitrary time limit on occupancy. The HUD report did not provide site-specific outcomes because all three sites were considered under the same rubric, even though only one adhered to all aspects of consumer choice and empowerment. Nevertheless, the report produced significant evidence favoring housing first and raised its profile considerably.

Another impetus toward housing first has come from the cost-effectiveness findings of Culhane, Metraux, and Hadley (2002), who found that targeting the highest-service-using homeless to receive immediate housing would likely lower costs substantially by reducing the number of emergency room visits, hospitalizations, and incarcerations. Because the costliest individuals are frequently heavy alcohol or drug abusers, the extension of housing first to non–mentally ill populations is a new approach awaiting further research (Kertesz et al., 2007). Several cities (most notably San Francisco) are implementing low-threshold housing programs for high users of services among the homeless.

Disentangling the elements of housing first (i.e., deciding which are essential ingredients and which are not) can be difficult when there is a lack of consensus on what the program means and how fidelity should be assessed. At this point in time, the Pathways (housing first) model has been replicated in Washington, D.C., and Philadelphia. In Canada, a large-scale experimental trial was launched in 2008 that will compare the Pathways approach with treatment-first programs in five cities across the nation.

Structural barriers can impede progress to implementing housing first. A lack of affordable housing makes the approach dependent on a scarce commodity, which results in scatter-site apartments. In addition, the lack of integration of service systems in mental health, substance abuse treatment, housing, and federal entitlements, such as Medicaid and SSI, diffuses responsibility and makes change difficult. Meanwhile, national advocacy groups such as the National Coalition for the Homeless (www.nationalhomeless.org) and the National Alliance to End Homelessness (www.endhomelessness.org) have been instrumental in calling attention to the problem and potential solutions including housing first. As the evidentiary foundation of housing first grows, advocacy efforts at the national, state, and local levels are increasing to support funding for these programs.

Practice Guidelines

As key members of the provider community—whether practitioners or administrators—social workers must grapple with these issues and make their own priorities and values evident. At present, practice guidelines in the field of mental health align closely with what is being promulgated as recovery-oriented practice (Davidson, O'Connell, Tondora, Lawless, & Evans, 2005). Although the housing first model was not developed explicitly as a recovery-oriented practice, its approach and value base embrace many aspects that are central to the recovery movement that is currently driving mental health reform in the United States (New Freedom Commission on Mental Health, 2003). Recovery principles and their application in practice can be applied to a broad range of services for homeless mentally ill adults. These principles include consumer choice and self-direction, person-centered care, empowerment rather than control, strengths-based rather than pathology-based orientation, mutual peer support, personal responsibility, and hope for the future.

Changes in frontline practice must also be accompanied by change at the organizational level. Housing first provides a valuable example of how structuring services in new ways enables recovery-oriented practice. Although the model has been established as evidence based, it integrates another evidence-based practice, assertive community treatment, into its structure to maximize its effectiveness in engaging with the hard-to-reach population of homeless adults who have a serious mental illness (Bond, Drake, Mueser, & Latimer, 2001). Other evidence-based practices often used within housing first are integrated treatment for dual diagnosis and supported employment (Drake et al., 2001).

The success of housing first is due, in large part, to its value-oriented philosophy, which acts as the organizing principle for service delivery. By applying the values of consumer choice and a right to housing, housing first is free from the rules and regulations that accompany many mental health programs that provide housing and treatment services. Without these programmatic constraints, social workers can genuinely engage with consumers and respond to their individual needs and preferences instead of having to hold them accountable to a system-defined standard of worthiness.

By removing the continuum approach based on sobriety and treatment adherence, social workers can embrace the nonlinear nature of recovery and offer services that are genuinely self-directed. Placing values first also has implications for the implementation of other evidence-based practices. For example, there is now a recognition that assertive community treatment needs some modification to give a greater sense of consumer choice and autonomy (Salyers & Tsemberis, 2007). In conclusion, changing the one-on-one interactions of social workers and consumers must be accompanied by organizational change that puts the consumer first and transforms the role of social workers from enforcers to empowering collaborators. In turn, administrators need to facilitate the opportunity and the challenge of using evidence to inform practice.

Publications from the New York Housing Study

Greenwood, R. M., Schaefer-McDaniel, N., Winkel, G., & Tsemberis, S. (2005). Decreasing psychiatric symptoms by increasing choice in services for adults with histories of homelessness. *American Journal of Community Psychology*, *36*(3–4), 223–238.

Gulcur, L., Stefancic, A., Shinn, M., Tsemberis, S., & Fischer, S. (2003). Housing, hospitalization, and cost outcomes for homeless individuals with psychiatric disabilities participating in continuum of care and housing first programmes. *Journal of Community and Applied Social Psychology*, *13*(2), 171–186.

Tsemberis, S., & Asmussen, S. (1999). From streets to homes: The pathways to housing consumer preference supported housing model. *Alcoholism Treatment Quarterly*, *17*(1–2), 113–131.

Tsemberis, S., Moran, L., Shinn, B., Shern, D., & Asmussen, S. (2003). Consumer preference programs for individuals who are homeless and have psychiatric disabilities: A drop-in center and a supported housing program. *American Journal of Community Psychology*, *32*(3–4), 305–317.

Yanos, P., Felton, B., Tsemberis, S., & Frye, V. (2007). Exploring the role of housing type, neighborhood characteristics, and lifestyle factors in the community integration of formerly homeless persons diagnosed with mental illness. *Journal of Mental Health*, *16*(6), 703–717.

Publications from the New York Services Study

Hawkins, R. L., & Abrams, C. (2007). Disappearing acts: Social networks of homeless individuals with co-occurring disorders. *Social Science and Medicine*, *65*(10), 2031–2042.

Henwood, B. F., & Padgett, D. K. (2007). The self-medication hypothesis revisited. *American Journal on Addictions*, *16*(3), 160–165.

Padgett, D. K. (2007). Ontological security in the third decade of the "homelessness crisis" in the United States. *Social Science and Medicine*, *64*(9), 1925–1936.

Padgett, D. K., Hawkins, R. L., Abrams, C., & Davis, A. (2006). In their own words: Trauma and substance abuse in the lives of formerly homeless women with serious mental illness. *American Journal of Orthopsychiatry*, *76*(4), 461–467.

Padgett, D. K., Henwood, B., Abrams, C., & Davis, A. (2008). Engagement and retention in care among formerly homeless adults with serious mental illness: Voices from the margins. *Psychiatric Rehabilitation Journal*, *31*(3), 226–233.

Shibusawa, T., & Padgett, D. K. (2009). Out of sync: A life course perspective on aging among formerly homeless adults with serious mental illness. *Journal of Aging Studies*, *23*(3), 188–196.

References

Allen, M. (2003). Waking Rip van Winkle: Why developments in the last 20 years should teach the mental health system not to use housing as a tool of coercion. *Behavioral Sciences and the Law*, *21*(4), 503–521.

American Psychiatric Association. (2000). *Diagnostic and statistical manual of mental disorders* (4th rev. ed.). Washington, DC: Author.

Bond, G. R., Drake, R. E., Mueser, K. T., & Latimer, E. (2001). Assertive community treatment for people with severe mental illness. *Disease Management and Health Outcomes, 9*(3), 141–159.

Bryk, A. S., & Raudenbush, S. W. (1992). *Hierarchical linear models.* Newbury Park, CA: Sage.

Carling, P. J. (1993). Housing and supports for persons with mental illness: Emerging approaches to research and practice. *Hospital and Community Psychiatry, 44*(5), 439–449.

Charmaz, K. (2006). *Constructing grounded theory.* Thousand Oaks, CA: Sage.

Ciarolo, J. A., Edwards, D. W., Kiresuk, T. J., Newman, F. L., & Brown, T. R. (1981). *Colorado Symptom Index.* Washington, DC: National Institute of Mental Health.

Culhane, D., Metraux, S., & Hadley, T. (2002). Public service reductions associated with placement of homeless persons with severe mental illness in supportive housing. *Housing Policy Debate, 13*(1), 107–163.

Dartmouth Psychiatric Research Center. (1995). *Residential follow-back calendar.* Lebanon, NH: Dartmouth Medical School.

Davidson, L., O'Connell, M. J., Tondora, J., Lawless, M., & Evans, A. C. (2005). Recovery in serious mental illness: A new wine or just a new bottle. *Professional Psychology: Research and Practice, 36*(5), 480–487.

Drake, R. E., Osher, F. C., & Wallach, M. A. (1991). Homelessness and dual diagnosis. *American Psychologist, 46*(11), 1149–1158.

Drake, R. E., Goldman, H. H., Leff, H. S., Lehman, A. F., Dixon, L. B., Mueser, K. T., et al. (2001). Implementing evidence-based practices in routine mental health service settings. *Psychiatric Services, 52*(1), 179–192.

Gladwell, M. (2006, February 13). Million dollar Murray: Why problems like homelessness may be easier to solve than to manage. *New Yorker,* 96–107.

Greenwood, R., Shaefer-McDaniel, N., Winkle, G., & Tsemberis, S. (2005). Decreasing psychiatric symptoms by increasing choice in services for adults with histories of homelessness. *American Journal of Community Psychology, 36*(3–4), 226–238.

Henwood, B. F., & Padgett, D. K. (2007). The self-medication hypothesis revisited. *American Journal on Addictions, 16*(3), 160–165.

Hopper, K., Jost, J., Hay, T., Welber, S., & Haugland, G. (1997). Homelessness, severe mental illness, and the institutional circuit. *Psychiatric Services, 48*(5), 659–665.

Kertesz, S. G., Mullins, A. N., Schumacher, J. E., Wallace, D., Kirk, K., & Milby, J. B. (2007). Long-term housing and work outcomes among treated cocaine-using homeless persons. *Journal of Behavioral Health Services and Research, 34*(1), 17–33.

Kessler, R. C., McGonagle, K. A., Zhao, S., Nelson, C. B., Hughes, M., Eshleman, S., et al. (1994). Lifetime and 12-month prevalence of DSM-III-R psychiatric disorders in the United States: Results from the national comorbidity survey. *Archives of General Psychiatry, 51*(1), 8–19.

Locke, G., Khadduri, J., & O'Hara, A. (2007, March 1–2). *Housing models.* Paper presented at the National Symposium on Homelessness Research, Washington, DC.

Lovell, A., & Cohn, S. (1998). The elaboration of "choice" in a program for homeless persons labeled psychiatrically disabled. *Human Organizations, 57*(1), 8–20.

McLellan, A. T., Alterman, A. I., & Woody, G. E. (1992). *Treatment services review.* Philadelphia: University of Pennsylvania Press.

Mueser, K. T., Drake, R. E., & Wallach, M. A. (1998). Dual diagnosis: A review of etiological theories. *Addictive Behaviors, 23*(6), 717–734.

New Freedom Commission on Mental Health. (2003). *Achieving the promise: Transforming mental health care in America. Final Report* (DHHS Pub. No. SMA-03–3832). Rockville, MD: U.S. Department of Health and Human Services.

Padgett, D. (2008). *Qualitative methods in social work research* (2nd ed.). Thousand Oaks, CA: Sage.

Padgett, D., Gulcur, L., & Tsemberis, S. (2006). Housing first services for people who are homeless with co-occurring serious mental illness and substance abuse. *Research on Social Work Practice, 16*(1), 74–83.

Padgett, D. K. (2007). There's no place like (a) home: Ontological security in the third decade of the "homelessness crisis" in the United States. *Social Science and Medicine, 64*(9), 1925–1936.

Padgett, D. K., Henwood, B., Abrams, C., & Davis, A. (2008). Engagement and retention in care among formerly homeless adults with serious mental illness: Voices from the margins. *Psychiatric Rehabilitation Journal, 31*(3), 226–233.

Patton, M. (2002). *Qualitative research and evaluation methods.* Thousand Oaks, CA: Sage.

Pearson, C. L., Locke, G., Montgomery, A. E., & Buron, L. (2007). *The applicability of housing first models to homeless persons with serious mental illness.* Washington, DC: Office of Policy Development and Research, U.S. Department of Housing and Urban Development.

Piat, M., Lesage, A., Boyer, R., Dorvil, H., Couture, A., Grenier, G., & Bloom, D. (2008). Housing for persons with serious mental illness: Consumer and service provider preferences. *Psychiatric Services, 59*(9), 1011–1017.

Regier, D. A., Farmer, M. E., Rae, D. S., Locke, B. Z., Keith, S. J., Judd, L. L., et al. (1990). Comorbidity of mental disorders with alcohol and other drug abuse: Results from the Epidemiologic Catchment Area (ECA) study. *Journal of the American Medical Association, 264*(19), 2511–2518.

Ridgway, P., & Zipple, A. (1990). The paradigm shift in residential services: From the linear continuum to supported housing services. *Psychiatric Rehabilitation Journal, 13*(1), 11–31.

Salyers, M. P., & Tsemberis, S. (2007). Act and recovery: Integrating evidence-based practice and recovery orientation on assertive community teams. *Community Mental Health Journal, 43*(6), 619–641.

Shibusawa, T., & Padgett, D. K. (2009). Out of sync: A life course perspective on aging among formerly homeless adults with serious mental illness. *Journal of Aging Studies, 23*(3), 188–196.

Sobell, L. C., Sobell, M. B., & Leo, G. I. (1988). Reliability of a timeline method: Assessing normal drinker's reports of recent drinking and a comparative evaluation across several populations. *British Journal of Addiction, 83*(4), 393–402.

Srebnik, D., Livingston, J., Gordon, L., & King, D. (1995). Housing choice and community success for individuals with serious and persistent mental illness. *Community Mental Health Journal, 31*(2), 139–151.

Stanhope, V., Henwood, B. F., & Padgett, D. K. (2008). *Understanding service disengagement from the perspective of case managers.* Unpublished manuscript, New York University.

Stefancic, A., Schaefer-McDaniel, N., Davis, A., & Tsemberis, S. (2004). Maximizing follow-up of adults with histories of homelessness and psychiatric disabilities. *Evaluation and Program Planning, 27*(4), 433–442.

Tanzman, B. (1993). An overview of surveys of mental health consumers' preferences for housing and support services. *Hospital and Community Psychiatry, 44*(5), 450–456.

Tompsett, C., Toro, P., Guzicki, M., Manrique, M., & Zatakia, J. (2006). Homelessness in the United States: Assessing changes in prevalence and public opinion, 1993–2001. *American Journal of Community Psychology, 37*(1–2), 47–61.

Tsemberis, S., Gulcur, L., & Nakae, M. (2004). Housing first, consumer choice, and harm reduction for homeless individuals with a dual diagnosis. *American Journal of Public Health, 94*(4), 651–656.

CHAPTER SEVEN

Collaborations among Diverse Organizations

Building Evidence to Support Community Partnerships

Sondra J. Fogel and Kathleen A. Moore

Statement of the Problem

Beginning with the Charitable Choice provisions in the Personal Responsibility and Work Opportunity Reconciliation Act of 1996 (Pub. Law No. 104–193), and strengthened through presidential executive orders, faith-based institutions have gained prominence as leaders in the administration and delivery of social services, particularly for vulnerable populations, such as the homeless (Ebaugh, Chafetz, & Pipes, 2005; Roberts-DeGennaro & Fogel, 2007). According to Stritt (2008), "The extant research unequivocally shows that they have and continue to make their primary contributions in the numerous 'gaps' of the American social safety net" (p. 730). Perhaps the most significant factor encouraging this development has been the declaration of religious organizations as eligible recipients of federal monies to provide social services, with the understanding that certain conditions are met (Tangenberg, 2005). Such conditions include enforcing nondiscrimination policies regarding client eligibility, refraining from any actions to convert or proselytize, and restricting the use of federal funds for specified program services.

As faith-based institutions have partnered with traditional nonprofits and governmental social services, there has been a great interest in learning whether the outcomes of services that such collaborations provide are different for clients served by secular organizations (Tangenberg, 2005). There is also growing interest in examining how faith-based and other diverse organizations work together to maximize opportunities for seamless service delivery (Ebaugh, Chafetz, & Pipes, 2007).

This chapter provides a case example of how a collaboration involving faith-based, secular, and government organizations formed to develop an innovative service for homeless adults living on the streets in a downtown area in Pinellas County, Florida. The chapter concludes with some guidelines for using evidence to inform practice in the area of supporting diverse collaborations. The information presented is part of a larger evaluation study of a "tent city" for homeless adults in Pinellas County. The chapter presents only the views of stakeholders who were involved in the collaboration process of building a tent-city program.

Literature Review

Increasingly, faith-based institutions have joined with other social service organizations and/or large-scale initiatives to address the welfare of vulnerable groups (Guo & Acar, 2005; Kegler, Kiser, & Hall, 2007). In fact, Tangenberg (2005) notes that "community practice networks between secular and faith-related providers may enhance service coordination when such coordination appears appropriate and consistent with client beliefs" (p. 200). Yet in general, knowledge regarding the collaboration between faith-based organizations and other providers in addressing desired client outcomes or client preferences is lacking. Likewise, literature in this area fails to differentiate the types of organizations that collaborate, as well as other numerous variables that distinguish organizational types and structures (Guo & Acar, 2005). The authors contend that collaborations with faith-based organizations are a unique type of partnership alliance.

COLLABORATION

Gray (1989) has defined collaboration as a "process through which parties who see different aspects of a problem can constructively explore their differences and search for solutions that go beyond their limited visions of what is possible" (p. 5). It is the work of Linden (2002), however, that is generally recognized to expand this idea to the nonprofit sector. Nonprofit collaboration "occurs when different nonprofits work together to address problems through joint efforts, resources, and decision making and shared ownership of the final project of service"

(Ebaugh et al., 2007, p. 178). This broad definition does not, however, address the extent of shared experience or the intensity of the collaboration (Guo & Acar, 2005). This has led to the development of different models to represent the continuum of collaboration on issues such as interdependence (Murray, 1998), resource sharing (Zajac & D'Aunno, 1993), and formality (Kohm, La Piana, & Gowdy, 2000).

Two theoretical frameworks that guide much of the current research on nonprofit collaborations are resource dependence theory (Pfeffer & Salancik, 1978) and transaction cost theory (Williamson, 1991). Briefly, resource dependence theory suggests that collaborations occur to sustain and/or advance an organizational mission, whereas transaction cost theory suggests that collaborations occur to promote efficiency and increase benefits in terms of economic or psychological outputs. Yet Gou and Acar (2005) note that these approaches fail to consider organizational environments and structural contexts, both of which affect the overall strategic choice made for or against participating in collaborations.

As stated earlier, there is also a need to develop a theoretical perspective on how to understand the collaboration between faith-based and secular organizations. Tangenberg (2005) suggests the use of Scott's (1981) open-system organizational perspective as a starting point. "The open systems perspective posits that a focal organization (such as a congregation or faith related agency) is a system of relationships that influences and is influenced by external environmental conditions" (Tangenberg, 2005, p. 200). To date, a limited number of studies have used this perspective. The case situation presented herein highlights how an open-systems framework may be useful in understanding how a collaboration evolves between a faith-based organization and other organizations in a community.

PROBLEM FORMULATION

As an emerging hub of urban activity, the vicinity in and around the downtown of St. Petersburg, Florida, has developed into an active commercial area supporting new businesses and high-end condominium housing. As these developments changed the landscape of the district, tolerance for homeless persons living on the streets in the downtown area began to falter. In response, a diverse group of local business leaders, city officials, and social service and faith-based advocates for the poor came together to discuss how to address the divergent needs of the downtown area. To guide their planned change efforts, they developed a practice question: what can be done to shelter the homeless and serve this vulnerable population? Using this question as their starting point for gathering data, group members began to research housing options for homeless adults living on the streets.

While these discussions were occurring, ongoing external events heightened the need for a coordinated response. Many homeless persons in the area were congregating at night and setting up tents at a waterfront location that was under consideration for a large municipal project. Under pressure to move to a new location, the tent dwellers were told that they were welcome to set up on a site in a lot next to a faith-based organization. In that contained area, many homeless were able to leave their tents up all day and obtain minimal supportive services. Perhaps most important, an oversight authority protected their possessions.

Although providing a place for homeless adults seemed to assuage the immediate need to ensure that they were safe and away from areas that affected future economic development considerations, it certainly did not address the long-term concern of how to care for and provide support for this vulnerable population. Given this, the initial group that formed the practice question, along with other county and homeless advocacy groups, assessed various shelter ideas that had emerged and used these ideas to inform their next set of actions.

After reviewing information as to how other cities shelter the homeless and assessing the strengths and capacity of the immediate region, the idea for a coordinated one-stop service center and temporary lodging site for homeless persons living on the street was proposed. Unfortunately, however, state and local budgets were projected to be significantly cut as a result of the recession. With this news, and considering the expense of providing these services, discussions to continue to pursue implementation of a one-stop service center ceased.

It might be expected that this would have stopped the effort to shelter the homeless living on the street. However, this was not the case. Building on the assessment of evidence from other metropolitan areas on how to serve the homeless, support from political leadership, and the daily visible workings of an existing and informal tent city, a proposal to provide a site for a pilot, 250-tent city emerged from the local Catholic Charities. It was willing to assume the lead role in organizing the housing and daily services for the tent city. However, Catholic Charities needed the help of other providers and government programs to serve the needs of this vulnerable population. With more discussions and support from the diverse members of the original convening group, a collaboration of providers and businesses formed to serve the homeless living on the street.

With the support of private donations from business leaders, social service agencies providing on-site assessment services, and local government support, Pinellas Hope developed as an innovative five-month tent shelter and one-stop service program for adults who were homeless. Site facilities were designated in the shelter for eating, meetings, and recreation. Bathroom, shower, laundry, and computer facilities were provided. In addition, trailers were set up to provide administrative and social services. Supported by multiple donors and government monies and with committed leadership from Catholic Charities, Pinellas Hope opened in December 2007 and was filled to capacity within one week. Individuals who lived on the street or couples without children were sheltered in 250 tents in a contained campsite.

Methodology

Given the lack of any systematic data to guide the implementation of this type of program, as well as lingering questions about the effectiveness of the type of housing service for this population, Pinellas Hope engaged in an outcome study. The principles of evidence-based practice (EBP) supported the collection of data from various data sources to inform decisions about whether the intervention produced the desired outcomes (McCracken & Marsh, 2008).

A two-stage, mixed-methods process evaluation was conducted to capture initial information regarding who used the services, how the participants were helped, and whether the program was an effective and cost-efficient option to consider for future efforts (Rallis & Rossman, 2003).

Process evaluations describe services and assess the resources and materials used in a program. It is appropriate to use this evaluative approach when programs are being implemented to understand the planning and implementation processes that lead to changes in the system. In fact, the approach is a necessary first step for understanding service components that may factor into projected outcomes (El Ansair, Phillips, & Hammick, 2001). A small research group, consisting of the authors, county employees, and a social service provider, was formed to provide oversight of the process evaluation and to assist staff in the Pinellas Hope program with data management.

A component of the first part of this process evaluation was the collection of qualitative data from interviews with various stakeholders of the tent city to gather their perceptions about the program. According to Anasta (2004), "Qualitative evaluation can illuminate the view of services held by users and nonusers, staff members who provide the service at all levels, collaborators and competitors, funders" (p. 58).

DATA COLLECTION

A total of twenty-seven respondents were interviewed. This purposive sample represented a diverse group of key informants, including social service providers, elected and government officials, Pinellas Hope staff and volunteers, and homeless advocates. These persons were involved in the decision-making processes of designing and/or providing services on site for residents of Pinellas Hope.

An interview schedule with closed- and open-ended questions was developed by the research group and approved by an institutional review board at a local university. Along with questions regarding the operation and resident population of Pinellas Hope, the exploratory study asked two key questions:

1. How would you describe the collaboration between the agencies that are involved in the Pinellas Hope program?
2. In what ways has the Pinellas Hope program been successful in meeting the needs of homeless persons?

Respondents were encouraged to expand on any topic that was presented to them and to address issues not covered in the interview. Comments were not taped but written as the interview was occurring, a noted limitation that may have altered exact quotes.

DATA ANALYSIS

Responses to the interviews were entered into a Microsoft Excel spreadsheet. As themes emerged, another section was added to the coding sheet. Data from the interviews were reviewed and categorized according to the themes. Three independent coders identified themes. After coding of all the interviews, the themes were condensed to reflect major areas of content in terms of their frequency by the same coders. Berg (2004) recommends this collaborative social research process for data collection and analysis.

Collaboration among agencies. Responses ranged from the complexity of providing services for this population to the challenges of collaboration in a declining fiscal environment. Three main themes emerged: (1) collaborative efforts appear to be effective in sustaining the Pinellas Hope program, (2) there is an increase in collaborative efforts as a result of the high visibility of the program in the downtown area, and (3) the declining government funding is creating a competitive environment that is promoting collaborative efforts among the service providers. Examples of responses included the following:

- "Pinellas Hope was an opportunity to get a lot done in one place."
- "The whole climate has changed because of the decreases in money."

- "The thought of collaboration means that [my agencies] might have to do more with less."
- "Everyone cooperates to get things done and the focus and best interest of the client is sought which incidentally is in the best interest of the public."
- "Every agency experiences [clients with] homeless issues so we all want to get it to work right."
- "There was an initial distrust of Catholic Charities among the players in the field."

What emerged from the interviews was the importance of the faith-based organization taking the lead in this operation. By adhering to the requirements for the receipt of government monies and providing an open but fairly private area on campsite grounds for providers to work with residents, the leadership of Catholic Charities increased the contacts and communication among the providers. As one respondent said, "There is no doubt that Pinellas Hope has helped to get agencies to work together."

Success of Pinellas Hope. Of the twenty-seven respondents, twenty-two suggested that the innovative, faith-based-led program was a success. The other five did not agree because of concerns that the use of tents would derail efforts to establish more permanent housing for the homeless. Yet the twenty-two who indicated that Pinellas Hope was a successful program broadly defined success. Examples of responses included the following:

- "It fulfills the basic human needs of homeless persons."
- "It offers respect, safety, and opportunities for homeless persons to build their self-esteem."
- "It provides a centralized location for homeless persons to come, assess their lives, find employment, and obtain a multitude of services."
- "It provides shelter and a safe place for homeless persons who would otherwise be living on the street."
- "It helps the public understand the plight of the homeless population."
- "It helps to mobilize the community around a social concern."

Many of the respondents did not know what the success outcome for the residents of Pinellas Hope was supposed to be. By default, the housing portion of the program (i.e., the use of tents on the contained campsite) became the desired outcome. Officially, the goal for the program was that 40 percent of residents regain a stable housing status.

In response to the question regarding success, many respondents suggested that operational, programmatic, and facility shortcomings needed to be addressed if the pilot program, Pinellas Hope, was to continue. For example, they raised questions about the continuation of funds for the program, both from private donors and from government sources. They were also concerned about how residents were being "helped" to regain self-sufficiency. Despite a less-than-perfect environment, respondents noted that the program filled an important gap in the community—the need for more shelter beds—but recognized that the residents of Pinellas Hope needed more services than were currently offered at the site.

Discussion

There is little evidence-based information regarding how to build and foster collaboration among diverse social service groups, particularly those that include faith-based organizations. However, this pilot project for the homeless population in Pinellas County became a catalyst for collaboration among service providers in the area. In addition, many stakeholders not previously involved with homeless issues became involved with Pinellas Hope.

From a resource-dependence theoretical perspective, respondents suggested that Pinellas Hope offered an additional resource to foster the mission of their agency. For example, police officers in the downtown area were able to reduce the number of arrests for various unlawful behaviors because many homeless persons living on the street relocated to Pinellas Hope. Other providers were able to recruit participants to underused service programs, as homeless persons were now in a place where they could access such programs. Many of the homeless were veterans who were identified during the intake process as eligible for health and mental health services. Other homeless persons were able to obtain entitlement program services because of their ability to stay in one place during the lengthy certification process.

Transaction cost theory suggests that collaborations can reduce the cost of services. For example, the cost of the service at Pinellas Hope was estimated to be $24.74 per day, significantly less than other shelter services in Pinellas County.

Because of the collaborative efforts between various secular service providers and Pinellas Hope, other community entities, such as local public school–supported hygiene drives, musical performances, and sponsorships to attend local events, provided additional unplanned services to residents. As open-systems theory suggests, the relationships that formed through the collaborative efforts at Pinellas Hope extended beyond the boundaries of the tent city.

Implications for Practice

As faith-based organizations become more prominent in the leadership of social services (Stritt, 2008), collaborations with other organizations in the community will likely increase. Consequently, faith-based organizations will need to strengthen their planned change efforts toward improving the efficiency and effectiveness of their services. In addition, they will need to strengthen their leadership skills in coordinating organizations with diverse missions and cultures. Even though there are many factors, including the desire to provide coordinated services for vulnerable populations, that can lead agencies to build collaborative relationships, with the decline of fiscal resources, increased dependency on other organizations, and political pressures, there remains little evidence to inform how to develop and sustain such partnerships. There is already growing recognition that collaboration can inspire competition and increase barriers to achieving desired client outcomes (Young & Denize, 2008). On the basis of the process evaluation of the Pinellas Hope program, we suggest the following guidelines for informing practice when building collaborations with faith-based organizations:

- Assess the motivating factors for the collaboration. Are there political pressures to collaborate? Are funders committed to participating in the collaborative process?
- Consider the mission of each agency in the collaboration. Will the agency be able to support its mission while collaborating? What is the responsibility of the faith-based organization to its congregation?
- Define program success and ensure that all collaborators agree to the desired outcome. What is the practice question that guides the decision-making processes? What are the desired program and client outcomes?
- Assess the involvement of providers in the collaborative. Are the agencies committed to achieving the desired outcome? What is the level of participation among the collaborators?
- Collect data to inform decisions and review this often with the collaborators. Is there a protocol for gathering information? What is the procedure for encouraging client participation in the decision-making processes?
- Provide opportunities to disseminate the full picture of how the collaboration is working to all involved, including recipients of service, staff and volunteers, stakeholders, and the greater community. Could community forums be scheduled to disseminate

information about the collaborative efforts? What role could the media perform in supporting the efforts of the collaborators?

Available evidence for use in making informed decisions regarding collaboration is in a nascent stage in terms of expanding the role of faith-based organizations as leaders in the provision of coordinated social services (Hula, Jackson-Elmoore, & Resse, 2007). Continued research is needed to build evidence to inform practitioners on effective approaches to develop and sustain collaborations among diverse organizations.

References

Anasta, J. W. (2004). Quality in qualitative evaluation: Issues and possible answers. *Research on Social Work Practice, 14*(1), 57–65.

Berg, B. L. (2004). *Qualitative research methods for the social sciences* (5th ed.). Boston: Pearson Education.

Ebaugh, H. R., Chafetz, J. S., & Pipes, P. F. (2005). Faith-based social service organizations and government funding: Data from a national survey, *Social Science Quarterly, 86*(2), 273–292.

Ebaugh, H. R., Chafetz, J. S., & Pipes, P. F. (2007). Collaborations with faith-based social service coalitions. *Nonprofit Management and Leadership, 18*(2), 175–191.

El Ansair, W., Phillips, C. J., & Hammick, M. (2001). Collaboration and partnerships: Developing the evidence base. *Health and Social Care in the Community, 9*(4), 215–227.

Gray, B. (1989). *Collaborating: Finding common group for multiparty problems.* San Francisco: Jossey-Bass.

Guo, C., & Acar, M. (2005). Understanding collaboration among nonprofit organizations: Combining resource dependency, institutional, and network perspectives. *Nonprofit and Voluntary Sector Quarterly, 34*(3), 340–361.

Hula, R., Jackson-Elmoore, C., & Resse, L. (2007). Mixing God's word and public business: A framework for the analysis of faith-based service delivery. *Review of Policy Research, 24*(1), 67–89.

Kegler, M. C., Kiser, M., & Hall, S. M. (2007, November–December). Evaluation findings from the Institute for Public Health and Faith Collaborations. *Public Health Reports, 122,* 793–802.

Kohm, A., La Piana, D., & Gowdy, H. (2000). *Strategic restructuring: Findings from a study of integration and alliances among nonprofit social service and cultural organizations in the United States* (Discussion Paper PS-24). Chicago: Chapin Hall Center for Children, University of Chicago.

Linden, R. W. (2002). *Working across boundaries: Making collaboration work in government and nonprofit organizations.* San Francisco: Jossey-Bass.

McCracken, S. G., & Marsh, J. C. (2008). Practitioner expertise in evidence-based practice decision making. *Research on Social Work Practice, 18*(4), 301–310.

Murray, V. V. (1998). Interorganizational collaborations in the nonprofit sector. In J. M. Shafirtz (Ed.), *International encyclopedia of public policy and administration* (Vol. 2, pp. 1192–1196). Boulder, CO: Westview.

Personal Responsibility and Work Opportunity Reconciliation Act of 1996, Pub. L. No. 104–193, 110 Stat. 2105.

Pfeffer, J., & Salancik, G. R. (1978). *The external control of organizations: A resource dependence perspective.* New York: Harper and Row.

Rallis, S. F., & Rossman, G. B. (2003). Mixed methods in evaluation contexts: A pragmatic framework. In A. Tashakkori & C. Teddue (Eds.), *Handbook of mixed methods in social and behavioral research* (pp. 491–512). Thousand Oaks, CA: Sage.

Roberts-DeGennaro, M., & Fogel, S. J. (2007). Faith-based and community initiative: Service providers and approaches to studying service outcomes. *Journal of Policy Practice, 6*(2), 45–62.

Scott, W. R. (1981). *Organizations: Rational, natural and open systems.* Englewood Cliffs, NJ: Prentice Hall.

Stritt, S. B. (2008). Estimating the value of the social services provided by faith-based organizations in the United States. *Nonprofit and Voluntary Sector Quarterly, 37*(4), 730–742.

Tangenberg, K. M. (2005). Faith-based human services initiatives: Considerations for social work practice and theory. *Social Work, 50*(3), 197–206.

Williamson, O. D. (1991). Comparative economic organization. The analysis of discrete structural alternatives. *Administrative Science Quarterly, 36*(2), 219–244.

Young, L., & Denize, S. (2008). Competing interests: The challenge to collaboration in the public sector. *International Journal of Sociology and Social Policy, 28*(1–2), 46–58.

Zajac, E. J., & D'Aunno, T. A. (1993). Managing strategic alliances. In S. M. Shortell & A. D. Kaluzny (Eds.), *Health care management: Organization design and behavior* (pp. 274–293). Albany, NY: Delmar.

Translation of Evidence into Community and Organizational Practice

The remaining chapters in this section focus on specific issues regarding how to implement and disseminate evidence-informed knowledge in communities or organizations. The chapters provide examples of an often forgotten part of evidence-informed practice: how are the principles of planned changed efforts implemented in community and organizational settings?

Section 2 begins with chapter 8, by Aimee N. C. Campbell, who frames evidence-informed practice in the larger context of translational research. These research activities include components that aid in the development and implementation of an innovation and activities that sustain the innovation in the practice community. Frequently, transmission of new evidence to support planned change does not get to those who are most likely to want and/or need the innovation. This chapter emphasizes the importance of sharing what is learned from using evidence to improve program and client outcomes. In this chapter, she provides two examples of how results from research programs are disseminated in communities and organizations.

Chapter 9, by Michael S. Kelly and Cynthia Franklin, provides a case example of how an organization can implement the steps in the process of evidence-informed practice to address a community problem related to students dropping out of high school. In this case study, administrators of a large, urban high school reflect on this problem, particularly for minority students. As the chapter demonstrates, using this process can increase the likelihood of support for a planned change effort. The authors offer practice guidelines in using a systematic approach to addressing problems that span both community and organizational issues.

Chapter 10, by Jean M. Kruzich and Pauline Jivanjee, emphasizes the importance of including client views and experiences when building evidence-informed information systems. The authors demonstrate the use of focus groups as a mechanism to engage youths with mental health issues to gain evidence for making decisions. Their work focuses on the client as the expert stakeholder in the evidence-informed process. Using the evidence gleaned from the focus groups, the authors offer guidelines for macro-oriented practitioners that might improve the decision-making processes related to achieving desired client outcomes. The chapter emphasizes the importance of diversity, the range of issues that shape a person's life, and how these perspectives are crucial to the development of culturally appropriate services.

Chapter 11, by Michiel A. van Zyl, Becky F. Antle, and Anita P. Barbee, provides empirical support for an effective dissemination strategy to improve worker outcomes in the area of child safety, permanency, and well-being through an empirically supported training program. Their research documents changes as a result of the training related to improvement in the level of knowledge among public child welfare workers, as well as improvements in other organizational outcomes. The research presented provides an outline for others on how to proceed in collecting evidence to evaluate the impact of a training program.

Chapter 12, by Paul W. Speer, N. Andrew Peterson, Allison Zippay, and Brian Christens, demonstrates how a mixed-methods research strategy can generate evidence to support a range of macro-practice activities. The authors investigate the efforts of a national organizing network to increase levels of civic engagement and empowerment and to influence local public policies. The authors investigate strategies the network uses to accomplish these outcomes using commonly available data sources that can be easily transported to other situations. For practitioners engaged in community activities, particularly those who promote empowerment in neighborhoods and local organizations, this research demonstrates how to analyze the impact of professional efforts using multiple sources of information.

Chapter 13, by Patricia Chamberlain, Lisa Saldana, C. Hendricks Brown, and Leslie D. Leve, addresses the important question of how larger systems responsible for the care of vulnerable youths can adopt and implement evidence-informed practice models. In particular, their focus is on understanding how to facilitate the adoption and full implementation of best practices. The authors used a randomized controlled trial to evaluate the implementation of an evidence-based practice, multidimensional treatment foster care, and then linked the evidence to develop a ten-stage implementation model. The research considered the important elements of both the implementation and dissemination of an empirically supported intervention, as well as the translation of knowledge into a set of practitioner skills.

CHAPTER EIGHT

Translational Research Model for Behavioral Interventions

Methodology of Dissemination and Implementation Research

Aimee N. C. Campbell

Statement of the Problem

Moving behavioral prevention and intervention research into practice settings suffers from long delays, and historically there has been little attention paid to the development of dissemination and implementation science. Furthermore, inconsistency; a failure to articulate specific stages within the process; limited theoretical development; and a lack of collaboration among researchers, providers, and communities have defined the components of the science-to-practice process.

The purpose of this chapter is to provide an overview of the core elements of translational research. The chapter presents a translational

This chapter was written under grant support from the National Institute on Drug Abuse (NIDA), Clinical Trials Network (CTN) (2U10DA013035-06, PI: Edward V. Nunes, MD), and the National Institute of Mental Health (1R25MH080665-01, PI: Nabila El-Bassel, DSW). The author acknowledges the review and invaluable feedback of Dr. Nabila El-Bassel; Dr. Denise Hien, principal investigator of the NIDA CTN Women and Trauma Study; Dr. Susan Witte, principal investigator of the Multimedia Connect Dissemination Study; and Dr. Rogério Pinto.

research model that consists of two phases of disseminating and implementing empirically supported behavioral interventions. Dissemination and implementation models are needed to further the development of using research to inform practice. The chapter highlights current barriers to disseminating empirically supported interventions into at-risk communities and provides suggestions for addressing those barriers to increase the visibility and use of dissemination and implementation research. The chapter concludes with two illustrations of methodologically innovative research studies. The first describes work to disseminate an empirically supported intervention for HIV prevention with heterosexual couples and subsequent research on implementation activities in AIDS services organizations throughout the state of New York. The second example presents a hybrid efficacy-effectiveness study conducted in the National Institute on Drug Abuse's Clinical Trials Network and specifies how this methodology can benefit dissemination and implementation research.

Defining Translational Research

Translational research is an umbrella term referring to the full intervention development process, from initial pilot testing to implementation research and sustainability of innovations in community organizations. The translational research model consists of two broad phases: phase 1, or basic science, which includes treatment development, efficacy, and effectiveness trials; and phase 2, or dissemination and implementation (Brekke, Ell, & Palinkas, 2007; Solomon, Card, & Malow, 2006; Woolf, 2008). Within each of the two phases of the model are specific stages. In behavioral research, Onken, Blaine, and Battjes (1997) describe three stages of phase 1: (1) intervention development, manual writing, and pilot testing; (2) efficacy testing; and (3) effectiveness trials examining transportability of the intervention into community settings (for an illustration of the two phases of the translational research model, see Figure 8.1).

Consensus on the definition and activities that constitute phase 2 dissemination and implementation research as well as who is responsible for championing the effort have been unclear. Terminological inconsistencies in this phase of the translational research model have been lamented for years (Backer, 2000; Kerner, Rimer, & Emmons, 2005). Many different terms have been used to describe dissemination, adoption, and implementation in the literature (e.g., *replication, technology transfer, translational research, transportability, adoption, adaptation*). Such terms are often used interchangeably to describe target

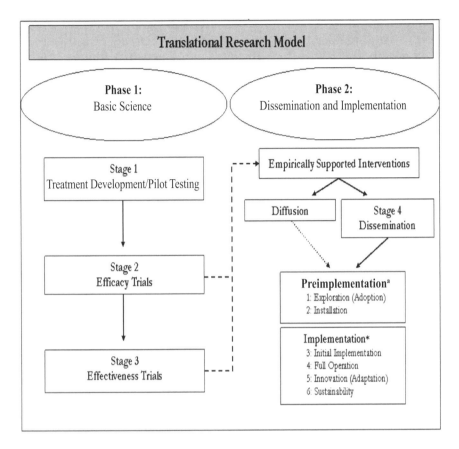

FIGURE 8.1.   *Translational research model*
[a]See Fixsen et al. (2005).

outcomes and process, and they have served to muddy the understanding of this key part of the translational research process.

However, a burgeoning consensus is beginning to emerge on the
terminology used and the parameters of dissemination and implementation research. One reason for this is the recent prominence that
the National Institutes of Health (NIH) has placed on dissemination
and implementation science. The NIH (2006) defines dissemination
as the "targeted distribution of information and intervention materials to a specific public health or clinical practice audience" (n.p.). Dissemination occurs through the active efforts of the researcher or other
representative of the intervention or innovation. This definition dis-
tinguishes dissemination from diffusion by using the word *targeted.*

The term *diffusion*, often still used interchangeably with *dissemination*, is the organic, unplanned, and passive spread of innovation information. Diffusion efforts include conference presentations, publications of outcome findings in journals, and other types of informational materials (Kerner et al., 2005) and are generally less likely to lead to implementation (Gotham, 2004), as the dashed line between diffusion and implementation notes in Figure 8.1.

Implementation occurs in collaboration with administrators, staff, and consumers in the specific target setting (e.g., schools, substance abuse treatment programs, community mental health clinics). The NIH (2006) defines implementation as the "use of strategies to adopt and integrate evidence-based health interventions and change practice patterns within specific settings" (n.p.). Thus, implementation encompasses the decision to adopt an intervention, preparation for delivery of the intervention, activities to deliver the intervention, and potential adaptation of the intervention to improve effectiveness. The NIH definitions of dissemination and implementation highlight the newly formed consensus of what constitutes phase 2 translational research (Brekke et al., 2007; Greenhalgh, Robert, Macfarlane, Bate, & Kyriakidou, 2004).

DISSEMINATION AND IMPLEMENTATION RESEARCH

The overall lack of understanding regarding the challenges and strategies used in research on dissemination and implementation has greatly hampered progress in the area (Kerner et al., 2005). Several recent conferences, including two held at the NIH, have highlighted the new emphasis on dissemination and implementation science, pulling together experts in the field to offer guidelines for moving forward and to more clearly outline the purpose of this research. The NIH convened conferences in the spring and fall of 2007: "Building the Science of Dissemination and Implementation in the Service of Public Health and Dissemination" and "Implementation Research Workshop: Harnessing Science to Maximize Health." After the second conference, the NIH (2007) summarized the current focus on dissemination and implementation to include the need to strengthen the science, improve the grant-review process for these types of studies, work to integrate and make innovations to theoretical models, and highlight the iterative processes of this research. The NIH also announced targeted funding opportunities specifically for research in dissemination and implementation research.

As these conferences suggest, one of the major tasks moving forward is to define and operationalize the phases of dissemination and implementation. Fixsen, Blase, Naoom, and Wallace (2007) state that the "missing link in the science to service chain is implementation" (p. 17). Studies are needed examining each component of dissemination and implementation. There have been multiple models put forth describing phases or stages of dissemination and implementation (e.g., Bhatta-charyya, Reeves, & Zwarenstein, 2007; Brekke et al., 2007; Kraft, Mezoff, Sogolow, Neumann, & Thomas, 2000; Wandersman et al., 2008).

A MODEL FOR IMPLEMENTATION

A conceptual framework is required because a single theory does not capture the complexity of the environment in which dissemination and implementation occur, including organizational characteristics, pro-vider attributes, training requirements, sustainability efforts, commu-nity capacity, and so on. Fixsen, Naoom, Blase, Friedman, and Wallace (2005) developed a six-stage model of implementation that encom-passes many of the ideas found throughout the literature. The model is sufficiently detailed but has flexibility as to who should fill different roles (e.g., trainer, technical assistance provider). Working under the premise that the implementation process represents multilevel behav-ioral change (Fixsen et al., 2005; Seidman, 2003), the model comprises preimplementation work, implementation activities, and maintenance and sustainability of the intervention in the adopting organization.

According to Gotham (2004), dissemination ends with the adoption of an innovation by an organization. Therefore, the initial stages of Fix-sen et al.'s (2005) model of implementation blend with the dissemina-tion activities. In this implementation model, stage 1 (exploration) and stage 2 (installation) can be thought of as preparatory work.

In stage 1, exploration includes the assessment of organizational and consumer needs to identify the most appropriate empirically supported intervention. Organizational and community capacity should be assessed for additional information on the fit of the innovation within the practice setting (Wandersman et al., 2008). The intervention repre-sentative collaborates with the organization to determine the best fit among intervention, capacity, and need. This is clearly an aspect of dissemination in that the intervention representative actively brings innovative interventions to organizations and providers. The explora-tion phase ends with the selection of a particular innovation by the organization.

Stage 2 involves activities required to prepare the organization to eventually implement the innovation. Installation activities include staff training, identification of evaluation methods and outcomes of interest, and realignment of organizational structures that may need modification to support the innovation. In addition, initial adaptation, or tailoring of the intervention to meet the needs or expectations of a particular population, may be required, especially if the adopting organization serves a client population that is significantly different from that included in the original testing of the intervention.

Core elements of empirically supported interventions must be retained with fidelity during implementation for the intervention to remain effective. Core elements typically derive from theory and previous testing experiences, and they are thought to be integral to producing the main effects of the intervention (e.g., Kelly, Sogolow, & Neumann, 2000). The intervention development team should specify the core elements.

Rotheram-Borus and Duan (2003) caution that focusing only on replication of an intervention with fidelity without taking into consideration the unique qualities of the communities and consumers is insufficient. Therefore, it is also important to maximize the appropriateness and relevance of noncore elements of the intervention that are based on population characteristics.

Stages 3–5 of the model—initial implementation, full operation, and innovation—comprise implementation efforts. Initial implementation involves feasibility testing of the intervention within the organization and is particularly critical (Fixsen et al., 2005). The introduction of change, especially while the innovation is new and staff members are not yet confident in their ability to effectively execute the innovation, is difficult for an organization. Glantz and Compton (2004) note that the likelihood of moving from adoption to implementation increases when the innovation is similar to current programs, existing resources are sufficient, additional training is kept to a minimum, and new procedures are easily put into practice. These characteristics are also similar to innovation qualities that Rogers (2003) described that increase the likelihood of an innovation being adopted. Further, in a recent systematic review of more than five hundred promotion and prevention programs, Durlak and DuPre (2008) found that level of implementation (i.e., fidelity and intervention dosage) was a strong predictor of program outcomes. This finding reinforces the need for the critical examination of implementation processes to maximize the opportunity for successful innovation integration.

Once the innovation is integrated into an organization's routine services, the model shifts into full operation. It is at this point that outcomes of the new innovation become evident through evaluation and the innovation obtains a treatment as usual status (Fixsen et al., 2005). Although the innovation should be implemented as faithfully as possible to how it was originally tested (i.e., efficacy and effectiveness trials), changes may be made once it is operational in the organization. Caution should be taken to discern whether changes are innovations to the intervention or merely natural drift. Assessment of client improvement can help with such determinations. Finally, sustainability (stage 6) of the innovation in an organization occurs approximately two to four years after initial implementation (Fixsen et al., 2005). Throughout the implementation process, sustainability activities can be introduced and discussed to ensure the longevity of the innovation in the organization if desired (e.g., setting aside resources for the maintenance of the innovation and ensuring that the innovation continues to meet the needs of clients, such as by assessing for shifts in client characteristics).

Although additional research is needed to flesh out specific activities essential to the implementation process, Fixsen et al. (2005) developed a comprehensive framework with which to ground research activities. Theoretical development within and between the stages is important to understanding and advancing the science of dissemination and implementation.

BARRIERS TO DISSEMINATION AND IMPLEMENTATION RESEARCH

The gap between phase 1, efficacy and effectiveness research, and phase 2, dissemination and implementation, has plagued many fields of study, including biomedical, addictions, and mental health (e.g., Institute of Medicine, 1998; Sprang, Craig, & Clark, 2008; Woolf, 2008). The research-to-practice gap results in the uneven distribution of empirically supported interventions in the community. Specifically, uneven adoption results in health disparities, whereby dissemination is done only in limited settings under the best of circumstances, where resources and time are more plentiful (Kerner et al., 2005). From an ethical standpoint, researchers have an obligation to enhance the dissemination of effective treatment into at-risk communities (Kerner et al., 2005). Treatment development, efficacy, and effectiveness outcomes are important, but only inasmuch as they are able to be transported and delivered to those in need.

Many obstacles have hindered dissemination and implementation research and the efficient transport of empirically supported intervention into at-risk communities. The following sections discuss five common areas described in the literature that slow the dissemination of promising interventions.

Linear Stage Model of Behavioral Research

The three-stage linear model of behavioral research includes (1) intervention development and pilot testing, (2) efficacy, and (3) effectiveness research. This model was employed as a mirrored approach to a medical or pharmacological model of research. The linear model is defined by specific guidelines using rigorous design and outcome assessment. Glasgow, Lichtenstein, and Marcus (2003) point to two influential papers published in the mid-1980s (see Flay, 1986; Greenwald & Cullen, 1985) that argued for the adoption of a structured, linear progression for scientific research—hypothesis development, methodological development, efficacy, effectiveness, and dissemination. Behavioral treatment researchers further specified how such models could translate more specifically to the social sciences (Onken et al., 1997; Rounsaville, Carroll, & Onken, 2001). However, the linear stage model limits the types of research questions, methods, and population characteristics under study and is less effective in understanding how to efficiently translate and disseminate findings.

The complexity of behavioral interventions complicates the ability to move innovative interventions into practice settings. Behavioral interventions take place in complex settings, involving multiple systems and often with competing needs (Brekke et al., 2007). Compared with medical innovations, for which it is easier to monitor objective symptoms and outcomes under tight controls, staff with diverse educational and training backgrounds, in organizations defined by a range of missions and resources, implement behavioral innovations to consumers with an infinite array of strengths and challenges (Glasgow et al., 2003). In addition, individuals are exposed to a host of outside variables (e.g., alternative treatments) that complicate treatment and assessment.

Effective interventions under strict sets of controls and with homogenous patient samples often fail to replicate positive outcomes in subsequent effectiveness trials with real-world parameters (Glasgow et al., 2003). Inconclusive research findings across efficacy and effectiveness studies, as well as inconsistent methodology, inclusion criteria, and assessment, make developing practice guidelines and conducting systematic reviews challenging (Glantz & Compton, 2004). Systematic reviews and meta-analyses can be rigorous and informative mechanisms by which practitioners are able to judge the merits of interventions. However, these methods can be compromised as a result of inconsistent reporting of outcomes and the restrictive guidelines placed on efficacy research. These issues challenge the current reliance on the linear stage model of research with behavioral treatments.

FUNDING BIAS TOWARD EFFICACY RESEARCH

There has been a strong bias toward funding developmental and efficacy studies and little historical emphasis on the study of dissemination and implementation science (e.g., Glasgow et al., 2003). Brekke et al. (2007) summarize several reports indicating that there is up to a twenty-year gap between scientific research and the implementation of findings into community organizations. The extent of this gap is partly related to the emphasis of federal funding dollars on treatment development and efficacy research as opposed to services and dissemination research. In an article published about this problem in biomedical research, Woolf (2008) suggests that phase 2, translational research, may result in more lives saved than phase 1, basic science or "bench-to-bedside" research (p. 212). He concludes that funding for research should be based on the proportion of health improvement that could result from an intervention, potentially shifting funds toward dissemination and/or services research. A parallel argument could be made for behavioral research. Efficacy and effectiveness studies are important, but until promising interventions are disseminated more broadly, the benefits to consumers and providers will be limited.

OUTCOME SELECTION

Relying on a narrow range of outcomes and treatment effects in the treatment development, efficacy, and effectiveness research can limit the utility of findings. The types of primary outcomes examined in efficacy and effectiveness research place less emphasis on individual change mechanisms. Although questions related to overall treatment effectiveness are vital, equally important questions as to for whom the treatment works best and how it works best can have far-reaching implications. Mediating and moderating analyses are key to understanding these types of questions (Glasgow et al., 2003; Kazdin, 1997; Kraemer, Wilson, Fairburn, & Agras, 2002; Rotheram-Borus & Duan, 2003) and may be more informative to practitioners than treatment by time analyses, which is often used as a primary outcome indicator (Rapkin & Trickett, 2005).

Rapkin (2002) suggests that reliance on general treatment effects in randomized control trials (RCTs) obscures contextual and historical elements that are important to consider for individual clients. For example, Kazdin (1997) developed a systematic research model for developing effective treatment that includes using diverse research designs, identifying change mechanisms, and using moderator analyses to answer practical questions with utility for providers and consumers. Finally, practical questions related to treatment attendance, time to complete treatment, long-term outcomes, and required supplies are essential in considering the appropriateness of an intervention for a target client population (Eke, Neumann, Wilkes, & Jones, 2006; Rotheram-Borus & Duan, 2003). Focusing on collecting data relevant to implementation activities will provide further information on which practitioners can draw to improve program outcomes and help clients achieve their desired outcomes.

Holding RCTs as the gold standard of research is frequently cited as a contributor to the science to practice mismatch (Glasgow et al., 2003; Rapkin & Trickett, 2005). Quasi-experimental designs, including two active experimental arms, nonrandomized intervention assignment and observational studies, hold promise in understanding how interventions work in community settings. Although quasi-experimental designs give up some internal validity controls, they more closely mimic the work done in community settings.

Rapkin and Trickett (2005) also argue that the complexities of behavioral research do not guarantee that randomization procedures result in comparable treatment arms in terms of combinations of variables. For example, allowing clients to self-select into two active treatment arms can answer relevant questions about who chooses certain treatment options, why, and for what desired outcome. Although this does not ensure comparability across treatment groups, careful planning, controlling for confounders, and advanced statistical techniques such as propensity score matching (see El-Bassel, Gilbert, Wu, Go, & Hill, 2005; Rosenbaum & Rubin, 1985) can allow for important questions to be answered.

DIFFUSION VERSUS DISSEMINATION ACTIVITIES

Behavioral intervention researchers have typically not been involved in dissemination and implementation research. In general, researchers practice diffusion, the passive distribution of innovations and information, which has shown limited success (Gotham, 2004). If one were to think about the spread of innovations on a continuum, diffusion of innovations through journals, conferences, or media outlets might fall into the category of "let it happen" rather than "helping it happen" or "making it happen" (Greenhalgh et al., 2004). Rotheram-Borus and Duan (2003) suggest that expecting researchers to disseminate interventions under current systems, rather than focusing direct efforts on the most effective ways to move research findings into communities, is misguided. Once findings from an efficacy or effectiveness trial are published, the researcher, often because of a lack of funding and appropriate resources, is unable to tackle dissemination activities that might increase the availability of the intervention to providers. Furthermore, researchers do not commonly view themselves as integral to the dissemination process. Their expertise is in design, methodological considerations, and statistical methods, not in collaborating with providers and communities on implementation efforts.

Problems in translating efficacy and effectiveness research into products that can be readily disseminated result in community providers' adopting of or continuing the use of interventions that lack empirical support. Glantz and Compton (2004) point to a number of reasons that this might be the case: lack of information about empirically supported interventions, lack of agency resources to enact change (e.g., funding and training opportunities), general belief among providers about the superiority of practice knowledge, and concerns about the appropriateness and adaptability of interventions with populations not represented in the original research. Further, many providers and consumers have a well-founded mistrust of research and researchers, especially in communities of color. Research that is not collaboratively developed with communities, that outsiders or funding sources impose, and that does not take into account unique community knowledge and characteristics will face limited acceptance (Dworkin, Pinto, Hunter, Rapkin, & Remien, 2008).

RESEARCHER-PRACTITIONER INTERACTION

Research on the dissemination and implementation of evidence-based practices should support opportunities for close collaboration among researchers and practitioners. Limited collaboration during early stages of research (e.g., intervention development, efficacy trials) can result in the research not reflecting the needs of the clients, as well as the practitioner's acceptability of required intervention skills. Efficacy and effectiveness research should be responsive to the types of resources available to providers (e.g., training, staffing) and to the heterogeneity of the client populations. Similarly, provider perception and client reactions to innovative interventions are powerful forces that can maintain the status quo if there are no interactions with the intervention representatives or purveyors. For example, in a study examining use of trauma treatment among mental health providers in a mostly rural Southern state ($N = 1,121$), researchers found that providers infrequently cited exposure therapy as a preferred treatment method, an empirically supported treatment for posttraumatic stress (Sprang, Craig, & Clark, 2008). The authors suggest several factors for the limited use of exposure therapy, including limitations in knowledge and training, discomfort with administering the treatment, and fear of negative client attitudes. These findings suggest that closer collaboration with clinicians in the development and dissemination of empirically supported interventions is necessary for widespread use.

AGENCY AND PROVIDER CHARACTERISTICS

Agency and provider characteristics also contribute to challenges in the dissemination and implementation of behavioral interventions. Organizational factors are important in determining how quickly new interventions or curricula can be adopted and integrated into agencies.

Rogers's (2003) diffusion-of-innovations theory details aspects of adopters versus nonadopters and of early versus late adopters. Those most likely to adopt an innovation are flexible, better equipped to deal with uncertainty and change, and hold attitudes favorable to change. With regard to the organization, programs that are larger, located in urban areas, have leadership marked by consensus building, and are motivated to make changes are more likely to adopt and implement innovations (Gotham, 2004; Rohrbach, Grana, Sussman, & Valente, 2006). Durlak and DuPre's (2008) systematic review of prevention and health promotion programs also confirms that multisystemic factors are integral to implementation at three levels, including (1) community (e.g., funding), (2) organizational (e.g., effective leadership, interagency coordination), and (3) provider (e.g., skill proficiency).

Promoting Dissemination and Implementation Research

This section addresses the promotion of dissemination and implementation research through the creation of vehicles for scientific development, environments to enhance collaboration, new researcher and provider roles, and innovative educational curricula.

SCIENCE, THEORY, AND METHODOLOGY

Although diffusion-of-innovation theory (Rogers, 2003) has done much to aid in the understanding of factors important to dissemination, it was not developed to fully delineate the implementation process. Translational research requires additional theoretical development and testing of promising preexisting theories (e.g., organizational, social network, social exchange) to further illuminate the stages of implementation. In a systematic review of health services diffusion of innovations, Greenhalgh et al. (2004) propose that new research should be based in theory; focused on process outcomes; and done in a collaborative, multidisciplinary manner. A broadening of implementation research to include cultural factors, analysis of multiple aspects of the same intervention across multiple agencies, and consumer subgroup analyses has also been suggested (Durlak & DuPre, 2008). The state of dissemination and implementation science is in an early phase, but there is a burgeoning awareness, coupled with commitment and motivation on both sides of the research-practice divide, to confront these new sets of questions.

Recently, several factors have converged that suggest that the time is right to more actively tackle the research-to-practice schism. Innovative research methodologies have been proposed that will facilitate dissemination and implementation research (see the section "Examples of Methodological Innovations" herein), and the NIH is targeting specific funding opportunities for such work. The push toward evidence-based practice (EBP) and the teaching of EBP in fields heavily involved in service provision, such as social work, has increased an interest in understanding how practitioners make practice decisions and the barriers to learning about and adopting empirically supported interventions. A bidirectional approach between practice and research will enhance scientific development. As Wandersman et al. (2008) note, bridging the science-to-practice gap will entail a detailed understanding of structural and functional elements (e.g., organizational and community capacity, synthesis of research findings) that are important to the dissemination and implementation processes. Service providers and consumers will play an integral role in communicating this information.

Given the lack of behavioral approaches tailored to ethnic minority populations, innovative designs and methodologies, as well as alternatives to RCTs, have been suggested as necessary to meeting diverse health needs. Often, RCTs are unable to fully assess differences across racial or ethnic subgroups because of small sample sizes or issues related to engaging communities of color. This has an impact on who eventually benefits from an empirically supported treatment. Bernal and Scharrón-del-Río (2001) suggest that equal emphasis (or integration) be placed on standard hypothesis testing and discovery-oriented research, including qualitative methods and process-oriented exploration. Within dissemination and implementation research, Castro, Barrera, and Martinez (2004) advocate for a systematic and thorough adaptation process by examining the fidelity-adaptation balance. Adaptation of a particular intervention is a specific process that requires collaboration among consumers, providers, and researchers and intervention developers to make the best implementation decisions. The adaptation phase of the implementation process is in need of research to appraise and select the best empirically supported interventions for working with diverse populations.

COLLABORATION BETWEEN RESEARCHERS AND PRACTITIONERS

The call for genuine collaboration between researchers and practitioners is not new (Kerner et al., 2005). For example, social work educators have been refining methods over the past thirty years to produce practitioners who can successfully evaluate their own practice, participate more fully in research activities, and communicate effectively with researchers. Proctor and Rosen (2008) suggest that research and practice are "often conducted 'in silo' form" (p. 289), with limited dialogue between researchers and service providers. They encourage an evaluation-feedback loop, whereby practitioners provide information to researchers on how effective the intervention actually is in a practice setting, and researchers share findings on promising new interventions (see also Ginexi & Hilton, 2006). The structures in which feedback loops occur, however, remain unclear. Enhancing opportunities for researchers and providers to collaborate on dissemination and implementation research may realistically come about through funding mechanisms directed toward translational research efforts (e.g., Kerner et al., 2005). As discussed earlier in the chapter, a variety of disciplines have questioned the utility of the current linear model of research for behavioral intervention research (Brekke et al., 2007; Ginexi & Hilton, 2006; Glasgow et al., 2003; Weisz, 2000), and researcher-provider collaboration is less likely under the isolating controls of efficacy RCTs.

Collaborative research philosophies and methods can be promising ways to move the science of dissemination and implementation research forward (Kerner et al., 2005). Brekke et al. (2007) suggest participatory research as a methodological alternative for behavioral research, as it does not conform to a linear scientific research model. Instead, participatory research emphasizes external validity, bidirectional communication with community stakeholders, and consensus building.

According to Israel, Schulz, Parker, and Becker (1998), community-based research includes basic tenets, such as using the community as the level of analysis, facilitating collaborative relationships in the community, prioritizing the mutual benefit of all parties in the research endeavor, promoting iterative feedback throughout the process, and ensuring the dissemination of findings to all involved members. Collaborating with communities to assess need, identify relevant research questions, and manage knowledge in the community is congruous to the aims of implementation research. Community-based research allows for better partnership from the onset (Kerner et al., 2005), thereby creating an environment in which research is more likely to be successful (e.g., recruitment of research participants that involves the community or treatment agency) and positive outcomes that are more likely to be sustained. The principles of community-based research can facilitate future dissemination and implementation efforts.

REDEFINING ROLES FOR PROVIDERS AND RESEARCHERS

It is also necessary to redefine the roles and expectations of researchers and providers. The construct of a purveyor, or supplier, has been presented in the literature using different terms, including *linking agent* (Kraft et al., 2000) and *change agent* (Rogers, 2003). A purveyor is "an individual or group of individuals representing a program or practice who actively work to implement that practice or program with fidelity and good effect" (Fixsen et al., 2005, p. 14). Specific purveyor activities might include identifying the need for change, helping establish relationships among stakeholders, enhancing organizational readiness and staff intentions to change, and facilitating sustainability activities.

The purveyor can be internal to the organization (e.g., on-site social worker) or external to the organization (e.g., researcher). The benefit of having an internal purveyor is that there will be ongoing expertise accessible to the organization. Internal purveyors can provide technical assistance, assess and monitor adherence drift, and help train new staff. External purveyors may have specific expertise with the intervention (i.e., intervention developer), which may be particularly helpful at the front end of the implementation process. Moving forward, it is necessary to redefine roles for researchers and providers that take into account specific dissemination and implementation activities (Kerner et al., 2005). In addition, education and training to fit the demands of these roles must be offered.

EDUCATION

Researchers can add integral information on how to adapt or integrate empirically supported interventions into diverse community settings. In 2007, the International Conference on Implementation and Translational Research in Stockholm highlighted the natural link between EBP and dissemination and implementation research. Work presented by leading researchers in these fields defined activities within dissemination and implementation research and the role it plays in teaching EBP (e.g., Manuel, Mullen, Fang, Bellamy, & Bledsoe, 2007).

In the field of social work, for example, curricula currently contain tools useful to dissemination and implementation research. Social work master's programs typically include skills training on how to conduct needs assessments, program evaluation, advocacy efforts, collaborative practice, and capacity building in organizations and communities. Social work researchers have also historically championed alternative research methodologies. Qualitative and participant observation methods can be useful at all stages of the dissemination and implementation processes.

Focus groups with staff, administrators, and consumers during pre-implementation can highlight needs and resources integral to adoption and implementation. Focusing specifically on such methods in educational programs and including material on dissemination and implementation research will help support a new generation of practitioners with the skills to collaborate in the research process, as well as client involvement in the decision-making processes.

Examples of Methodological Innovations

Although there is still much work to be done, there are many examples of innovation already taking place across the translational research process. Two examples are presented here, including a newly funded dissemination and implementation study and an example of a hybrid efficacy-effectiveness study.

MULTIMEDIA CONNECT: DISSEMINATION AND IMPLEMENTATION RESEARCH

The Connect curriculum is a six-session HIV-prevention intervention for heterosexual couples developed by the Social Intervention Group at Columbia University School of Social Work. Given the increasing rates of HIV transmission among women, it is important to consider the context in which sexual risk behaviors are negotiated. As such, the Connect curriculum was developed to intervene at the couple level with the goal of increasing communication and awareness of risk behaviors for HIV and to teach skills to reduce such behaviors. An additional goal related to community-level change was to encourage couples to share Connect information with their family and friends—to act as health educators.

Connect was found to be efficacious (El-Bassel et al., 2003) and has been packaged for dissemination with funding from the Centers for Disease Control and Prevention (CDC) as a Diffusion of Effective Behavioral Interventions (DEBI) program. The CDC dissemination efforts include three strategies: (1) identifying best evidence interventions by reviewing recent science on prevention program efficacy and recommending dissemination of these programs, (2) funding evidence-based programs for packaging through Replicating Effective Programs (REP), and (3) packaging and disseminating evidence-based programs using the DEBI mechanism. A total of thirteen programs have gone through REP (CDC, 2008b), and eighteen programs have gone through DEBI (CDC, 2008a). REP programs, once cleared by the CDC, are then tracked to become DEBIs. The CDC funds community-based organizations (CBOs) directly to provide these interventions. The CDC also provides funding to regional training programs and capacity-building agencies to work with local CBOs and assist them with training and technical assistance so that the CBOs can adopt and implement the interventions.

In addition to packaging a traditional version of Connect using CDC funding, the Social Intervention Group received funding from the

National Institute of Mental Health (R01-MH80659) to translate Connect into a multimedia version for ease of dissemination (i.e., the Multimedia Connect Dissemination Study). The multimedia, Internet-based version of Connect will be tested against the traditional version in an RCT comparing rates of adoption. Eighty community-based HIV/AIDS organizations in the state of New York will be randomized to implement either the original version of Connect or the multimedia version. Implementation processes will be evaluated during the course of the study to include training of community clinicians, agency use of expert technical assistance offered by the researchers, level of fidelity with which the interventions are implemented, staff attitudes toward the innovation, and organizational characteristics such as budget and agency size. The primary outcome of the study is the frequency with which organizations adopt and implement the Connect intervention (either manual or multimedia) into the treatment curriculum. An important innovation of this study is the ability to answer research questions regarding the effectiveness of the two treatment delivery options.

The Multimedia Connect Dissemination Study is an excellent example of dissemination and implementation research using an empirically supported intervention with a focus on community-based principles of research. The active dissemination of the intervention into the community, collaboration with administrators and staff at each organization, and systematic evaluation of the implementation processes will provide valuable information on implementation research efforts.

WOMEN AND TRAUMA STUDY: HYBRID EFFICACY-EFFECTIVENESS MODEL

A promising methodological innovation that addresses some of the challenges to translating and disseminating promising interventions is the combination of elements of efficacy and effectiveness trials. The practical clinical trial (Glasgow, Magid, Beck, Ritzwoller, & Estabrooks, 2005; March et al., 2005; Tunis, Stryer, & Clancy, 2003) and the hybrid efficacy-effectiveness model (Carroll & Rounsaville, 2003) have similar characteristics. However, the hybrid model was developed specifically with behavioral interventions in mind (i.e., in addictions research). The hybrid model can inform directions for further behavioral intervention development and test the efficacy of interventions in a real-world context, allowing for greater dissemination efficiency.

In comparison to the standard efficacy RCTs, a hybrid model decreases the amount of time between developmental and effectiveness research while answering questions relevant to community providers. The main characteristics are increased attention to training with clinicians of diverse backgrounds, diversity in study setting and patient characteristics, attention to relevant multisystemic outcomes (e.g., cost-effectiveness, patient acceptability, patient and provider satisfaction), and retention of key scientific design features (Carroll & Rounsaville, 2003). As in efficacy trials, the model retains randomization and keeping staff blind to study hypotheses and participant treatment assignment. It also includes methodological features, including objective outcome measures and close monitoring of treatment adherence and fidelity. Finally, statistical analysis based on intention to treat samples is used to hold outcomes to stringent efficacy benchmarks.

The hybrid model simultaneously highlights external validity concerns. For example, Carroll and Rounsaville (2003) suggest employing diverse counselors to test how the intervention will be implemented in the community and to assess both clinician and participant satisfaction with the intervention as a whole and with individual components. By attending to these questions during earlier stages of the research, both researchers, who participate in the dissemination, and providers, who are responsible for implementing innovative interventions, will have access to more information (Glasgow et al., 2003; Schoenwald & Hoagwood, 2001).

The Women and Trauma Study (WTS), funded by the National Institute on Drug Abuse (NIDA), is an example of the hybrid model (Carroll & Rounsaville, 2003) executed in community settings with a complex clinical population. Since 2000, NIDA has funded the Clinical Trials Network (CTN), a multisite research network charged with the development and implementation of research protocols in collaboration with community-based treatment programs. An important feature of the CTN is addressing the critical need to adopt new and effective treatments, using research and practice as a vehicle for conveying knowledge, and promoting dissemination. In the CTN context, clinicians reported the need for interventions that address co-ocurring trauma symptoms and addiction that many of the women experienced in their community-based treatment programs. The WTS was developed from this collaboration. The main purpose of the WTS was to assess the effectiveness of an integrated trauma and addiction cognitive behavioral treatment, Seeking Safety (SS) (Najavits, 2002), to a psychoeducational health group, the Women's Health Education (WHE), for treatment-seeking women with comorbid posttraumatic stress and substance use disorders (see Hien et al., 2009).

Following the guidelines set forth by Carroll and Rounsaville (2003), the WTS retained several key characteristics of efficacy trials. Participants were randomized to receive one of the two study interventions (SS or WHE), thus allowing researchers to answer causal questions about treatment effectiveness under the assumption that treatment groups were alike on key characteristics. Second, the study monitored clinician adherence and fidelity to the manualized treatments through videotaping and rating clinician performance. Finally, outcome measure data (substance use and posttraumatic stress severity) were collected using assessments both during and posttreatment with strong psychometric properties and with trained, reliable interviewers blind to participant treatment condition. The level of scientific rigor, although more burdensome to staff, allowed for increased confidence in the usefulness of the findings and the interpretation of the findings.

Elements of effectiveness trials were included to extend external validity and generalizability to a broader sample of programs working with this population of women. Each of these elements is discussed in the following sections.

Collaboration. Community-based treatment programs worked with the research team during protocol development to make necessary adaptations to the procedures of the study and intervention format prior to implementation. On the basis of this feedback, several modifications to the study treatment and research design were implemented (i.e., akin to adaptations to innovations made by agencies during the implementation process). First, the number of intervention sessions was reduced from twenty-five to twelve to better fit with the service delivery systems operating in the programs. For these programs, twenty-five sessions (standard length of SS) was greater than the typical number of sessions provided in a specialized group. The interventions were provided in group format and operated on rolling admission rather than as closed groups (e.g., participants could start with session 4 and end with session 3). The adjustments were congruent with current group structure and enabled the programs to serve more clients and reduce wait time for the starting group.

Counselor selection and training. Counselors and supervisors were selected from the treatment programs and received training from the coordinating site. Using community treatment staff enhanced the diversity of educational levels and treatment experience and allowed the study to monitor whether representative community treatment staff could be trained to deliver the interventions with fidelity. For example, 5 percent of the counselors had earned less than a bachelor's degree; 39 percent had a bachelor's-level degree; and 56 percent had at least a master's degree. Counselors and supervisors were selected to participate in the study on the basis of interest and the ability to conduct manualized treatment protocols. This was assessed before training through a recorded individual session using structured relapse prevention material (97 percent successfully completed this task). Centralized training occurred over three days using a combination of didactic review of manualized intervention, observation of trainer-conducted mock intervention sessions, and trainee-conducted mock intervention practice sessions. After the training, counselors and supervisors conducted practice sessions that lead site experts reviewed to receive certification to conduct the intervention. During the study, counselors received weekly individual supervision and supervisors rated videotaped intervention sessions for adherence. Contingency measures were in place should the counselor have fallen below the standard of meeting the minimum adherence levels.

Eligibility criteria. The WTS used the diagnostic criteria from the *Diagnostic and Statistical Manual of Mental Disorders* (DSM-IV) (American Psychiatric Association [APA], 1994) to characterize the study participants, but with broadened inclusion criteria to allow for maximum participation by program participants. Because many women who do not meet full criteria for the disorder often have functional impairment that is clinically indistinguishable from those meeting full criteria, women with subthreshold posttraumatic stress disorder (PTSD) were also included. Subthreshold PTSD is defined as meeting DSM-IV (APA, 1994) criteria A (exposure to a traumatic stressor), B (reexperiencing symptoms), E (symptom duration of at least one month), and F (significant distress or impairment of functioning), and either C (avoidance and numbing symptoms) or D (symptoms of increased arousal), but not both as in the full diagnosis of PTSD.

The number and type of substances used and/or abused were not limited; neither were other existing psychopathologies (except for history of psychotic disorders). Participants were free to take medications of any kind while participating in the clinical trial. Flexibility of sample characteristics is uncommon in traditional RCTs but essential when working in collaboration with community-based providers and clients. In addition, there were no restrictions on attending additional addiction or trauma specific or informed behavioral treatments. Nonstudy service utilization was monitored throughout the study to examine differences and predictors of treatment outcomes in later analyses.

Sustainability. Finally, using several criteria, each site determined whether and how to incorporate the two interventions after completion of the study, including outcomes (i.e., which intervention was effective?), ability to train staff (i.e., what skills training is needed?), acceptability of the intervention for clients (are clients motivated to participate in the intervention?), program resources (are appropriate staffing and financial resources available?), and motivation of staff (do staff understand the importance of using the evidence to inform practice?).

All six sites that completed the study integrated at least one of the interventions into their service curricula. To aid training capacity, the coordinating site offered a workshop to all study counselors and supervisors to develop skills to successfully assume the role of trainer. Four sites conducted on-site training and one site offered training to other agencies in the community. Specific challenges for sites at poststudy included maintaining adequate levels of supervision, continuing to evaluate client outcomes, and motivating staff and clients to try a new treatment approach.

The WTS illustrates the ways efficacy and effectiveness research can be modified to be more collaborative and inclusive of providers and consumers while still being able to answer important questions about behavioral intervention effectiveness. Conducting the study in community-based treatment programs created the opportunity to recruit a large treatment sample ($N = 353$) and allowed for the examination of contextual factors that influence treatment outcomes. The outcomes from this study support the use of innovative methodologies to enhance the ecological validity of efficacy and effectiveness research.

Implications for Practice Decisions

The translational research model suggests that intervention development, efficacy, and effectiveness research can be responsive to practice. Dissemination and implementation research efforts need to be more clearly conceptualized and championed by federal funding agencies, educational and training programs, and individual researchers. In addition, there needs to be an effort to include participation in the research from community-based agencies, frontline staff, and consumers. There has been an influx of attention and research over the past ten years on how to define and advance the study of dissemination and implementation. Major advances in translational research are now needed to inform practitioners in their efforts to improve program outcomes and help clients achieve desired outcomes.

References

American Psychiatric Association (APA). (1994). *Diagnostic and statistical manual of mental disorders* (4th rev. ed.). Washington, DC: Author.

Backer, T. E. (2000). The failure of success: Challenges of disseminating effective substance abuse prevention programs. *Journal of Community Psychology, 28*(3), 363–373.

Bernal, G., & Scharrón-del-Río, M. R. (2001). Are empirically supported treatments valid for ethnic minorities? Toward an alternative approach for treatment research. *Cultural Diversity and Ethnic Minority Psychology, 7*(4), 328–342.

Bhattacharyya, O., Reeves, S., & Zwarenstein, M. (2007, October 15–16). *What is implementation research? Rationale, concepts and practices.* Paper presented at the International Conference on Implementation and Translational Research, Stockholm.

Brekke, J. S., Ell, K., & Palinkas, L. A. (2007). Translational science at the National Institute of Mental Health: Can social work take its rightful place? *Research on Social Work Practice, 17*(1), 123–133.

Carroll, K. M., & Rounsaville, B. J. (2003). Bridging the gap: A hybrid model to link efficacy and effectiveness research in substance abuse treatment. *Psychiatric Services, 54*(3), 333–339.

Castro, F. G., Barrera, M., Jr., & Martinez, C. R. (2004). The cultural adaptation of prevention interventions: Resolving tensions between fidelity and fit. *Prevention Science, 5*(1), 41–45.

Centers for Disease Control and Prevention, Division of HIV/AIDS Prevention, and National Center on AIDS and Community Health at the Academy for Educational Development. (2008a). *Diffusion of effective behavioral interventions.* Retrieved August 5, 2008, from http://www.effectiveinterventions.org.

Centers for Disease Control and Prevention, Division of HIV/AIDS Prevention, and National Center for HIV/AIDS, Viral Hepatitis, STD, and TB Prevention. (2008b). *Replicating effective programs plus.* Retrieved August 5, 2008, from http://www.cdc.gov/hiv/topics/prev_prog/rep/index.htm.

Durlak, J. A., & DuPre, E. P. (2008). Implementation matters: A review of research on the influence of implementation on program outcomes and the factors affecting implementation. *American Journal of Community Psychology, 41*(3–4), 327–350.

Dworkin, S. L., Pinto, R. M., Hunter, J., Rapkin, B., & Remien, R. (2008). Keeping the spirit of community partnerships alive in the scale up of HIV/AIDS prevention: Critical reflections on the roll out of DEBI (Diffusion of Effective Behavioral Interventions). *American Journal of Community Psychology, 42*(1–2), 51–59.

Eke, A. N., Neumann, M. S., Wilkes, A. L., & Jones, P. L. (2006). Preparing effective behavioral interventions to be used by prevention providers: The role of researchers during HIV prevention research trials. *AIDS Education and Prevention, 18*(Suppl. A), 44–58.

El-Bassel, N., Gilbert, L., Wu, E., Go, H., & Hill, J. (2005). Relationship between drug abuse and intimate partner violence: A longitudinal study among women receiving methadone. *American Journal of Public Health, 95*(3), 465–470.

El-Bassel, N., Witte, S. S., Gilbert, L., Wu, E., Chang, M., Hill, J., et al. (2003). The efficacy of a relationship-based HIV/STD prevention program for heterosexual couples. *American Journal of Public Health, 93*(6), 963–969.

Fixsen, D. L, Blase, K. A., Naoom, S. F., & Wallace, F. (2007, October). *Core implementation components.* Paper presented at the International Conference on Implementation and Translational Research, Stockholm.

Fixsen, D. L, Naoom, S. F., Blase, K. A., Friedman, R. M., & Wallace, F. (2005). *Implementation research: A synthesis of the literature* (FMHI Publication

#231). Tampa: University of South Florida, Louis de la Parte Florida Mental Health Institute, National Implementation Research Network.

Flay, B. R. (1986). Efficacy and effectiveness trials (and other phases of research) in the development of health promotion programs. *Preventive Medicine, 15*(5), 451–474.

Ginexi, E. M., & Hilton, T. F. (2006). What's next for translation research? *Evaluation and the Health Professions, 29*(3), 334–347.

Glantz, M. D., & Compton, W. M. (2004). Mental health and substance abuse innovations: Issues of diffusion and adoption. *Clinical Psychology: Science and Practice, 11*(2), 183–185.

Glasgow, R. E., Lichtenstein, E., & Marcus, A. C. (2003). Why don't we see more translation of health promotion research to practice? Rethinking the efficacy-to-effectiveness transition. *American Journal of Public Health, 93*(8), 1261–1267.

Glasgow, R. E., Magid, D. J., Beck, A., Ritzwoller, D., & Estabrooks, P. A. (2005). Practical clinical trials for translating research to practice: Design and measurement recommendations. *Medical Care, 43*(6), 551–557.

Gotham, H. J. (2004). Diffusion of mental health and substance abuse treatments: Development, dissemination, and implementation. *Clinical Psychology: Science and Practice, 11*(2), 160–176.

Greenhalgh, T., Robert, G., Macfarlane, F., Bate, P., & Kyriakidou, O. (2004). Diffusion of innovations in service organizations: Systematic review and recommendations. *Milbank Quarterly, 82*(4), 581–629.

Greenwald, P., & Cullen, J. W. (1985). The new emphasis in cancer control. *Journal of the National Cancer Institute, 74*(3), 543–551.

Hien, D. A., Wells, E. A., Jiang, H., Suarez-Morales, L., Campbell, A., Cohen, L. R., et al. (2009). *Effectiveness of behavior therapy groups for co-occurring PTSD and substance use disorders: Primary outcomes from the NIDA clinical trials network "Women and Trauma" multi-site randomized control trial.* Manuscript submitted for publication.

Institute of Medicine. (1998). *Bridging the gap between practice and research: Forging partnerships with community-based drug and alcohol treatment.* Washington, DC: National Academies Press.

Israel, B. A., Schulz, A. J., Parker, E. A., & Becker, A. B. (1998). Review of community-based research: Assessing partnership approaches to improve public health. *Annual Review of Public Health, 19*, 173–202.

Kazdin, A. E. (1997). A model for developing effective treatments: Progression and interplay of theory, research, and practice. *Journal of Clinical Child Psychology, 26*(2), 114–129.

Kelly, J. A., Sogolow, E. D., & Neumann, M. S. (2000). Future directions and emerging issues in technology transfer between HIV prevention researchers and community-based service providers. *AIDS Education and Prevention, 12*(Suppl. A), 126–142.

Kerner, J., Rimer, B., & Emmons, K. (2005). Dissemination research and research dissemination: How can we close the gap? *Health Psychology, 24*(5), 443–446.

Kraemer, H. C., Wilson, T., Fairburn, C. G., & Agras, S. (2002). Mediators and moderators of treatment effects in randomized clinical trials. *Archives of General Psychiatry, 59*(10), 877–883.

Kraft, J. M., Mezoff, J. S., Sogolow, E. D., Neumann, M. S., & Thomas, P. (2000). A technology transfer model for effective HIV/AIDS interventions: Science and practice. *AIDS Education and Prevention, 12*(Suppl. A), 7–20.

Manuel, J. I., Mullen, E. J., Fang, L., Bellamy, J. L., & Bledsoe, S. E. (2007, October). *Preparing social work practitioners to use evidence-based practice: A comparison of experiences from an implementation project.* Paper presented at the International Conference on Implementation and Translational Research, Stockholm.

March, J. S., Silva, S. G., Compton, S., Shapiro, M., Califf, R., & Krishnan, R. (2005). The case for practical clinical trials in psychiatry. *American Journal of Psychiatry, 162*(5), 836–846.

Najavits, L. M. (2002). *Seeking safety: A treatment manual for PTSD and substance abuse.* New York: Guilford Press.

National Institutes of Health (2006). *Dissemination and implementation research in health (R01).* Retrieved December 30, 2007, from http://grants.nih.gov/grants/guide/pa-files/PAR-07-086.html.

National Institutes of Health (2007). *Building the science of dissemination and implementation in the service of public health.* Retrieved December 30, 2007, from http://conferences.thehillgroup.com/conferences/di2007/meeting summary110707.pdf.

Onken, L. S., Blaine, J. D., & Battjes, R. J. (1997). Behavioral therapy research: A conceptualization of a process. In S. W. Henggeler & A. B. Santos (Eds.), *Innovative approaches for difficult-to-treat populations* (pp. 477–485). Arlington, VA: American Psychiatric Press.

Proctor, E. K., & Rosen, A. (2008). From knowledge production to implementation: Research challenges and imperatives. *Research on Social Work Practice, 18*(4), 285–291.

Rapkin, B. D. (2002). Ecologically-minded reconstruction of experiments in HIV prevention: Reduce, reuse, and recycle. *Journal of Primary Prevention, 23*(2), 235–250.

Rapkin, B. D., & Trickett, E. J. (2005). Comprehensive dynamic trial designs for behavioral prevention research with communities: Overcoming inadequacies of the randomized controlled trial paradigm. In E. J. Trickett & W. Pequegnat (Eds.), *Community interventions and AIDS* (pp. 249–277). New York: Oxford University Press.

Rogers, E. M. (2003). *Diffusion of innovations* (5th ed.). New York: Free Press.

Rohrbach, L. A., Grana, R., Sussman, S., & Valente, T. W. (2006). Type II translation: Transporting prevention interventions from research to real-world settings. *Evaluation and the Health Professions, 29*(3), 302–333.

Rosenbaum, P. R., & Rubin, D. B. (1985). Constructing a control group using multivariate matched sampling methods that incorporate the propensity score. *American Statistician, 39*(1), 33–38.

Rotheram-Borus, M. J., & Duan, N. (2003). Next generation of preventive interventions. *Journal of the American Academy of Child and Adolescent Psychiatry, 42*(5), 518–526.

Rounsaville, B. J., Carroll, K. M., & Onken, L. S. (2001). A stage model of behavioral therapies research: Getting started and moving on from stage I. *Clinical Psychology: Science and Practice, 8*(2), 133–142.

Schoenwald, S. K., & Hoagwood, K. (2001). Effectiveness, transportability, and dissemination of interventions: What matters when? *Psychiatric Services*, 52(9), 1190–1197.

Seidman, E. (2003). Fairweather and ESID: Contemporary impact and a legacy for the twenty-first century. *American Journal of Community Psychology*, 32(3–4), 371–375.

Solomon, J., Card, J. J., & Malow, R. M. (2006). Adapting efficacious interventions: Advancing translational research in HIV prevention. *Evaluation and Health Professions*, 29(2), 162–194.

Sprang, G., Craig, C., & Clark, J. (2008). Factors impacting trauma treatment practice patterns: The convergence/divergence of science and practice. *Anxiety Disorders*, 22(2), 162–174.

Tunis, S., Stryer, D., & Clancy, C. (2003). Practical clinical trials: Increasing the value of clinical research for decision making in clinical and health policy. *Journal of the American Medical Association*, 290(12), 1624–1636.

Wandersman, A., Duffy, J., Flaspoher, P., Noonan, R., Lubell, K., Stillman, L., et al. (2008). Bridging the gap between prevention research and practice: The interactive systems framework for dissemination and implementation. *American Journal of Community Psychology*, 41(3–4), 171–181.

Weisz, J. R. (2000). Agenda for child and adolescent psychotherapy research: On the need to put science into practice. *Archives of General Psychiatry*, 57(9), 837–838.

Woolf, S. H. (2008). The meaning of translational research and why it matters. *Journal of the American Medical Association*, 299(2), 211–213.

CHAPTER NINE

Bringing the Village Together to Prevent High School Dropout

Using the Process of Evidence-Based Practice

Michael S. Kelly and Cynthia Franklin

Statement of the Problem

This chapter presents a case study that used the process of evidence-based practice (EBP) to search, appraise, and select a "best" intervention to prevent students from dropping out of high school—specifically, the process model advocated by EBP scholars in the fields of social work and school mental health (Gambrill, 2007; Gibbs, 2003; Kelly, 2008; Raines, 2008). This five-step process model is based on work at McMaster University in Canada and led by Gordon Guyatt in 1992 (Straus, Richardson, Glasziou, & Haynes, 2005). Various authors later imported this process model into the social work profession. The EBP process follows an information-processing and decision-making model for appraising and selecting the best intervention. The five-step process model is currently a widely accepted approach for EBP training that numerous disciplines have embraced (e.g., psychology, social work, medicine). This process model eschews an emphasis on specific empirically supported interventions that fail to meet standards of social validity, community relevance, and cultural competence (Kelly, 2008). By integrating the best available evidence with community resources and preferences, this chapter describes a case study in which the decision-making processes of EBP were used to select the best intervention for preventing students from dropping out of high school.

Problem Formulation

Helen Sanders, the principal at Forest Grove North High School moved quickly into the pupil personnel services (PPS) team meeting and sat down at the head of the table. Principal Sanders didn't mince words as she spoke to her team of deans, school social workers, school psychologists, and guidance counselors. "We are not doing enough to stop our students from dropping out. The school board has put me and this team on notice and we can't keep doing the same things we've been doing and expecting a new result. It's time to make some changes in our dropout interventions and do it now."

The room fell silent. This was not a complete surprise to the team, as the dropout rate of Forest Grove had been revealed in the local paper after the school district reported it to the state and federal departments of education. This Chicago suburb, a mixture of working-class and middle-class white, Hispanic, and African American families, had two high schools, Forest Grove North (FGN) and Forest Grove South (FGS). Both FGS and FGN had recently announced that they had, for the first time since the passage of the 2002 No Child Left Behind (NCLB) legislation, met the NCLB-imposed standards of Average Yearly Progress. However, the local newspaper found evidence that the schools had experienced a dramatic increase in their dropout rates in the last five years, particularly in the African American and Hispanic student populations. School parent groups had criticized the school district in the local paper, saying that FGN and FGS had, in the words of one parent advocate, "pushed kids out to pump up their test scores." There was talk in the community about possible civil rights legal challenges to the school district for its high dropout rate and "pushouts" of minority students.

Principal Sanders and her team didn't believe that they were trying to push kids out, but there was no denying that in the past ten years, the dropout rate had risen dramatically for minority students. In 1998, FGS and FGN had an average dropout rate of 12 percent a year, roughly spread equally across all three racial groups in the schools. The dropout rate, though not great, was lower than that of many other suburbs in the Chicago area. In 2008, 24 percent of all FGS and FGN students failed to finish high school in four years; among African American and Hispanic students, the percentage was 35 percent. The team had periodically discussed the issue of students who were dropping out, but to date, there had been limited schoolwide programming devoted to keeping students in school. In addition, the level of community involvement in addressing the problem was minimal, usually conducted on a case-by-case basis by individual PPS team members with a student's church or an outside mental health provider.

Principal Sanders told her team that members needed to report back to the school board in a month about their plan to address the dropout problems at the school. After she had left the room, the team turned to one another, and after a few moments of awkward silence, one of the deans said, "Okay, now what?"

This case study is based on a composite of several cases that the first author worked on as a research consultant and practitioner over the past decade in the Chicago suburbs. That said, the majority of what follows is a summary of how a PPS team might put the EBP process into action in its specific school context, and thus extra effort is made to show both the practical applications of this approach and a warts-and-all attitude in describing the pluses and minuses of trying to do this kind of evidence-informed prevention work.

Literature Review

WHY USE THE EBP PROCESS?

Throughout this chapter and the case study example, there will be an effort to describe the evidence as clearly and accurately, and in as useful a manner, as possible. The lack of clear communication about the quality and relevance of evidence is one of the main reasons that there are not more mutually beneficial collaborations between practitioners and researchers to search and select empirically supported interventions (Franklin & Hopson, 2007). Research on the adoption of research-based interventions in schools reveals that researchers often feel frustrated that practitioners do not implement interventions with adequate fidelity, whereas practitioners find the interventions designed and tested by researchers to be ultimately ineffective, unless they can adapt and modify them to fit their practice setting (Walker, 2004). Add to this situation the already-strained practitioner-researcher relationship and the fact that many problems existing in schools have little solid empirical research to support change efforts.

School-based settings need a better process for parents, teachers, administrators, and researchers to work together in searching and using the best evidence (Raines, 2008). That process can happen in many different ways, but ultimately the process comes down to this: how can practitioners quickly and simply access current research and use it for the specific clients they serve, and furthermore improve services based on that evidence? The EBP process, with its emphasis on collaborating with clients to design questions about problems they face, finding and appraising the best available research, and implementing interventions based on those research findings, presents a solid opportunity for school social workers to use this process in responding to school-related problems (Dupper, 2003; Franklin, Harris, & Allen-Meares, 2006; Gibbs, 2003; Raines, 2004).

This chapter demonstrates the EBP process in some detail. The authors contend that the process can become a straightforward and user-friendly way for school social workers to enhance their practice to address (and even solve) community and organizational-level problems, such as high school dropout.

DEFINITION OF EVIDENCE-BASED PRACTICE

Evidence-based practice is a decision-making process that is transparent, culturally sensitive, and uses the best available evidence to help clients solve their problems. In a school context, the EBP approach is particularly useful in helping various key stakeholders understand the complex problems that exist in school settings. Although EBP is often caricatured as rigid or dependent solely on manualized treatments or protocols, the EBP approach described in this chapter is more flexible and dynamic than those caricatures of EBP. From the efforts of social work scholars, such as Gambrill (2003) and Gibbs (2003), EBP is characterized by the use of evidence to inform practice choices that ultimately are implemented by a collaboration between the social work practitioner and his or her client while also considering cultural, developmental, and ethical factors.

EBP AS A PROCESS

Although the EBP process can differ in small but significant ways for each client and problem context, the overall EBP process tends to follow similar steps based on Gibbs's (2003) conceptual framework and includes the following five elements: (1) identification of a problem that the client (in this case, the PPS team and Principal Sanders) wants to resolve and the creation of an answerable question related to the problem that engages the interest of the client; (2) consultation either by designated members of a team or by an outside consultant (usually consultation of online research databases and journal articles) to identify the best-available evidence to address the problem; (3) critical appraisal of the evidence in light of the research's methodological rigor and the research's applicability to the specific client's problem; (4) presentation of that evidence in future meetings to the client in concise and culturally relevant language to help the client make decisions about next steps to take, including information on interventions that address the problem; and (5) evaluation of the intervention plan and the consideration of either termination or a repeat of this five-step process to address another problem that has arisen in the community.

Interestingly, the aforementioned approach has been used sparingly thus far in designing and implementing empirically supported interventions for community change, though there is no scientific barrier to doing this type of EBP process with problems that have a macro-practice component, such as dropout prevention (Dupper, 2006; Thyer, 2007).

CASE STUDY

Searching for Evidence

CLIENT OUTCOMES

To prepare for the EBP process, the school social worker did some initial digging to find research to underline the severity of the school's dropout problem and how it compared with other urban and suburban school contexts. She consulted the *School Services Sourcebook* (Franklin et al., 2006), which disseminates research evidence to practitioners, and found a list of resources on the risks associated with high school dropout. One of those resources, the National Dropout Prevention Center/Network, had a set of fact sheets that she found accessible and useful (see www.dropout prevention.org/stats/quick_facts.htm).

Although none on the PPS team would disagree that high school dropouts are a serious issue, the team was shocked at how poor the outcomes were for youth who drop out, and how at-risk poor and minority youth were becoming dropouts in both urban and suburban areas.

CONSEQUENCES FOR HIGH SCHOOL DROPOUTS

Some of the information that was uncovered in the team's research for evidence included the American Youth Policy Forum (2006), which quoted statistics suggesting that a youth drops out of school every nine seconds. Another finding showed that only about 70 percent of youths complete high school and receive a regular diploma (Reimer & Smink,

2005). Even though there are startling numbers like these, a reading of dropout reports suggested that everybody wanted to debate about how many young people drop out of high school. However, the truth is that no one really knows for sure what the exact statistical counts are. The different statistics largely depended on what statistical data the researchers examined, and scholars often debated the meaning or interpretation of those numbers (e.g., Chaddock, 2006).

What the team found with more certainty than the debates about numbers were the horrific consequences of dropout. This is what really caught their attention and motivated them to participate in solving the problem. It is no longer possible to build a viable adult life, for example, without a high school diploma, because recent data suggest that, on a set of economic measures, students who drop out of school and never return to graduate or earn their certificate of General Educational Development (GED) are at risk of a host of negative social, economic, and health outcomes in adulthood compared to peers who graduate from high school. They earn less, have poorer job prospects, have poorer health, and are overrepresented in the U.S. prison population (National Center for Education Statistics, 2005).

The team also discovered that in a recent analysis of graduation data in large cities, such as Chicago, the graduation rates were much lower than had been previously thought. In America's largest cities, only about half (52 percent) of students in the principal school systems of the fifty largest cities complete high school with a diploma. This essentially amounts to a coin toss in terms of predicting high school graduation rates (Swanson, 2008). Conventional wisdom had indicated that students graduated at a rate of roughly 85 percent, but Swanson's (2008) report suggested that a graduation crisis was prevalent in America's cities. There is even a larger gap for ethnic minorities and males, as well as a fifteen-percentage-point gap between the suburbs and urban areas, with urban areas having much worse dropout rates (Swanson, 2008). This information certainly fit with the experience of Principal Sanders and the team.

The Swanson (2008) research report, however, is not without its critics, who suggest that the way the researchers calculated the data is flawed and exaggerates the numbers of dropouts (Mishel & Joydeep, 2007). Other longitudinal analyses of dropout data suggest that the dropout crisis is more concentrated in lower socioeconomic areas and mostly exists in about 20 percent of America's high schools (Mishel & Joydeep, 2007). It is interesting to note that low socioeconomic status was associated with dropout status regardless of ethnic group. Even though the two research reports that Principal Sanders and the team examined disagreed on some points, where the reports appeared to converge is on the fact that high dropout rates existed in urban school districts and lower income areas. This information certainly hit home. The team found that poverty is a risk factor for all youths. As school leaders, the team members would have to tackle the risk factors associated with residing in low-income areas if they were serious about solving the dropout crisis. Some of the highest dropout rates, for example, are among Hispanics and immigrant and African American populations. These youths need special attention and support in their schools to help them graduate from high school. The risk factor of poverty often over shadows their lives, especially in urban school districts.

REASONS FOR DROPOUT

It is important to know what the risk factors for dropout are and what leads a young person to drop out of high school. The team found that the answers to those questions, however, were complicated by the many reasons that converge and contribute to a young person's decision to leave school. On the basis of a survey of recent research (Bridgeland, DiUlio, & Morrison, 2006), it appears that every youth has his or her own story and set of reasons. Franklin et al.'s (2006) *School Services Sourcebook* presents the research related to the reasons students drop out of school. Table 9.1 provides a summary of these reasons, related to individual, family, peer, and school and/or academic problems. It is not uncommon for these problems to overlap.

TABLE 9.1. Reasons for dropping out of high school

Individual reasons	Family reasons	School-related and academic reasons
• Poor daily attendance	• Parents not engaged in	• Student-to-teacher ratio
• Misbehavior	child's schooling	(too big)
• Alcohol and drug use	• Teen pregnancy	• Failure to be promoted to
• Feeling alienated from	• Students getting married	next grade
other students	• Financial and work	• Quality of teachers
• Mental health issues	responsibilities	• Want smaller school size
• Special education	• Permissive parenting style	• School safety concerns
• High mobility and frequent	• Negative emotional	• Not feeling welcomed at
moves	reactions and sanctions	school
• Trouble with the law or	for bad grades	
juvenile justice	• Child abuse and neglect	
involvement	• Foster care placement	

CASE STUDY

Research Methods and Data Analysis

ASKING THE EBP QUESTION

The PPS team at Forest Grove North High School collaborated with research consultants to develop a programmatic response to its high school dropout problem by using the EBP process in constructing a practice question. This question was based on the Client Oriented Practical Evidence Search (COPES) question framework that Gibbs (2003) and other EBP researchers (Sackett, Richardson, Rosenberg, & Haynes, 1997) have advanced. In the COPES sequence, social workers can help clients identify the major issues they want to learn more about or interventions that they want to evaluate and decide to pursue (e.g., deciding between different treatments for a psychiatric condition, learning about the major risk factors for suicide). After some spirited discussion, the PPS team decided that there was an urgent need to find out about what works to prevent teen dropout and to compare whether it was better to advocate for a totally new school-based approach or simply to do more of what they already had been doing but with more resource support. The COPES question that the team developed is as follows: If students deemed at risk for dropping out of high school are given a specific school-based dropout intervention program or standard school-based intervention, such as counseling and academic advising, will the school-based dropout program produce better outcomes, specifically helping youths stay in school and graduate on time?

ANSWERING THE EBP QUESTION

The EBP search process addressed whether specific school-based programs are more effective than regular school-based counseling and academic advising. In the spirit of practicing what we preach in terms of using the EBP process, we detail from the outset how we went about compiling the evidence and clarify the choices made related to searching and appraising the evidence. We used the following resources in the search:

- Five online clearinghouses, including the National Registry of Evidence-Based Programs and Practices (http://nrepp.samhsa .gov/find.asp), the U.S. Department of Education's What Works Clearinghouse (www.whatworks.ed.gov/), the National Dropout Prevention Center (www.dropoutprevention.org/ndpcdefault .htm), the Office of Juvenile Justice and Delinquency Prevention Web site (www.ojjdp.ncjrs.gov/programs/mpg.html), and the

Campbell Collaboration Web site (www.campbellcollaboration .org). We chose these five sites because all are at least partially grounded in school-based research and demonstrate high standards for evaluating the potential effectiveness of interventions.

- Three major school social work textbooks, all of which had presumably updated findings through the year before they were last published, including: Constable, Massat, McDonald, and Flynn's (2006) *School social work: Practice, policy and research*, Dupper's (2003) *School social work: Skills and interventions for effective practice*, and Franklin et al.'s (2006) *School services sourcebook.*
- An electronic database search of the following common article databases, using the following keyword search terms based on the tools from leading social work EBP resources (e.g., Gibbs, 2003): "effective school dropout prevention programs," "school dropout and prevention," "social skills deficits," "effective social skills programs schools," and "social skills training school interventions." As the textbooks had updated resources through 2005, we searched databases from January 2006 to August 2008. The databases were contained in the helpful mega-database tool qUICsearch at the University of Illinois at Chicago, which provides a comprehensive search of EBM Reviews (collection of systematic reviews, for example, from the Cochrane and Campbell collaborations), PsycInfo, Academic Search Premier (EBSCO), and Social Work Abstracts.

We collected all of the hits from each of the foregoing resources and read the articles, searching for studies of programs that met the following four criteria (some of these are based on criteria from *Blueprints for Violence Prevention Selection Process* [Center for the Study and Prevention of Violence, 2006] and Stone and Gambrill's [2007] review of school social work textbooks):

1. The program being studied had an experimental or quasi-experimental design with a control or comparison group and a sample size that allowed for statistical power.
2. The studies had been conducted with students that had similar demographics (low to middle-income socioeconomic status [SES] white, African American, and Hispanic) and could be generalized to the specific FGN and FGS student population.
3. Findings from the programs in the study showed sustained treatment effects after a minimum of a one-year follow-up.
4. The study had materials that could be easily accessed for implementation via Web site or contact person with clear instructions on how to receive training related to the intervention.

TABLE 9.2. Dropout prevention and intervention programs: Selected results from the EBP search

Effective programs and interventions	Program contacts
Career Academies Career development/job training Mentoring Other: Alternative programs	National Partnership for Careers in Law-Public Safety, Corrections, and Security
Project Graduation Really Achieves Dreams (Project GRAD) Academic support Case management Family strengthening School/classroom environment Other: College preparation and scholarships	Project GRAD USA
Advancement via Individual Determination (AVID) Academic support Family strengthening Structured extracurricular activities Other: College preparation	AVID Center Headquarters
Check and Connect Academic support Behavioral intervention Case management Family strengthening Mentoring Truancy prevention	Institute on Community Integration, University of Minnesota
Functional family therapy Behavioral intervention Family therapy	FFT Communications
Multidimensional family therapy Behavioral intervention Court advocacy/probation/transition Family strengthening Family therapy Mental health services Structured extracurricular activities Substance abuse prevention	University of Miami, Medical Center

TABLE 9.2. (Continued)

Effective programs and interventions	Program contacts
Quantum Opportunities Academic support After school Life skills development Mentoring Structured extracurricular activities Other: Planning for future	Office of National Literacy Programs, Opportunities Industrialization Centers of America

If all four criteria were met, we judged the intervention to be effective. If any combination of the criteria were met, we judged the intervention to be promising. If none of the criteria were met but the intervention had some research support (e.g., single-subject designs, pre- and post-test with no control group), we judged the intervention to be emerging. Often in a search for evidence, it is hard for any empirically supported intervention to meet the criteria of an effectiveness rating; fortunately in this case study, however, the search suggested that a sizable number of interventions had been empirically tested.

RESULTS OF THE SEARCH FOR EVIDENCE

Table 9.2 shows some of the results from the EBP search for interventions that met the "effective" criteria. There were twelve interventions we judged to be effective. Each of those programs met the criteria of having a rigorous research design, including a one-year follow-up and of working with relevant ethnic-minority and white populations from low-SES and middle-class backgrounds. This evidence was reported to the PPS team during an hourlong PPS meeting. After that meeting, the PPS team chose to explore the Quantum Opportunities Program (QOP).

CASE STUDY
Discussion

At the FGN pupil personnel team meeting, Principal Sanders opened the discussion by cutting right to the main issue and asking, "Did you find something that works?" The research consultants discussed the information depicted in Table 9.2 and presented a Microsoft PowerPoint report and presentation. They outlined various programs, including their strengths and potential weaknesses in being adapted to the specific context of FGN. The team members listened, took notes, and asked questions. They were given a copy of the PowerPoint presentation and asked to reflect on the information until the next meeting, which was scheduled for the following week to consider the next steps.

At the next meeting, the FGN pupil personnel team was surprised by the number of programs that were rated "effective." One PPS team member voiced a new concern: "It's almost as if now we have too many choices." The team returned to their COPES question for guidance and agreed that they would favor the approach that best allowed them to change their focus and emphasis without having to totally revamp all the organizational structure or staffing of the PPS team. In assessing the QOP, the team perceived this program to be feasible to implement given the PPS structure in the school.

The QOP is an intensive four-year program that combines life skills training, mentoring, community service, financial incentives, and case management to enable at-risk students to stay in school and graduate on time (Redd, Brooks, & McGarvey, 2002). The QOP has been shown to decrease dropout, increase high school graduation rates, and increase community engagement for students (Hahn, Leavitt, & Aaron, 1994). It is primarily organized around a case manager and/or counselor who remains with the QOP students (called associates in the program) for the entire four years of high school. Students also complete ninety-six computer-based life-skills training courses during their four years of school that take place in a computer lab and are paced for each student's individual learning style. Students are compensated for their time in the QOP. For example, they receive a bonus for completing the program each semester, which is paid into an account that the student can use for future training or college education.

Initially, the question of how to implement the program seemed to be a problem. As with all the other programs, QOP seemed to be too big and overwhelming for the PPS team to view as working at their school. However, Principal Sanders reminded the team that she had been given authority ("more like pressure," she joked) to use her resources to tackle the dropout problem. The question she asked the group was, "How can we take the faculty resources we already have and possibly redirect those resources to the program we choose?" After some further discussion, the head of the counseling department shared that he believed that their current counseling caseload could be reconfigured to free up two counselors to be QOP case managers and/or counselors. The school social worker added that with the two interns she had each year, she would be able to work with the two QOP counselors to act as a site manager for the program and to make sure that the high school students were completing their life-skills courses. The team then brainstormed that they could tap the job coaches who were part of the school's school-work transition program to develop community service internships that QOP students could complete. By the end of the meeting, the basic elements of an organizational structure were in place to begin planning for the implementation of the QOP for the next school year. Principal Sanders thanked the PPS team and told the group, "I think we've got something I can sell to the superintendent and school board."

Implications for Practice Decisions

Rigorous criteria need to be used in assessing and appraising sources of evidence. The nature of evidence is constantly evolving and changing, so rating an intervention as effective is, at best, solid only for the time frame that an EBP search process is conducted. It is entirely possible that future evaluation research shows the QOP or other programs evaluated in this case study to have less robust outcomes than the research from the past two decades.

One heartening outcome from this EBP search was how many options were available. We often have been unable to find many (or in some cases, any) programs that we would be able to judge effective on the basis of rigorous criteria, and thus we face the challenge of how to best adapt an intervention or program to a school or community context (Kelly, 2008). Even with the relative wealth of options we had for this case study, the actual discussion of implementing the QOP program revealed how challenging it is to translate effective interventions into an actual practice setting (Franklin & Hopson, 2007).

Principal Sanders gave both concrete and symbolic encouragement at key moments in the EBP search process by reminding the PPS team of their charge and encouraging them to think creatively. Without her leadership, the PPS team could have easily become bogged down in arguing over how realistic it was to implement any of the programs at FGN. In addition, a key advantage of the specific program that the PPS team chose was that current members of the FGN faculty could deliver some elements of it. This is a persistent issue in the implementation of effective programs in schools, as faculty and administration are likely to resist programs that appear to require large start-up costs in terms of new faculty, training, and support (Kelly, 2008). The whole issue of how to do the QOP was as important to the frontline practitioners of the PPS team as were the rigorous criteria in searching for the intervention.

Equally important to the decision-making processes in searching, appraising, and selecting an intervention is the evaluation of an evidence-based practice. Principal Sanders's commitment to expend resources to address the dropout problem is helpful in that she is under a mandate to show some difference in the school's dropout statistics and is very interested in collecting ongoing data to evaluate the effectiveness of the intervention.

Practicing the EBP process in a school- and community-based context requires a deliberative approach as summarized in this case study. Principal Sanders could have done some research herself or could have deputized some member of her team to find out what programs work. This research could have led her to the same "best" program. By using the EBP process, clients, including the PPS team and representatives from the parent community, participate in the decision-making processes. Without their investment and input, the program would have been hard to implement given the many new roles and responsibilities the team was going to have to assume. Similarly, this process is much more difficult without taking the time to specify a well-constructed COPES question and the criteria for appraising the evidence. The use of an expert research consultant was also a wise investment on the part of the principal.

Many school and community settings are strapped for time to do their regular work, let alone conduct systematic, time-intensive EBP searches. We suggest that if a school does not have the resources to hire a research consultant to help with the search, then the school needs to appoint an in-house staff member to become the point person for conducting the EBP searches and carve out a day of staff time per week to complete the searches and compile the evidence into an accessible format for the key stakeholders. As this may not be possible in many settings, organizations at least need to carve out time for using the EBP process when major issues are presented to a school or community to select a best practice.

Practice Guidelines

The following practice guidelines might provide direction to school and community-based practitioners in using the EBP process to conceptualize and support a planned change effort.

Define the problem. Work with community partners and stakeholders. Define the nature and scope of the problem to be addressed. Gather data from the community (through quantitative data surveys and administrative records, as well as qualitative data from focus groups and in-depth interviews). Share problem definition with key stakeholders and integrate their input into the decision making.

Design a well-built EBP question and research strategy. Following the definition of the problem, devise a question that adheres to the COPES framework (Gibbs, 2003) and allows for the researcher or practitioner to adequately appraise the best available evidence. Decide in advance how the evidence will be appraised. For prevention questions (e.g., the one in this case study), decide how the effectiveness of the programs will be assessed (e.g., ease of adoption, rigorous research design, follow-up data showing effectiveness of intervention). Seek, locate, document, and compile the sources of evidence. Assess the credibility and quality of these sources based on a set of criteria.

Share findings and design interventions based on the EBP search. Gather key stakeholders and those who are likely to implement the proposed intervention and review the EBP search findings. Revisit the COPES question to clarify the ultimate goals for the EBP search and to make decisions related to which interventions are most likely to change the practice situation, taking into account the implementation and transla-tional issues identified through the EBP search. In addition, discuss the transportability issues related to the chosen intervention and develop plans with relevant stakeholders to design a framework for implement-ing the intervention with fidelity.

Conclusion

An EBP process that uses the best available evidence to answer impor-tant practice questions represents a vital new tool in efforts to bridge the gap between research and actual day-to-day practice. In the case study here, a large suburban high school was able to search through the evidence on effective dropout prevention programs and choose a program that best fit its needs and capacity. The high school dropout rate continues to be a significant problem for many large metropolitan areas, and the evidence that intensive, multicomponent interventions appear to work is encouraging. What is not clear yet is how to engage schools and communities in implementing a best practice with fidelity, considering the realities of the practice world.

References

American Youth Policy Forum. (2006). *Whatever it takes: How twelve communities are reconnecting out-of-school youth.* Retrieved June 24, 2008, from http://www.aypf.org/publications/WhateverItTakes/WITfull.pdf.

Bridgeland, J. M., DiUlio, J. J., & Morrison, K. B. (2006). *The silent epidemic: Per-spectives of high school dropouts.* Retrieved July 10, 2008, from http://www.civicenterprises.net/reports.php.

Center for the Study and Prevention of Violence (2006, August). *Blueprints for violence prevention selection process.* Retrieved September 28, 2008, from http://www.colorado.edu/cspv/infohouse/publications.html#blueprintsfacts.

Chaddock, G. R. (2006, June 21). High school dropout rate: High but how high? *Christian Science Monitor*, p. 3.

Constable, R., Massat, C., McDonald, S., & Flynn, J. P. (2006). *School social work: Practice, policy and research* (6th ed.). Chicago: Lyceum Books.

Dupper, D. (2003). *School social work: Skills and interventions for effective practice*. Hoboken, NJ: Wiley.

Dupper, D. (2006). Guides for designing and establishing alternative school programs for dropout prevention. In C. Franklin, M. B. Harris, & P. Allen-Meares (Eds.), *School services sourcebook: A guide for school-based professionals* (pp. 413–422). New York: Oxford University Press.

Franklin, C., Harris, M., & Allen-Meares, P. (2006). *School services sourcebook*. New York: Oxford University Press.

Franklin, C., & Hopson, L. (2007). Facilitating the use of evidence-based practices in community organizations. *Journal of Social Work Education, 43*(3), 377–404.

Gambrill, E. (2003). A client-focused definition of social work practice. *Research on Social Work Practice, 13*(3), 310–323.

Gambrill, E. (2007). Views of evidence-based practice: Social workers' code of ethics and accreditation standards as guides for choice. *Journal of Social Work Education, 43*(3), 447–462.

Gibbs, L. E. (2003). *Evidence-based practice for the helping professions: A practical guide with integrated multimedia*. Pacific Grove, CA: Brooks/Cole-Thomson Learning.

Hahn, A., Leavitt, T., & Aaron, P. (1994). *Evaluation of the Quantum Opportunities Program (QOP). Did the program work? A report on the post secondary outcomes and cost-effectiveness of the QOP program (1989–1993)*. Waltham, MA: Brandeis University, Heller Graduate School. (ERIC Document Reproduction Service No. ED385621).

Kelly, M. S. (2008). *The domains and demands of school social work practice: A guide to working effectively with students, families, and schools*. New York: Oxford University Press.

Mishel, L., & Joydeep, R. (2007). Where our high school dropout crisis really is. *Education Digest, 72*(6), 12–21.

National Center for Education Statistics. (2005). *Youth indicators 2005: Trends in the well-being of American youth*. Retrieved June 28, 2008, from http://nces.ed.gov/pubsearch/pubsinfo.asp?pubid=2005050.

Raines, J. C. (2004). Evidence-based practice in school social work: A process in perspective. *Children and Schools, 26*(2), 71–85.

Raines, J. C. (2008). *Evidence-based practice in school mental health*. New York: Oxford University Press.

Redd, Z., Brooks, J., & McGarvey, A. (2002). *Educating America's youth: What makes a difference* [Research brief]. Washington, DC: Child Trends.

Reimer, M., & Smink, J. (2005). *Information about the school dropout issue: Selected facts and statistics*. Retrieved June 2, 2008, from http://www.dropoutpreven tion.org/ndpcdefault.htm.

Sackett, D. L., Richardson, W. S., Rosenberg, W., & Haynes, R. B. (1997). *Evidence-based medicine: How to practice and teach EBM*. New York: Churchill Livingstone.

Stone, S., & Gambrill, E. (2007). Do school social work textbooks provide a sound guide for education and practice? *Children and Schools, 29*(2), 109–118.

Straus, S. E., Richardson, W. S., Glasziou, P., & Haynes, R. B. (2005). *Evidence-based medicine: How to practice and teach EBM* (3rd ed.). New York: Churchill Livingstone.

Swanson, C. B. (2008). *Cities in crisis: A special analytic report on high school graduation.* Bethesda, MD: Editorial Project in Education.

Thyer, B. (2007). *Evidence-based macro-practice: Addressing the challenges and opportunities for social work education.* Retrieved July 2, 2008, from http://www.utexas.edu/ssw/ceu/practice/articles.html.

Walker, H. (2004). Commentary: Use of evidence-based interventions in schools: Where we've been, where we are, and where we need to go. *School Psychology Review, 33*(3), 398–407.

CHAPTER TEN

Using Evidence from Youths to Guide Improvements in the Mental Health System

Jean M. Kruzich and Pauline Jivanjee

Statement of the Problem

In the field of child and youth mental health, there have been significant changes in service delivery in the past twenty-five years. The Comprehensive Community Mental Health Services for Children and Their Families Initiative has funded community-based systems of care in many communities across the United States and has influenced family-centered service delivery in other communities (Osher, Penn, & Spencer, 2008). Along with these developments, there has been a shift in the philosophy underlying mental health services to a recovery model that

This research was conducted with funding from the National Institute of Disability and Rehabilitation Research (NIDRR), U.S. Department of Education, and the Center for Mental Health Services Substance Abuse and Mental Health Services Administration (NIDRR Grant No. H133B990025). The content does not necessarily represent the views or policies of the funding agencies. The authors with to thank Nancy Koroloff, Lyn Gordon, youth research assistants, and members of the project advisory groups for their assistance, and research participants for sharing their experiences and perceptions.

emphasizes mental health services that are youth guided, individualized, and culturally competent. In this model, the focus extends beyond the management of the illness to client-oriented outcomes, such as independence, employment, satisfying relationships, and quality of life (Frese, Stanley, Kress, & Vogel-Scibilia, 2001). At the same time, legislators and funding agencies increasingly expect these services to be based on empirically supported interventions (Waddell & Godderis, 2005). Evidence-based practice (EBP) is the integration of the best research evidence with practice expertise while considering the client's unique values and circumstances (Sackett, Straus, Richardson, Rosenberg, & Haynes, 2000).

Despite the movement toward using research to inform practice, many young people aged seventeen to twenty-four are not receiving mental health services. Other young people who are in the process of transitioning from child mental health services to receiving services in the adult system are at high risk for a range of adverse outcomes. This chapter examines the potential for improving services for this vulnerable population through seeking information about their experiences and perspectives on services. A participatory action research study is presented in which transition age youths (seventeen to twenty-four) with mental health needs participated in focus groups. In these groups, youths identified their preferences, concerns, and expectations related to their interactions with service providers (Institute of Medicine, 2000). Participants reflected on their experiences and offered recommendations on how to improve services for young people with mental health needs.

Literature Review

There has never been a nationally representative survey of the prevalence of child and adolescent psychiatric disorders in the United States. Screening tools have been used to provide approximations (Costello, Egger, & Angold, 2005). Recent estimates suggest that 20 percent of U.S. children between the ages of nine and seventeen have a diagnosable mental or addictive disorder associated with at least minimum impairment. When the federal definition for serious mental disorder is used, 11 percent of these children, which translates to 4 million youths, suffer from a major mental illness that results in significant impairments at home, at school, and with peers (U.S. Department of Health and Human Services, 1999).

Students with emotional or behavioral disorders (EBDs) consistently have a lower high school graduation rate than any other subgroup of students with disabilities. Statistics from 2002 to 2003, which represent the most recently available data, suggest that 35 percent of students with EBD graduated from high school, compared to 52 percent for all students with disabilities and 71 percent for all public school students (Greene & Winters, 2005; U.S. Department of Education, Office of Special Education and Rehabilitative Services, Office of Special Education Programs, 2007). Because of their psychosocial problems, youths with EBD are at high risk for attempting suicide, engaging in acts of aggression and violence, having unprotected sex, and using drugs and alcohol (Armstrong, Dedrick, & Greenbaum, 2003). Compared with youths in the general population, youths with serious emotional disturbance are overrepresented among low-income families and African American or Hispanic families (Mark & Buck, 2006).

Studies have demonstrated consistently that many of the children and youths who need mental health services do not receive them. For those who do receive treatment, the research suggests that premature termination from treatment is high. For example, Kazdin (1993) estimated that between 50 percent and 75 percent of the children who need mental health services never have contact with providers or terminate treatment prematurely. In another study, Kazdin, Holland, and Crowley (1997) found that 40–60 percent of families who begin treatment withdraw before their therapist thought they were ready to terminate. Armbruster and Fallon (1994) found that the great majority of children who enter outpatient treatment attend for only one or two sessions. Only one in five children with a serious emotional disturbance used mental health specialty services (Burns et al., 1995; Farmer, Burns, Phillips, Angold & Costello, 2003). It is estimated that about 75 percent of children with emotional and behavioral disorders do not receive specialty services, and most of those children fail to receive any services at all, as reported by their families (Huang et al., 2005).

Studies identify a variety of barriers to mental health services for children and adolescents. Parents' perceptions play an important role, particularly for younger children, in whether they receive mental health services. A recent study of 878 sixteen-year-olds suggests that parental attitudes continue to be important influences even when youths are old enough to seek out services themselves. Of the teens who said they would be unwilling to use mental health services, 36 percent cited "didn't want parents to know'" as a barrier to accessing mental health services (Samargia, Saewyc, & Elliott, 2006). Parents of youths with special care needs reported relatively high levels of barriers to accessing mental health care for their children, including difficulties finding providers with skills or experience, trouble obtaining referrals, and problems with paying for the services (Warfield & Gulley, 2006).

Historically, professionals have developed mental health and social service programs and policies. The assumption has been that experience in designing programs and policies and extensive knowledge of the population served and/or setting for service delivery represented the necessary requisites for developing programs that would meet client needs (Bloor, Frankland, Thomas, & Robson, 2001). However, in recent years, studies have begun to identify the importance of family involvement in service delivery, with results suggesting that family participation changes service providers' approaches to service delivery, providers' views of their work, and families' approaches to treatment (Jivanjee, Friesen, Kruzich, Robinson, & Pullmann, 2002). The few studies that have been done indicate that involving youths in the decision-making processes helps them feel more confident about controlling their own lives in a positive way and avoid risky behaviors (Matarese, Carpenter, Huffine, Lane, & Paulson, 2008; Walker & Child, 2008).

Increasingly, there is recognition that youth and family involvement is important to creating systems of care that better meet client needs. The federal Center for Mental Health Services of the Substance Abuse and Mental Health Services Administration introduced requirements for family involvement in developing, implementing, and evaluating systems of care. Starting in 1993, the federal Comprehensive Community Mental Health Services Program for Children and Their Families required federally funded programs to actively seek out family members to help implement requirements. By 2005, applicants for services were required to demonstrate full participation in service planning and in the development of local services (Osher et al., 2008).

The phrase "family and consumer driven" moved into the public lexicon as noted in the New Freedom Commission on Mental Health (2003) report. Subsequently, the Federation of Families for Children's Mental Health initiated a process that resulted in the development of a working definition of family- and consumer-driven services. It was viewed as an approach to service delivery in which goals are established in true partnership with families and grounded in the experiences, expertise, strengths, hopes, dreams, desires, and needs of the children, youths, and families being served (Osher, Quinn, & Hanley, 2002).

In spite of supportive funder requirements and a developing youth and family movement, a true partnership among families, youths, and professionals has not been achieved (Huang et al., 2005). The question remains as to how to include a wide range of family and youth voices so they can shape systems of care for children and youths with mental health needs. Evidence-based practice is intended to help macro practitioners enhance the quality of the decision-making processes in program design and service delivery, manage constantly evolving research knowledge, and incorporate client values and expectations into mental health services (Mullen, Shlonsky, Bledsoe, & Bellamy, 2005). A key aspect of EBP is the integration of client preferences, needs, strengths, and values as part of a contextual assessment (Gambrill, 2006). The greatest barrier to drawing consumers into collaborative decision making is the socialization from professional training and education in which mental health professionals are supported to act as the experts (Sabin & Daniels, 2002). The prevailing paradigm for the design of human service programs is provider driven and not a shared process with those who have vital information that no other source can provide, namely the consumers.

Methodology

The purpose of the present study was to gain an understanding of youth, young adult, and family perspectives on social, psychological, cultural, and economic barriers, as well as supports to community integration for youths with mental health needs. This evidence was expected to inform the decision-making processes in designing an intervention aimed to increase the participation of youths and family members in their care plan.

RESEARCH METHOD

Focus groups were used to collect the data. The groups were based on an inductive, qualitative research methodology that is particularly helpful in understanding participants' cognitive and emotional perceptions in a relaxed, nonthreatening environment (Heary & Hennessy, 2002). Participants in the focus groups were selected because of common experiences related to a topic of interest. The focus group allows for interaction and stimulation of thought during the group process, thus producing rich descriptive data (Peterson-Sweeney, 2005). The groups provide a less formal, relatively unstructured process that is particularly valuable when discussing emotionally sensitive topics with youths who might be uncomfortable discussing such issues in a one-on-one interview (Giacomini & Cook, 2000; Jones & Broome, 2001). The study reported here is part of a larger study that included focus groups with the youths' family members (see Jivanjee, Kruzich, & Gordon, 2009)

Participatory research teams were formed in two cities. Each team included a young-adult research assistant who had experience with mental health services and was trained in focus group methodology, ethical aspects of research such as confidentiality and informed consent, and skills in data entry and qualitative data analysis. In addition, local advisory groups that included young adults with mental health needs were created. The teams consulted with advisory group members at all stages of the project and received assistance in developing the recruitment tools, a pre–focus group questionnaire, and focus group questions, as well as advice about interpretation of the findings and dissemination strategies.

STUDY POPULATION AND SAMPLING

To obtain the best possible representation of youths' views, a sample was selected of youths who varied in age, gender, ethnicity and/or race, and socioeconomic status (Blankertz, 1998). At both research sites, transition-age youths (seventeen to twenty-four years old) with mental health difficulties were recruited through contacts with schools; colleges; family support organizations; youth employment and alternative educational programs; and agencies serving homeless and gay, lesbian, bisexual, transgender, and queer youths. Project staff distributed brochures, electronic message board announcements, and flyers inviting youths who had experienced mental health needs and were between the ages of seventeen to twenty-four to contact the project staff. In some agencies, staff shared project materials with youths being served by their program, and parent-support groups invited their members to pass along project information to their children. All focus group participants were identified either as someone who had received mental health services or as someone who had mental health needs that interfered with their functioning.

DATA COLLECTION AND MEASURES

Twelve ninety-minute focus groups with young people were held in a variety of community settings in the Seattle and Portland metropolitan areas, including public libraries, human service agencies, offices of family support organizations, and a university. Before the start of each focus group, participants completed a pre–focus group questionnaire that included questions related to demographics; living arrangements; participation in school and work; and their use of, need for, and access to mental health services. Participants also signed consent forms to participate in the focus group and to have their comments audiotaped. Young-adult research assistants assumed the lead role in facilitating the groups, and a principal investigator or project manager assumed a secondary role of taking notes and taping the session with two cassette recorders. Following the focus group, participants received $30 in cash.

The guide for conducting the focus group interviews with the youths included five major areas of questions: (1) understanding of community integration and a successful life in the community, (2) perceptions of the barriers to community integration, (3) perceptions of the supports for community integration, (4) their hopes for the future, and (5) advice to another young person who was struggling with similar challenges.

On the basis of the results of earlier focus groups and identification of issues that youths reported, questions were modified for later focus groups and other questions were added that were more specific (e.g., How did the topic of depression initially arise with a primary care provider?). In early focus groups, it became apparent that participants were unfamiliar with the concept of community integration, so the team revised the question to ask participants to identify those places and situations in which they felt a sense of belonging.

DATA ANALYSIS

Responses from the pre–focus group questionnaire were entered into SPSS for computation of descriptive statistics. Focus groups were recorded and transcribed verbatim. This material was analyzed using the N6 Qualitative Software System (QSR International, 2002), which aids in coding, organization, and retrieval of text for qualitative analysis. With the assistance of the software, the research team analyzed the data using Glaser and Strauss's (1967) constant comparative method.

The process of analysis began with developing a framework based initially on the main topics covered in the focus group. Each team member was assigned several transcripts to read independently, using the aforementioned five major areas of questions to guide the preliminary analysis. Within these areas, team members identified themes in an inductive analysis process, and a preliminary code list was developed through negotiation during a series of team meetings. Within the initial categories, multiple subcategories emerged from the data. For example, within the category of supports for a successful life in the community, participants' comments were coded as related to opportunities to achieve goals, effective services, accurate information about mental health, understanding mental health difficulties, supportive relationships, empowerment, and choice. Next, all team members independently assigned these preliminary codes to the transcripts and added additional codes where needed.

As the team members became more familiar with the data, further categories emerged that enabled the team to construct a more detailed framework, which was then transposed into the N6 Qualitative Software System and became the "tree" used to code all the data. Once this was complete, a separate report on each index was produced that illustrated all relevant data. These were then analyzed further to establish patterns and associations across themes.

Credibility of interpretations was enhanced by investigator triangulation, with more than one investigator collecting and analyzing the raw data, such that findings emerged through consensus between investigators. Team members shared with a sample of participants a draft of the study findings to inquire whether their viewpoints were faithfully interpreted and whether the account made sense to participants with different perspectives. In addition, the team members were involved in developing an audit trail, peer debriefing, and sharing preliminary findings with members of the family and youth advisory group (Giacomini & Cook, 2000; Rodwell, 1998).

Findings

Fifty-nine youths (thirty-six males and twenty-three females) participated in twelve focus groups. The racial and/or ethnic breakdown of the participants was as follows: 66 percent European American, 15 percent African American, 10 percent multiracial, 7 percent Pacific Islander, and 2 percent Native American. In response to other youths who heard about the focus groups from mental health providers and expressed interest in the study, the age range of youth participants was expanded from the range of seventeen to twenty-four to the range of fifteen to twenty-eight. The mean age of participants was 19.5 years, with a standard deviation of 2.45.

Of the fifty-nine young adults who participated in the study, 41 percent had dropped out of high school, 39 percent had graduated from high school or gained a General Education Diploma (GED), 14 percent had some college education, 5 percent were enrolled in high school, and 2 percent had completed a four-year college degree.

The living arrangement for the participants in the study was as follows: 42 percent lived with parents, 21 percent lived with roommates, 16 percent lived alone, 10 percent lived with other extended family members, 9 percent lived in a homeless shelter, and 7 percent lived with a partner or spouse.

On the pre–focus group questionnaire, participants were asked to check their most recent diagnosis, as well as other diagnoses, that they had received from their clinical assessments. The four most frequently selected diagnoses were depression (38 percent), bipolar disorder (28 percent), anxiety (22 percent), and ADD/ADHD (17%). Fifty-three percent of the youths identified two or more diagnoses, and 22 percent of the youths did not report a diagnosis.

POSITIVE EXPERIENCES WITH MENTAL HEALTH SERVICES

Personal qualities of service providers. Young people described positive experiences in receiving services that were mostly characterized by warm relationships with supportive service providers who showed that they cared and who seemed to understand their difficulties. Examples of these perceptions included the following:

> I was really excited that he was coming over that day, to be with him, to take me out and do stuff. He helped me get my first job. He made it fun. We would goof around. He was like a buddy. That is what makes it work. People don't like to hang out with people who are just like adults, because adults are boring.

> She said, 'Life is sometimes not fair, get over it.' That was it. I was like, 'Okay, thank you for being honest with me.' It was pure honesty on her part and before that nobody was ever honest.

> She has always been there for me. She is like my rock, so I feel comfortable here.

> Don't hire old social workers. You have to have young people. So J. is more like a friend and that is what makes it work. He helped me more because he let me make myself better. He didn't try to force me. He was more like a friend.

> She really is awesome. She helped me a lot through a lot of this stuff, and she is still helping me. She just gives me that little glimmer of hope and that's cool. She understands.

> The best support I've gotten is from people who have the same problem as me, because they can relate to it. My therapist was only a couple of years—she is twenty-six—older than me. She had gone through the same things.

Helpful programming. The focus group participants appreciated the practical assistance they received with independent living skills, such as money management, education, independent living arrangements, and leadership training. Examples of these perceptions included the following:

> They taught me how to manage a checkbook. How to manage money. I really didn't learn how to manage a checkbook or how to manage money till I had just completely dropped out of high school and went to try to get my GED. While I was getting my GED they gave me an independent living

skills book. Through that it taught you how to look for transportation, and get a job. It taught you how to find a house.
Taught you how to look in the paper for a job.

If you have problems going back home, they help you. They
listen to you. They actually help the youth try to get up on
their feet and get their education. So, it is really good.

They give us, like, leadership training. They give us a lot of
training that relates to the job, so we already have stuff
behind us.

We will go to legislative meetings, like when there is a bill
and it has something to do with youth. We are a group that
goes there and figures stuff out.

CHALLENGES IN GETTING NEEDS MET THROUGH THE SERVICE SYSTEM

Lack of information about support. Participants reported that no one
had told them about support available through their high school.
For example, several participants commented that they had no knowledge that school counselors could assist teens who experienced mental health difficulties. Examples of these perceptions included the
following:

I needed something, some kind of counseling or something
like that. I didn't even realize that the counselors in high
school were actual counselors. I thought they were like secre-
taries who did your schedule.

It would be nice if they were like, 'Hey, this is your counselor.
They don't just help you with figuring out what class you
want to take your sophomore year. They can also help you
with blah, blah, blah, if you just want to talk.'

Complaints about the quality and relevance of services. Focus group participants complained about inappropriate mental health services
related to inaccurate diagnoses. Many participants had been given multiple diagnoses over the years, and they believed they had been prescribed inappropriate medications. Other participants complained
about the attitudes of the service providers. Examples of some of these
perceptions included the following:

They have changed my diagnosis probably on an annual
basis for five years. Finally everyone has agreed on one that

explains everything. I have been on a ton of different meds. I have been on meds that made me worse.

They try to refute any sort of objectives that I had personally, like to go to college. They tell me things like, 'You are going to be on meds the rest of your life. Here is your prognosis. You are going to be in and out of hospitals, in and off the streets and have problems as well, blah, blah, blah.' They will train you for working at McDonalds which is kind of what they are insinuating that that is the only work you will be able to obtain.

I felt she was really manipulative and I think she jumped to a lot of conclusions really quickly after one or two sessions. She would talk to me for a while and then she would have me leave the room and have my mother come in and talk to her. I have no idea what she said to my mother. I have no idea if she interpreted things right or wrong. My mother always came out crying. That was a red flag right there. I have no idea why my mother is crying. 'What did you tell her?' There was no trust.

They weren't productive because it seemed like much of the group time was spent on people trying to compare horror stories or compare sob stories. The people who were there trying to use it as a therapeutic tool were outnumbered. Groups can bring out the best or the worst and it is hard for facilitators to keep control of the group.

My teacher, the people that have my case, my case manager, I guess they are supposed to tell my other teachers. And I don't know if they tell my other teachers or if my other teachers just don't listen to them.

They don't know how to help with long-term diagnosis or short-term diagnosis. They have to do more with the world of education and whether I can pass an exam on time.

Concerns about not being heard by service providers. A common theme among participants who had participated in a treatment program was their perception that they were not listened to during therapy. As a result, they felt that providers responded inappropriately and often did not know what was going on in the lives of the participants. Examples of these perceptions included the following:

They were all thinking I was suicidal, jumping to conclu-sions. I wasn't at all. I feel like they weren't really listening to what the real problems were.

It was really bad because the counselor would always listen to my parents and would never listen to anything that came out of my mouth.

Everyone had control of my mental health except me, because it was like the doctors, my parents, they were run-ning the show. They were making the decisions. They thought they knew what was best for me. I think a lot of times kids may know what is best for them.

Skepticism about whether service providers had their interests at heart. Some participants were cynical about the motives of service providers and suspicious that they were working with them only because they were being paid, as the following comment exemplifies: "I'm skeptical of people that don't really have an interest in my well-being. Like you go to a therapist and you talk to them, but they're getting paid $200 to listen an hour. Are they actually giving me good advice or they just sit-ting there for the money?"

Lack of access to mental health services. Although participants had many criticisms of the services they had received, some youths expressed concerns because they could not access mental health services. Some youths lacked health insurance, and others could not use services because they did not have transportation. Younger participants feared losing services at the age of eighteen and were afraid that they would not have their needs met in the adult mental health system. Examples of these perceptions included the following:

I am being told that some of my supports are going to just disappear because I will be turning eighteen. They can't work with me anymore. They are trying to transition me into adulthood but it is a hard road.

I know once I turn eighteen it is not going to—it is not like I am never going to have a crisis again—I know there is a pos-sibility that I could go through another crisis after I turn eigh-teen. I won't have the support I had before I turned eighteen.

IDEAL SUPPORTS

When participants were asked to identify ideal supports, they had many ideas about how to improve their use of services, such as receiving information about existing services, as well as more accessible services. In addition, they wanted to interact with service providers whom they could feel comfortable with during their treatment. Examples of these perceptions included the following:

> A way to access or like a list of psychiatrists near here. It is so hard to figure it out. Someone that can help you find the right one or one who takes your insurance. Counselors, the same thing, what are ways to access them, or to find out about them, and get information? Also support groups are needed.

> I guess if I was able to create a university therapy system. I wouldn't make patients feel like they are not supposed to be getting service.

> Somewhere you can go, like when you are about to fall through the cracks, and be kind of taken care of.

> I get the most help out of being able to talk to people who are kind of on my level and just sit down and talk about it.

Discussion

Focus groups represent a tool that can be used to access the perceptions of youths toward their system of care. Although initially developed to access consumers' evaluation of a service or product (Bloor et al., 2001), focus groups have been used as a valuable tool for gathering information from consumers at the front end, where policies and services are designed. Using focus groups in the present study resulted in a rich opportunity for transition-age youths with mental health disorders to give input about their experiences receiving mental health and school-based services and to share their ideas about how services could be improved. However, because the groups are not representative samples, results cannot be generalized to a larger population. Nevertheless, the findings from this exploratory focus group research can generate important hypotheses for further testing; pave the way for subsequent, quantitative studies; and provide valuable information for program planners and managers.

As has been demonstrated frequently in the literature (see Gambrill, 2006; Hepworth, Rooney, Rooney, Strom-Gottfried, & Larsen, 2006; Shulman, 1999), the quality of the client-worker relationship is central to young people's perception of the helpfulness of a service provider.

The participants in this study particularly appreciated and felt connected to providers who were warm and friendly, who were informal in their approach, who showed that they really cared, and who had experiences that allowed them to understand the challenges in their lives. They liked social workers, therapists, and other providers who were close to them in age, who offered assistance in ways that included fun, and who demonstrated genuine care. Young people felt that they could trust providers if they demonstrated warmth and genuineness. They appreciated providers who went beyond the call of duty to really listen to them and to focus on their needs. Without these qualities, service providers were perceived as motivated by self-interest and not competent, and young people reported being unwilling to engage with them.

The voices of youths need to be considered in the decision-making process when selecting providers, to ensure that they have the qualities and skills with which young people with mental health needs will engage. Professional education may need to promote the training of peer helpers and mentors who have experienced mental health difficulties or who have observed the struggles of close family members with mental illness. Empirically supported interventions that meet high levels of scientific rigor will be ineffective if delivered by service providers with whom young people do not engage.

Transition-age participants in the present study also appreciated services that addressed their basic needs for education, job training, employment, accommodation, and material needs, as well as mental health symptom relief. Participants reported many challenges to accessing and receiving appropriate services, and made recommendations to increase the accessibility and availability of relevant assistance. Some young people wanted assistance negotiating complex service systems and wanted information about accessible services. A few youths reported that they gained skills through leadership training and had participated in advocacy activities to improve services. Given the concerns participants expressed about the lack of responsiveness of services and poor communication between providers, improved coordination of services between the youth and adult mental health systems is obviously a need that has to be addressed to better serve this population.

Implications for Organizational Decision Making

Marsh (2002) suggests that learning from clients is crucial to planning effective services for a number of reasons. First, ethical and effective

practice is based on learning from the client through his or her involvement in developing and seeking solutions. Second, service providers
need to involve clients who have been silenced or marginalized to
increase their voice in the decision-making processes, as well as in the
institutions that can bring resources and recognition to their concerns.
Third, interventions and services can be refined and improved on the
basis of client experiences and feedback.

If macro practitioners are serious about developing empirically supported interventions, then not only does the research literature need to
be culled for rigorously conducted studies that identify techniques that
can be investigated quantitatively, but it also is critical to research evidence-based processes that cut across interventions, such as relationship building or the wraparound approach to service delivery (Huang
et al., 2005; Waddell & Godderris, 2005). Young people who participated
in the present study expressed appreciation for being asked about their
opinions of services and for being listened to and taken seriously. Service providers need to listen to their clients to improve services so that
transition-age youths can achieve their desired outcomes. Youths are
more likely to engage in the decision-making processes if service providers collaborate with the youths in designing programs that are relevant in meeting their needs. Focus groups are a cost-effective medium
for gaining in-depth feedback from service users and have the potential
to engage the client in the decision-making processes related to designing, implementing, and evaluating programs.

Practice Guidelines

We suggest four guidelines in using evidence from clients to inform
practice for community and organizational change.

1. RECOGNIZE CLIENTS AS THE EXPERTS OF THEIR EXPERIENCE.

Peter Senge (1990) noted that the ability to achieve the results truly
desired is eroded by feelings that our beliefs are the truth, that the truth
is obvious, that our beliefs are based on real data, and that the data we
select are the real data.

One long-held assumption has been that program design decisions
require professional expertise that only trained planners, professional
elites, administrators, and faculty possess (Mulroy, 2008). Not including
those we serve in the decision-making processes is to assume that their
perspective is not significantly different from ours or that it is not relevant. Although program directors are generally quick to acknowledge
the importance of assessing the needs of a target population, why is it

not equally important to involve those who receive the services in designing programs that will best meet their needs? Have we gathered information from current or potential clients to identify what aspects of the program are crucial components for them?

2. CHALLENGE ASSUMPTIONS REGARDING CLIENT PARTICIPATION AND INVOLVEMENT

A number of agencies have begun hiring consumers as providers of mental health services. Although not without its challenges, the benefits are many, including instilling hope in consumers, helping professionals become aware of their own prejudices, and shifting professionals' attitudes about the prognosis of people with mental illness (Carlson, Rapp, & McDiarmid, 2001). Conducting focus groups to inform program decisions (Fogel, 2004) and developing interventions that support shared decision making between professionals and clients in treatment decisions (Deegan, Rapp, Holter, & Riefer, 2008) are examples of other means for increasing consumer voices. Regardless of the approach, to create room at the table for meaningful client involvement requires changes in organizational culture and climate. Organizational assessment tools could be used to guide an agency in changing its decision-making processes, such as *Is Your Organization Supporting Meaningful Youth Participation in Collaborative Team Planning?* (Research and Training Center on Family Support and Children's Mental Health, 2008) and *Achieving Quality Services: A Checklist for Evaluating Your Agency* (Hamner, Timmons, & Hoff, 2002).

3. EMPOWER CLIENT SELF-DETERMINATION

The assumptions organizational members hold about influence or power have practical consequences for their willingness to work collaboratively with those they serve. If a program administrator believes there is a fixed amount of power available in relationship to a program—in other words, if it is viewed as a zero-sum relationship—then an increase in the power or influence held by the client will result in decreased influence on the part of the professional (Tannenbaum, 1968). However, organizational theory suggests that power or influence can also be viewed as expandable, so that service users, if they feel valued, are likely to increase their involvement leading to increased program effectiveness, thus resulting in both parties having greater power than before participants became involved in program design (Price & Mueller, 1986).

4. CONSIDER THE ROLE OF ALLY AS WELL AS ADVOCATE.

Although much is written about the role of the service provider as an advocate, little attention has been given to the role of ally. An ally is a member of a dominant group who works to dismantle any form of oppression. Allied behavior means taking personal responsibility for the changes that are needed in our society. It is intentional, overt, consistent activity that challenges prevailing patterns of oppression, makes privileges that are so often invisible visible, and facilitates the empowerment of persons targeted by oppression (Ayvazian, 2001). Participatory program planning can help empower participants and provide an opportunity for them to develop useful skills in making decisions related to their system of care (Nichols, 2002).

Conclusions

The incorporation of client preferences and values has been identified as a key aspect of evidence-based practice (Gambrill, 2006; Marsh, 2002). However, as human service organizations increasingly adopt and implement empirically supported interventions, it appears that there has been little attention to involving clients in the decision-making processes in selecting and appraising those interventions. Without information from clients about the types of services they find helpful or the attributes of service providers they prefer to engage with, it is less likely that clients will complete treatment. If decision makers in human service organizations promote methods, such as focus groups, to gain client perspectives on their preferences and needs, service providers will gain information that will assist them to provide interventions that are more appropriate and relevant to meeting client needs. As a result, practitioners will be more likely to engage clients in the helping relationship and assist clients in achieving their desired outcomes.

References

Armbruster, P., & Fallon, T. (1994). Clinical, socio-demographic, and systems risk factors for attrition in a children's mental health clinic. *American Journal of Orthopsychiatry, 64*(4), 577–585.

Armstrong, K. H., Dedrick, R. F., & Greenbaum, P. E. (2003). Factors associated with community adjustment of young adults with serious emotional disturbance: A longitudinal analysis. *Journal of Emotional and Behavioral Disorders, 11*(2), 66–77.

Ayvazian, A. (2001). Interrupting the cycle of oppression: The role of allies as agents of change. In P. S. Rothenberg (Ed.), *Race, class, and gender in the United States: An integrated study* (5th ed., pp. 809–815). New York: Freeman.

Blankertz, L. (1998). The value and practicality of deliberate sampling for heterogeneity: A critical multiplist perspective. *American Journal of Evaluation*, 19(3), 307–324.

Bloor, M., Frankland, J., Thomas, M., & Robson, K. (2001). *Focus groups in social research*. Thousand Oaks, CA: Sage.

Burns, B. J., Costello, E. J., Angold, A., Tweed, D., Stangl, D., Farmer, E. M., et al. (1995). Children's mental health service use across service sectors. *Health Affairs*, 14(3), 147–159.

Carlson, L. S., Rapp, C. A., & McDiarmid, D. (2001). Hiring consumer-providers: Barriers and alternative solutions. *Community Mental Health Journal*, 37(3), 199–213.

Costello, J., Egger, H., & Angold, A. (2005). Ten-year research update review: The epidemiology of child and adolescent psychiatric disorders: I. Methods and public health burden. *Journal of the American Academy of Child and Adolescent Psychiatry*, 44(10), 972–986.

Deegan, P. E., Rapp, C., Holter, M., & Riefer, M. (2008). Best practices: A program to support shared decision making in an outpatient psychiatric medication clinic. *Psychiatric Services*, 59(6), 603–605.

Farmer, E. M. Z., Burns, B. J., Phillips, S. D., Angold, A., & Costello, E. J. (2003). Pathways into and through mental health services for children and adolescents. *Psychiatric Services*, 54(1), 60–66.

Fogel, S. J. (2004). Risks and opportunities for success: Perceptions of urban youths in a distressed community. *Families in Society: The Journal of Contemporary Social Services*, 85(3), 335–344.

Frese, F. J., Stanley, J., Kress, K., & Vogel-Scibilia, S. (2001). Integrating evidence-based practices and the recovery model. *Psychiatric Services*, 52(11), 1462–1468.

Gambrill, E. (2006). *Social work practice: A critical thinker's guide*. New York: Oxford University Press.

Giacomini, M. K., & Cook, D. J. (2000). Qualitative research in health care; Part A: Are the results of the study valid? *Journal of the American Medical Association*, 284(3), 357–362.

Glaser, B. G., & Strauss, A. L. (1967). *The discovery of grounded theory: Strategies for qualitative research*. Chicago: Aldine.

Greene, J., & Winters, M. (2005). *Public high school graduation and college-readiness rates: 1991–2002* (Education Working Paper No. 8). New York: Center for Civic Innovation, Manhattan Institute. Retrieved September 10, 2008, from http://www.manhattan-institute.org/pdf/ewp_08.

Hamner, D., Timmons, J., & Hoff, D. (2002). *Achieving quality services: A checklist for evaluating your agency*. Boston: Institute for Community Inclusion. Retrieved September 10, 2008, from http://www.communityinclusion.org/pdf/ib15.pdf.

Heary, C. M., & Hennessy, E. (2002). The use of focus group interviews in pediatric health care research. *Journal of Pediatric Psychology*, 27(1), 47–57.

Hepworth, D. H., Rooney, R. H., Rooney, G. D., Strom-Gottfried, K., & Larsen, J. (2006). *Direct social work practice* (7th ed.). Pacific Grove, CA: Brooks/Cole.

Huang, L., Stroul, B., Friedman, R., Mrazek, P., Friesen, B., Pires, S., et al. (2005). Transforming mental health care for children and their families. *American Psychologist, 60*(6), 615–627.

Institute of Medicine. (2000). *Crossing the quality chasm: A new health system for the 21st century.* Washington, DC: National Academies Press.

Jivanjee, P., Friesen, B. J., Kruzich, J. M., Robinson, A., & Pullmann, M. (2002, January–February). Family participation in system of care: Frequently asked questions (and some answers). *California Institute for Mental Health, 5*(1), 1–7. Retrieved October 19, 2008, from http://www.cimh.org/downloads/Jan-Feb02.pdf.

Jivanjee, P., Kruzich, J. M., & Gordon, L. (2009). The age of uncertainty: Parent perspectives on the transitions of young people with mental health difficulties to adulthood. *Journal of Child and Family Studies, 18*(4), 435–446.

Jones, F. C., & Broome, M. E. (2001). Focus groups with African American adolescents: Enhancing recruitment and retention in intervention studies. *Journal of Pediatric Nursing, 16*(2), 88–96.

Kazdin, A. (1993). Premature termination from treatment among children referred for antisocial behavior. *Journal of Child Psychology and Psychiatry, 31*(3), 415–425.

Kazdin, A. E., Holland, L., & Crowley, M. (1997). Family experience of barriers to treatment and premature termination from child therapy. *Journal of Consulting and Clinical Psychology, 65*(3), 453–463.

Mark, T. L., & Buck, J. A. (2006). Characteristics of U.S. youths with serious emotional disturbance: Data from the national health interview survey. *Psychiatric Services, 57*(11), 1573–1578.

Marsh, J. C. (2002). Learning from clients. *Social Work, 47*(4), 341–343.

Matarese, M., Carpenter, M., Huffine, C., Lane, S., & Paulson, K. (2008). Partnerships with youth for youth-guided systems of care. In B. A. Stroul & G. M. Blau (Eds.), *Transforming mental health services for children, youth and families* (pp. 275–300). Baltimore: Paul H. Brooks.

Mullen, E., Shlonsky, A., Bledsoe, S., & Bellamy, J. (2005). From concept to implementation: Challenges facing evidence-based social work. *Evidence and Policy, 1*(1), 61–84.

Mulroy, E. (2008). University community partnerships that promote evidence-based macro practice. *Journal of Evidence-Based Social Work, 5*(3–4), 497–517.

New Freedom Commission on Mental Health. (2003). *Achieving the promise: Transforming mental health care in America. Final report* (DHHS Pub. No. SMA-03-3832). Rockville, MD: U.S. Department of Health and Human Services.

Nichols, L. (2002). Participatory program planning: Including program participants and evaluators. *Evaluation and Program Planning, 25*(1), 1–14.

Osher, D. M., Quinn, M. M., & Hanley, T. V. (2002). Children and youth with serious emotional disturbance: A national agenda for success. *Journal of Child and Family Studies, 11*(1), 1–11.

Osher, T., Penn, M., & Spencer, S. (2008). Partnerships with families for family-driven systems of care. In B. A. Stroul & G. M. Blau (Eds.), *Transforming mental health services for children, youth and families.* (pp. 249–273). Baltimore: Brookes.

Peterson-Sweeney, K. (2005). The use of focus groups in pediatric and adolescent research. *Journal of Pediatric Health Care, 19*(2), 104–110.

Price, J. L., & Mueller, C. W. (1986). *Handbook of organizational measurement.* Cambridge, MA: Ballinger.

QSR International (2002). *N6 qualitative analysis software.* Melbourne, Australia: Author.

Research and Training Center on Family Support and Children's Mental Health. (2008). *Is your organization supporting meaningful youth participation in collaborative team planning? A self-assessment quiz* [Brochure]. Portland, OR: Portland State University. Retrieved September 10, 2008, from http://www.rtc.pdx.edu/PDF/pbAMPQuizBrochure.pdf.

Rodwell, M. K. (1998). *Social work constructivist research.* New York: Garland.

Sabin, J. E., & Daniels, N. (2002). Managed care: Strengthening the consumer voice in managed care: Helping professionals listen. *Psychiatric Services, 53*(7), 805–811.

Sackett, D. L., Straus, S. E., Richardson, W. S., Rosenberg, W., & Haynes, R. B. (2000). *Evidence based medicine: How to practice and teach EBM* (2nd ed.). New York: Churchill Livingstone.

Samargia, L. A., Saewyc, E. M., & Elliott, B. (2006). Foregone mental health care and self-reported access barriers among adolescents. *Journal of School Nursing, 21*(1), 17–24.

Senge, P. M. (1990). *The fifth discipline: The art and practice of the learning organization.* New York: Doubleday.

Shulman, L. (1999). *The skills of helping individuals, families, groups, and communities* (4th ed.). Itasca, IL: Peacock.

Tannenbaum, A. S. (1968). *Control in organizations.* New York: McGraw-Hill.

U.S. Department of Education, Office of Special Education and Rehabilitative Services, Office of Special Education Programs. (2007). *27th (2005) annual report to Congress on the implementation of the Individuals with Disabilities Education Act* (Vol.Ê1). Washington, DC: Author.

U.S. Department of Health and Human Services. (1999). *Mental health: A report of the surgeon general.* Rockville, MD: U.S. Department of Health and Human Services, Substance Abuse and Mental Health Services Administration, Center for Mental Health Services, National Institutes of Health.

Waddell, C., & Godderis, R. (2005). Rethinking evidence-based practice for children's mental health. *Evidence-Based Mental Health, 8*(3), 60–62.

Walker, J. S., & Child, B. (2008). *Involving youth in planning for their education, treatment and services: Research tells us we should be doing better.* Portland, OR: Portland State University, Research and Training Center on Family Support and Children's Mental Health. Retrieved September 10, 2008, from http://www.rtc.pdx.edu/PDF/pbAMP-YouthParticipationResearchSummary.pdf.

Warfield, M. E., & Gulley S. (2006). Unmet need and problems accessing specialty medical and related services among children with special health care needs. *Maternal and Child Health Journal, 10*(2), 201–216.

CHAPTER ELEVEN

Using Training to Change the Learning Environment in Public Child Welfare Organizations

Michiel A. van Zyl, Becky F. Antle, and Anita P. Barbee

Statement of the Problem

The field of child welfare has been charged with protecting children from abuse and neglect. There is a growing emphasis on the importance of program outcomes in child welfare, such as child safety, permanency, and well-being (Gendell, 2001). Child welfare agencies are being held accountable for these outcomes through legislation such as the Government Performance and Results Act of 1993 (Kautz, Netting, Huber, Borders, & Davis, 1997) and the Adoption and Safe Families Act (ASFA) of 1997 (Gendell, 2001). The ASFA identified key outcomes of child safety, permanency, and well-being for state child welfare agencies, and these states are held accountable for such outcomes through the Child and Family Service Reviews (CFSR) process.

The CFSRs, authorized by the 1994 amendments to the Social Security Act and administered by the Administration for Children and Families, require the federal government and state child welfare agencies to

Support for this research was provided by a grant from the U.S. Department of Health and Human Services, Administration for Children and Families, Administration on Children, Youth, and Families, Children's Bureau (CFDA #90CT0079).

work as a team in assessing states' capacity to promote positive out-comes for children and families served in the child welfare system. The CFSRs emphasize four areas: (1) family-centered practice, (2) commu-nity-based practice, (3) individualized services, and (4) strengthening parental capacity (for additional information, see www.acf.hhs.gov /programs/cb/cwmonitoring/tools_guide/hand-2.htm). This process includes statewide assessment prepared by the state child welfare agency; state data profile prepared by the Children's Bureau of the U.S. Department of Health and Human Services; reviews of fifty cases at three sites throughout the state; and interviews or focus groups (con-ducted at all three sites and the state level) with stakeholders, including but not limited to children, parents, foster parents, all levels of child welfare agency personnel, collaborating agency personnel, service pro-viders, court personnel, and attorneys.

One strategy to promote best practice and positive outcomes in child welfare is the use of training and evaluation (Scale, 1997; Tracy & Pine, 2000). In fact, the CFSRs have included training as one of seven core systemic factors related to the key outcomes of safety, permanency, and well-being. In addition to this policy impetus for an outcomes focus on child welfare training systems, a second factor is the competency-based foundation of child welfare training. The competency-based approach to training evaluation refers to the belief that child welfare training should be designed, delivered, and evaluated to tie worker performance to the goals of the organization (Tracy & Pine, 2000).

In the field of child welfare, title IV-E funds support training evalua-tion for child welfare agencies in all fifty states (Miller & Dore, 1991). Title IV-E provides matching funds to states for foster care and adop-tion maintenance payments, administration, and training of workers. Yet funding for child welfare training is decreasing (Tracy & Pine, 2000). Not all training positively affects child welfare outcomes (Gleeson & Philbin, 1996). Eighteen of the fifty states reviewed through the first CFSR process between 2001 and 2006 failed to be in substantial con-formity with basic standards for their child welfare training systems.

The purpose of the present research study was to examine the rela-tionship between training in public child welfare agencies and child welfare outcomes, specifically child safety, permanency, and well-being. The research examined the training process and effects from the training that contribute to building an evidence base for promoting organizational change.

Literature Review

THEORETICAL MODELS

One of the earliest and most influential models of training evaluation was proposed by Kirkpatrick (1959), who identified four levels at which training should be evaluated. Level 1 refers to the reactions of trainees to the training. Most research for level 1 evaluation has operationalized these reactions as to whether or not the trainees liked the training. Level 2 refers to the learning of training concepts and has been evaluated through tests of recall of training content. Recall tests might include a test of knowledge following training or tests that evaluate changes in knowledge before and after training.

Level 3 of the Kirkpatrick (1959) model refers to training transfer, which is defined as the application of the learning to the job (Burke, 1997). Training may result in positive, negative, or zero transfer of skills. Positive transfer involves an increase in essential job skills as a result of training. Negative transfer refers to the decrease in job skills or loss of skills following training. Zero transfer is defined as the absence of any effect of training on job skills.

Level 4 of Kirkpatrick's (1959) model evaluates the impact of training on the organization. As previously mentioned, there has been very little evaluation at this level to date (Shelton & Alliger, 1993). However, Phillips (1996a) describes return on investment (ROI) analysis with conversion of soft outputs to hard outputs for fiscal outcomes as one application of level four evaluation.

Kaufman and Keller (1994) suggested several modifications of Kirkpatrick's (1959) taxonomy of training outcomes. The authors proposed the expansion of level 1 evaluation to include the value of training content and methods, as well as the availability of resources. They also added a fifth level that evaluates the impact of training on society. General recommendations by Kaufman and Keller (1994) include the framing of results-oriented questions and the application of training evaluation concepts to program evaluation.

Phillips (1996b) proposed a model with slight modifications to the four levels of Kirkpatrick's original work, as well as the addition of an analysis of the ROI for training. In Phillip's five-level framework, level 1 corresponds to the reactions and planned actions of trainees. Level 2 refers to attitude change and the learning of specific skills and knowledge. Level 3 includes the frequency and use of skills from training on the job. Level 4 corresponds to business results, such as outputs, quality, costs, time, and customer (client) satisfaction. Finally, Phillips argues that there should be an analysis of the ROI or monetary value for training. What percentage of the training costs is recouped through business gains?

Another set of adaptations to the Kirkpatrick (1959) model was made by Alliger and Tannenbaum (1997) in their meta-analysis of the literature related to training. The purpose of the meta-analysis was to assess the degree of relationship between levels of the Kirkpatrick taxonomy.

Yet in this process, the authors greatly increased the specificity of Kirkpatrick's constructs. Alliger and Tannenbaum (1997) operationalized level 1 trainee reactions as affective reactions, utility reactions, and combined reactions. Affective reactions refer to whether the trainees liked the training material. In contrast, utility reactions refer to whether the trainees perceived training material to be useful for their work. Combined reactions refer to a combination of the affective and utility reactions.

Alliger and Tannenbaum (1997) operationalized level 2 learning outcomes as immediate recall, long-term retention, and behavioral demonstration. Immediate recall is measured through a posttest administered immediately following training. Long-term retention is measured through a posttest administered at a specified time in the future (e.g., six months following training). Behavioral demonstration refers to the use of role play or some other in-training observation of skills being taught.

Alliger and Tannenbaum (1997) did not modify the existing definition of level 3 evaluation or training transfer. However, they did specify level 4 organizational outcomes as productivity, customer satisfaction, cost savings, and morale.

LOUISVILLE CHILD WELFARE TRAINING EVALUATION MODEL

On the basis of this evolution of core training evaluation models, the present authors developed a comprehensive model to examine the relationship between child welfare training and organizational outcomes (on the Louisville Child Welfare Training Evaluation Model, see Figure 11.1). This model includes predictor variables, training cycle, training outcomes, and organizational outcomes.

Three units of analysis were studied in the present research: (1) individual learners, (2) teams, and (3) organizations. In the first unit of analysis, there are two constructs, learning readiness and personality type. Previous research by Ford, Quinones, Sego, and Sorra (1992) identified the importance of the individual's learning readiness for training outcomes such as reactions and learning. Research by Barbee, Bledsoe, Antle, and Yankeelov (1999) found that there are significant relationships among education level, personality type, and job satisfaction of workers to the transfer of training. For example, workers who have the personality trait of conscientiousness, according to the Big Five Questionnaire (Caprara, Barbaranelli, Borgogni, & Perugini, 1993), are significantly more likely to transfer training to the job.

In the second unit of analysis, there are two constructs, team attitude and management support (Ford et al., 1992). Team attitude can be measured by the team's reaction to training material. Changing attitudes is

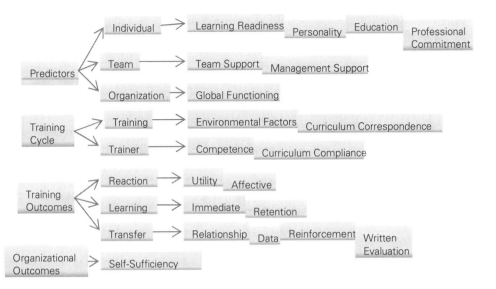

FIGURE 11.1. *Louisville Child Welfare Training Evaluation Model*

an important precursor to changing practice (Pecora, Delewski, Booth, Haapala, & Kinney, 1985).

Organizational support is the primary construct in the third unit of analysis, which includes organizational cohesion, policy and procedure concordance, and other dimensions as measured by the Global Scale of Organizational Functioning (Coetsee, 1998). An organizational culture that supports learning and outcome achievement is essential to quality child welfare practice (Moore, Rapp, & Roberts, 2000).

In the Louisville Child Welfare Training Evaluation Model, there are two levels of analysis for the training cycle, the training and the trainer. At the training level of analysis, there are two constructs, curriculum correspondence and environmental factors. Curriculum correspondence refers to the degree to which the training curriculum addresses the key goals and objectives of the organization. Environmental factors are variants in the training environment, such as season, comfort of training location, and so on.

There are also two constructs, compliance with the curriculum and competence, at the trainer level of analysis. Compliance with curriculum refers to whether the trainer teaches the material directly from the training manual or changes the material. Competence refers to the trainer's speaking ability and skill to engage the training audience.

The training outcomes included in the Louisville Child Welfare Training Evaluation Model are trainee reactions, learning, and transfer.

Trainee reactions are classified as utility reactions (e.g., Is the training material useful?) and affective reactions (e.g., Do trainees like the material?) (Alliger & Tannenbaum, 1997). Learning is categorized as immediate, retention, and behavioral demonstration (Alliger & Tannenbaum, 1997). Transfer refers to the use of new skills on the job. The transfer of training to the workplace is a key consideration in evaluating the effectiveness of training (Delewski & Pecora, 1986).

Federal policy has identified child safety, permanency, and well-being as organizational outcomes for child welfare agencies (ASFA, 1997). Child safety is defined as the absence of subsequent incidents of child maltreatment, and permanency refers to the length of time in out-of-home care or number of placements. Child well-being is generally measured through standardized scales that assess functioning across a set of domains.

TRAINING EVALUATION LITERATURE

There are a number of studies that document high levels of satisfaction with child welfare training (Cauble & Thurston, 2000), as well as significant increases in knowledge (e.g., Smith, Schinke, & Springer, 2000) and transfer of skills as a result of training (e.g., Curry, McCarragher, & Dellman-Jenkins, 2005; Yankeelov, Barbee, Barber, & Fox, 2000). However, studies on the organizational impact of training are rare in the training literature because of the difficulty of collecting data for organizational outcomes (Shelton & Alliger, 1993).

A study by Curry et al. (2005) built on previous research (see Curry, 2001; Curry, Caplan, & Knuppel, 1994) that focused on the transfer of training. Through Curry et al.'s (2005) research, the following transfer variables were identified: supervisory support, coworker support, application planning, and caseload size. The results of this latter study demonstrated that all variables affected training transfer and, subsequently, staff retention.

Another study by Jones and Biesecker (1980) evaluated training for permanency planning skills. Their study contributed to building an evidence base for reducing the caseload size of foster-care workers, as well as fiscal savings associated with better permanency planning. Given this paucity of evidence, there is a great need for more research on the use of training to improve organizational outcomes.

RESEARCH PURPOSE

The overall purpose of this present research study was to examine training as a mechanism for change in public child welfare organizations.

More specifically, the purpose was to evaluate the acquisition of knowledge and skills; transfer of case-planning skills; and the impact of those skills on casework outcomes related to child safety, permanency, and well-being through routinely generated state reports. This research study was funded by a federal grant through the U.S. Department of Health and Human Services, Administration for Children and Families, Children's Bureau, which provided supervisor-team training to more than forty child welfare teams in the state of Kentucky. The purpose of the grant was to prepare teams for the CFSRs through training in core casework skills to promote ASFA outcomes of child safety, permanency, and well-being.

The research questions explored in this study including the following:

- What are the individual, team, and organizational predictors of training outcomes?
- How do trainee attitudes affect training outcomes?
- Which factors contribute to an increase in knowledge and retention of learning over time?
- What are the factors that enhance transfer skills from training to practice?
- What is the most effective training delivery method to promote training outcomes?
- What is the impact of training on federally mandated outcomes of child safety, permanency, and well-being?
- What is the best training delivery method to promote child welfare outcomes?

Methodology

DESIGN

The research was based on three phases of data collection. The first phase consisted of training evaluation survey research. The second phase consisted of a chart file review study. The third phase consisted of acquisition of state-level management data on organizational outcomes.

The study used an experimental-control group posttest-only design. For the training evaluation survey research, there were two groups: an experimental (training) group and a control group. The classroom training consisted of five days focusing on solution-based casework (SBC) practice skills and the link to federal child welfare outcomes of child safety, permanency, and well-being. The SBC practice model is an evidence-supported practice model that Kentucky's public child welfare system has adopted (see Antle, Barbee, Christensen, & Martin, 2008a). The SBC model combines elements of relapse prevention, solution-focused therapy, and family development theory in working collaboratively with families in the system (Christensen, Todahl, & Barrett, 1999). The federal definitions of child safety, permanency, and well-being established by the ASFA and the CFSRs were used in this training. Child welfare workers were trained together with their supervisors in key casework skills, such as engagement, assessment, case planning, and ongoing casework. The training also emphasized the supervisor-worker relationship, federal legislation, and outcomes accountability. The control group received neither training nor reinforcement after training. The research study used a waiting list control group, which allowed teams assigned to this latter group to participate in the training following completion of the study.

For the chart file review of training transfer and organizational outcomes, there were three groups: (1) experimental training group, (2) experimental training-plus-reinforcement group, and (3) control group. The training-plus-reinforcement group received a half day of face-to-face case consultation. During this session, participants processed case examples and learned to use skills from the training. The classroom training and training-plus-reinforcement groups were conducted by trainers with graduate degrees (master's and doctoral degrees) in social work and related fields. Elements of the training cycle (e.g., curriculum compliance and trainer competence) were assessed. Data were collected to assess the fidelity and accuracy with which the training curriculum was delivered. The same trainers provided the training interventions for all groups. Training was voluntary, but all regions ultimately chose to participate in the training in preparation for the CFSRs.

SAMPLE

In the first phase of the training evaluation survey research, there were seventy-two supervisors who participated in the study. As Table 11.1 notes, forty-two supervisors were in the training group, and thirty supervisors were in the control group. The supervisors were drawn from six geographically representative regions, three urban and three rural regions. Data from the caseworkers were also collected (e.g., reinforcement of casework practice, supervisor-worker relationship) so all members of the supervisor's team were included in the study. There were a total of 195 caseworkers in the two experimental training groups and 136 caseworkers in the control group.

For the chart file review evaluation of training transfer and organizational outcomes, a random sample of cases was drawn from each of the

TABLE 11.1. Numbers of supervisors, their teams, and caseload in three urban and three rural regions

Training method	Training evaluation		Chart file review	
	Supervisors	Team caseworkers	Caseload	Sample
Training and reinforcement	42	195	339	40
Training only			412	40
Control group	30	136	421	40
Total	72	331	1172	120

three groups using a list of cases that were opened for each team following completion of the training (or the date equivalent for the control group). There were forty cases from each of three groups (training-plus-reinforcement group, training-only group, and control group), for a total sample size of 120 cases. Cases were selected that had been opened within six months of the completion of training plus having received the reinforcement.

All cases for the three groups that were in an open status during the target date range were included in the study. The total number of cases by group was as follows: training plus reinforcement ($n = 339$), (2) training only ($n = 412$), and (3) control ($n = 421$). The total sample size of cases for the organizational outcome assessment was 1,172.

VARIABLES AND MEASUREMENT: PREDICTOR VARIABLES

Individual. All predictor variables were measured before training only. The first individual variable measured was learning readiness. Learning readiness incorporates such concepts as transfer of learning skills, use of feedback, learning as a life skill, support for learning, and self-directedness in learning (van Zyl & van Zyl, 2000). Learning readiness was measured using van Zyl and van Zyl's (2000) Learning Benefit Inventory. This scale contains seventy items to which subjects respond on a five-point Likert scale, ranging from "none of the time" to "all of the time." The internal consistency reliability of the scale was determined to be satisfactory, with Cronbach's alpha scores of factors or subscales ranging from 0.75 to 0.89. The construct validity (unidimensionality) of the scale was established using structural equation modeling.

The second individual variable was personality. The short version of the Big Five Questionnaire was used to measure personality. The scale measured five personality traits, including (1) extraversion, (2) conscientiousness, (3) openness to experience, (4) agreeableness, and (5) neuroticism (Caprara, Barbaranelli, Borgogni, & Perugini, 1993). This short version contains forty adjectives. On a five-point Likert scale, respondents rated the degree to which each adjective accurately described them. The average weighted mean coefficient for the five subscales was 0.75 (Viswesvaran & Oanes, 2000). Construct validity of the scale was supported through high correlations with the similar NEO Personality Inventory (NEO-PI) scale (Barbaranelli, Caprara, & Maslach, 1997).

Team. Team variables included both team support and supervisor support. Team support was measured using the team learning conditions subscale of the Training Transfer Inventory (Coetsee, 1998). Coetsee (1998) validated the Training Transfer Inventory through a study of 2,810 mine workers, supervisors, and managers in South Africa. The team learning conditions subscale measures the degree to which the team is open to or supportive of new information and processes in the workplace. This scale contains thirty items to which subjects respond on a five-point Likert scale, ranging from "strongly disagree" to "strongly agree." This subscale has acceptable internal consistency, with a Cronbach's alpha of 0.778. The construct validity of the subscale was tested using structural equation modeling.

Supervisor support of training and/or learning was measured using the supervisor subscale of the Training Transfer Inventory (Coetsee, 1998). This subscale measures the degree to which the supervisors support new learning or training material. Supervisors completed this subscale in reference to their immediate managers, the service region administrative assistants. The subscale contains fourteen items with which respondents rated their degree of agreement on a five-point Likert scale. The internal consistency of the subscale is acceptable, with a Cronbach's alpha of 0.884. Construct validity was supported through structural equation modeling analysis in which supervisor support of training and/or learning emerged as an independent factor.

Organization. The variable of organizational support was measured using the organizational learning conditions and support subscale of the Training Transfer Inventory (Coetsee, 1998). This subscale assesses the degree to which the organization supports or maintains an environment of learning. The subscale contains seventeen items to which subjects respond on a five-point Likert scale, ranging from "strongly disagree" to "strongly agree." This subscale has acceptable internal consistency, with a Cronbach's alpha of 0.789. The construct validity of the subscale was tested using structural equation modeling. The items on this subscale emerged as a single factor and were not combined with any other subscales.

TRAINING OUTCOMES

Training outcomes were measured at pre- and posttraining. Trainee reactions were measured only at posttraining. Learning of training material and transfer of skills and/or behaviors from training were measured at both pre- and posttraining.

Reactions. Trainee reactions were measured along the dimensions of utility and affective reactions. Utility reactions refer to the degree to which trainees find the training material useful. Affective reactions refer to the degree to which trainees like the training. Both of these reactions were measured using a scale adapted for this study—the twelve-item Level 1 Training Evaluation Scale. For each item, respondents indicated their degree of agreement on a five-point Likert scale. A similar scale was previously used for the evaluation of substance abuse training in child welfare (Barbee & Barber, 1995).

Learning. Learning of training material was measured using a test of the training curriculum. This knowledge-based test was developed specifically for this research and consisted of both multiple choice questions and open-ended questions. There were thirty-nine items on the test that covered material from each of the key content areas of the training.

Transfer. There were two primary skill areas assessed for the transfer of skills and/or behaviors from the training. The first skill area was the supervisor-worker relationship. The supervisor-worker relationship was measured with a subscale, Consideration of the Supervisory Behavior Description Questionnaire (Fleishman, 1957). There have been a number of studies on the reliability and validity of this latter research instrument. One study by Szilagyi and Sims (1974) found that the internal consistency reliability coefficients were very high (.93). Furthermore, the construct validity of the subscale was confirmed through factor analysis, which found factor congruency indices (phi coefficients) of .95. The subscale contains twenty-eight items to which respondents rate their degree of agreement on a five-point Likert scale.

The second skill area was supervisor feedback. A subscale of the Training Transfer Inventory was developed that assessed the degree of reinforcement or demonstration of specific skills and/or behaviors from the training. Coetsee (1998) used a similar procedure when he added a subscale based on specific goals and curricula from the training being evaluated.

Chart File Review. The transfer of skills from the training were assessed through a review of the chart files and derived from the SBC model of case planning. This model provides a tool for examining the presence and appropriateness of key components of assessment and case planning. The assessment components include maltreatment and/or presenting problem, sequence of events, family development stages, family choice of discipline, individual patterns of behavior, child and/or youth development, and family support. The case-planning components include the case plan itself, prevention plans, family-level objectives, individual-level objectives, and permanency goal.

CHILD WELFARE OUTCOMES

The variables for the child welfare outcomes component of this research include child safety, permanency, and well-being. Child safety was operationalized as recidivism among existing or recently closed permanency and protection cases. This definition is derived from the state of Kentucky, and the data are routinely collected through the *Recidivism Referral Report*. Permanency was operationalized as the number of children who left out-of-home care. This definition is also derived from the state of Kentucky, and the data are routinely collected through the TWS-Q187 report (percentage of children leaving out-of-home care). Child well-being was measured through the following indicators: period of time since last visit with biological parents, frequency of worker visits, and period of time since the last dental visit (Sullivan & van Zyl, 2008).

PROCEDURE

Per the requirements of the institutional review board that reviewed the proposal for this study, all participants in the research (supervisors and workers) completed informed consent forms before completing the surveys. The pretraining measures of predictor variables and knowledge of training content were distributed to supervisors in the experimental group on the first day of supervisor training. Supervisors in the control group received these measures from a regional administrator, who was responsible for administering the tests. The pretraining measures of the supervisor-worker relationship and reinforcement and/or demonstration of curriculum-based skills were administered to caseworkers in the experimental group on the first day of team training. The measures were administered to caseworkers in the control group at the same time. The response rates for pretraining measures were are follows: 73 percent for supervisors in the experimental group, 95 percent for caseworkers in the experimental group, 81 percent for supervisors in the control group, and 88 percent for caseworkers in the control group.

The posttraining measures of training outcomes were collected at several points in time. First, reactions from the experimental group supervisors to training and immediate learning of material were measured on the final day of training. Regional administrators administered the tests to supervisors in the control group at the same time. The retention of material learned in training was measured one month after the completion of training. Tests were mailed to both experimental and control group supervisors. Other transfer variables, such as supportive supervisor relationship and supervisor reinforcement, were measured at one month to allow time for transfer of learning. These tests were also mailed to the experimental and control group caseworkers.

The response rates for the immediate posttraining measures were as follows: 78 percent for supervisors in the experimental group, 40 percent for caseworkers in the experimental group, 58 percent for supervisors in the control group, and 22 percent for caseworkers in the control group. In contrast, the response rates for the one-month posttraining measures were as follows: 41 percent for supervisors in the experimental group and 31 percent for supervisors in the control group.

Data on the transfer of skills and behavior from the learning were collected through a chart file review process. Researchers obtained electronic copies of records and reviewed these using a data abstraction tool. The data on casework outcomes were collected through routine state reports. The requested parameters for the reports (teams and date ranges) were provided to state information systems personnel, and reports were then sent via e-mail to the researchers for analysis.

Results

LEARNING

There was a significant, positive correlation between utility reactions to training and learning, $r(22) = .51$, $p < .05$. The more favorably the participants rated the training, the more they learned. Repeated-measures analyses of variance were performed to determine whether there was a significant change in knowledge between pretraining, immediately at posttraining, and one month after training, as well as a difference in this change between the experimental and control groups. There was a significant change in knowledge (learning) between pretraining and immediately at posttraining, $F(1, 31) = 5.66$, $p < .05$. The mean total score on the Supervisor Level 2 Knowledge Test before training was 31.04 (standard deviation [SD] = 2.58, range = 25–37), and the mean on the test immediately after training was 32.30 (SD = 3.10, range = 25–37). There was no significant main effect of group (experimental versus control), and no significant interaction between learning and group (experimental versus control).

RETENTION

Retention was measured as the change in knowledge between immediately after training and one month after training. There was not a significant main effect for knowledge or for group status, and the interaction between the two variables was also nonsignificant. The overall mean score on the Supervisor Level 2 Knowledge Test immediately after training for the experimental group was 32.75 (SD = 3.26, range = 25–37), and the mean score one month after training was 33.24 (SD = 2.25, range = 26–37). The mean score for the control group immediately after training was 31.14 (SD = 2.54, range = 25–37), and the mean score one month after training was 31.25 (SD = 2.53, range = 25–37). This difference was not statistically significant, indicating that the knowledge demonstrated immediately following the training was maintained over time.

SURVEY RESEARCH: PREDICTORS OF TRANSFER

To measure predictors of the transfer of learning to practice, a standard multiple regression analysis was performed that used the marker variables of learning readiness, management training support, and learning as predictor variables. The outcome variable was transfer, measured by the caseworker ratings of supervisor reinforcement of casework skills covered in the training. Caseworkers evaluated their supervisors' reinforcement of casework skills before training and one month after training. A difference score was entered into the model, and data were aggregated across caseworkers to maintain supervisors as the unit of analysis. This research intended to explore whether learning of training material affects the transfer of trained skills. Therefore, immediate learning (pretraining to immediate posttraining) was included as a predictor. Learning readiness and training support were also included as predictors. The outcome variable was the supervisor reinforcement of casework skills (difference score). R for regression was significantly different from zero, $F(3, 38)$ = 20.18, $p < .001$. Only training support contributed significantly to prediction of learning transfer (sr^2 = .559). Independent variables in combination contributed only 0.015 in shared variability. Altogether 61 percent (58 percent adjusted) of the variability in learning transfer was predicted by knowing scores in training support, immediate learning, and learning readiness.

CHART FILE REVIEW: TRANSFER OF CASEWORK SKILLS

The mean scores on assessment skills for the three groups of casework-ers were as follows: training-plus-reinforcement group, $M = 6.43$; (2) training-only group, $M = 5.59$; and control group, $M = 6.08$. The differ-ence between the composite scores between groups was not statisti-cally significant, $F (2,108) = 2.043$, $p = .135$. The mean score on case-planning skills for the three groups of caseworkers were as follows: training-plus-reinforcement group, $M = 5.34$; training-only group, $M = 5.14$; and control group, $M = 4.77$. The difference between these com-posite scores between groups was not statistically significant, $F (2,107) = 0.867$, $p = .423$.

Differences in assessment skills. There was a positive impact of training noted on certain assessment skills (assessment of family development). The training-plus-reinforcement group correctly completed the family development assessment at a significantly higher rate, $\chi^2(2, N = 111) = 32.43$, $p < .0001$, than the training-only group and the control group. Percentages were used as basis for comparison, as workers did not complete the same number of assessments or handle the same number of cases in their caseloads, although the range of numbers was relatively similar. Each case was reviewed on a pass-fail basis. The percentage of cases in which workers correctly completed the family development assessment were as follows: training-plus-reinforcement group, 46.8 percent of cases; training-only group, 20.3 percent; and control group, 32.9 percent.

Differences in case-planning skills. The training had a positive impact on certain case-planning skills (completion of secondary family objec-tives and out-of-home care goals). Percentages were also used for the analyses in this section, the rationale being similar to the reasons given in the previous section (i.e., dissimilar number of cases and ratings on a pass-fail basis). The training-plus-reinforcement group correctly completed secondary family objectives related to well-being at a sig-nificantly higher rate, $\chi^2(2, N = 101) = 8.93$, $p < .05$. The percentage of cases in which workers correctly completed the secondary family objec-tives were as follows: training-plus-reinforcement group, 59.1 percent of cases; training-only group, 13.6 percent; and control group, 27.3 percent.

In addition, the training-plus-reinforcement group correctly com-pleted out-of-home care goals for children at a significantly higher rate, $\chi^2(2, N = 82) = 8.33$, $p < .05$. The percentage of cases in which case-workers correctly completed the out-of-home care goals were as fol-lows: training-plus-reinforcement group, 50.9 percent of cases; training-only group, 11.3 percent; and control group, 37.7 percent.

The training did not appear to have an impact on the writing of correct permanency goals by the caseworkers. The training-only group correctly documented permanency goals at a significantly lower rate than the other groups, $\chi^2(2, N = 104) = 10.46$, $p < .01$. The percentage of cases in which workers had correctly documented the permanency goals were as follows: training-plus-reinforcement group, 38.6 percent of cases; training-only group, 18.2 percent; and control group, 43.2 percent.

OUTCOMES: CHILD SAFETY

There was a positive impact from the training on child safety. Both the training-plus-reinforcement group and the training-only group had significantly fewer recidivism referrals for child maltreatment than did the control group, $F(2, 112) = 18.63$, $p < .0001$. The training-plus-reinforcement groups had 349 referrals for recidivism, the training-only group had 350 referrals, and the control group had 538 referrals.

There were significant relationships between child safety and other predictor variables and/or training outcomes. There was a significant, positive correlation between supervisor learning self-direction and a change in recidivism referrals for maltreatment, $r(113) = .293$, $p < .01$. There was a significant, positive correlation between organizational learning conditions and a change in recidivism referrals for maltreatment, $r(113) = .609$, $p < .0001$. There was a significant, positive correlation between supervisor transfer of casework reinforcement skills and change in recidivism referrals, $r(77) = .794$, $p < .0001$.

OUTCOMES: PERMANENCY

The training did not appear to have an effect on the outcomes related to permanency. Notably, there was a significant, negative correlation between the number of out-of-home placements and the number of strengths identified for the case, $r(105) = -.199$, $p < .05$.

OUTCOMES: WELL-BEING

There was a significantly longer period of time between the visits with the child and the biological parents for the control group ($M = 2.17$ months) than for either of the training groups (training plus reinforcement and training only, $M = 1.17$ months, $t(30) = -5.48$, $p < .0001$). For this analysis, well-being data were obtained from the Kentucky Foster Care Census, which was performed on only out-of-home care cases. In the chart review, in- and out-of-home care cases were included. Groups were collapsed to provide sufficient power for the analysis.

Therefore, clients whose workers participated in the training had more frequent visits than did those whose workers did not participate in the training. Also, there was a significantly longer period of time since the child's last dental visit for the control group than for either of the training groups, $t(30) = -18.45$, $p < .0001$. For example, in the training group, the mean length of time since the child's last dental visit was 1.53 months, whereas the control group's mean was 3.4 months.

Discussion

There are a number of key findings from this research that contribute to the understanding of how training can be used as a mechanism for organizational change in public child welfare. First, there were significant findings related to training outcomes. The present research study suggests that there is a significant, positive correlation between utility reactions and immediate learning. This finding is consistent with the meta-analysis conducted by Alliger and Tannenbaum (1997), which suggested that utility reactions are a strong predictor of learning from training. First, participants in the present research study experienced significant increases in knowledge and retained that knowledge over time. One positive finding from the present research study was that immediate learning and retention of acquired knowledge did occur after the training.

Other evaluations of child welfare training have also found that training produces significant knowledge gains (e.g., Cauble & Thurston, 2000). Although the knowledge gain immediately after training and one month after training in the present research study was statistically significant, one must question whether it was practically significant. McCowan, McGregor, and LoTempio (1989) raised a similar concern following child welfare training that produced an increase in knowledge but not an increase in achieving a mastery level. The present study suggests that supervisor knowledge was fairly high before training (mean score on the test was thirty-one of a possible thirty-nine), suggesting that knowledge of the material might not be the best area to focus on when evaluating outcomes from training for experienced supervisors.

One major finding from the present study is that management's support of its supervisors predicts learning and transfer. This finding builds on the work of Ford et al. (1992), who reported that supervisor attitudes toward trainees were one of the strongest predictors of the transfer of learning to practice.

Another key finding from this research was a significantly higher rate of training transfer when training plus reinforcement was provided than with classroom training only. Participants in the training-plus-reinforcement group used correct assessment and case-planning skills at a significantly higher level. There was no difference in the skill level of participants between the classroom training only and the control group. Although significant differences were detected between the training plus reinforcement and training-only group in assessment and most case-planning skills, no such differences were detected in permanency-related case-planning skills. This finding may be because of the limited emphasis of the curriculum on permanency issues. More attention was given to child safety and well-being concerns through this training intervention. The finding that training plus reinforcement produced higher training transfer is consistent with studies by Miller and Dore (1991) and Leung, Cheung, and Stevenson (1994) on the importance of training reinforcement for the transfer of skills in child welfare practice. Alvarez, Salas, and Garofano (2004) also found that posttraining interventions (along with other factors such as individual self-efficacy and posttraining mastery orientation) consistently influence training outcomes.

Most important, this research demonstrated that there was a significant impact of training on organizational outcomes of child safety and well-being. There were fewer recidivism referral reports for the training group. The training group had more recent visits with biological parents and dental professionals. Child safety was related to supervisor learning readiness and transfer, as well as organizational learning conditions. Although there was no impact of training on permanency outcomes, this may be because the training did not target these outcomes. In the chart file review assessment of casework skills, there was no significant difference in permanency-related case-planning skills. One distinction between the findings of this organizational outcomes assessment and the chart file review study on training transfer was that the type of training intervention was no longer significant. Although training plus reinforcement produced significantly greater results for the transfer of assessment and case-planning skills than classroom training alone, any exposure to the training (training plus reinforcement or classroom training only) had a significant impact on outcomes of child safety and well-being. This may be explained by the very strong and consistent emphasis of the training curriculum on the federal outcomes related to child safety, permanency, and well-being.

Implications for Decision Making

There are a number of implications from this present study for making decisions in public child welfare organizations, particularly in relationship to the design of training systems. First, if scarce resources are to be devoted to training as a mechanism to promote effective practice and positive outcomes of child safety, permanency, and well-being, administrators and trainers should consider the following:

- Explain utility and relevance of training to promote learning and transfer.
- Reinforce training material following the training, such as with training refreshers or booster sessions.
- Enhance organizational support to promote training transfer. When supervisors and workers believe that there are high levels of management support for what is being trained, they are more likely to use and transfer the skills from the training.
- Attend to elements of the training cycle, including curriculum development, fidelity of the training intervention, and trainer competence. Use adult learning theories, a team-based approach to training, and ongoing reinforcement of key concepts and skills to maximize outcomes. Assess fidelity of the training model through recording compliance with the curriculum guidelines, as well as participant and expert assessments of trainer competence.
- Link training to organizational outcomes. Evaluate the entire chain of evidence, starting with individual and organizational predictor variables, the training cycle, intermediate training outcomes, and large-scale organizational outcomes. For the latter, make use of standard data elements that all states are now required to produce for the CFSR process.

Conclusions

This present research study supports the use of the Louisville Training Evaluation Model for training and evaluation in public child welfare. This model includes individual, team, and organizational variables, as well as guidelines for delivering the training. The model also tracks participant satisfaction, learning, and the transfer of skills to practice. Last, the model provides a base for collecting data to demonstrate whether the training has a measurable impact on achieving federally mandated child welfare outcomes. The research discovered that, although participants are satisfied with training and learn the material, their individual learning readiness and management support of training predicts whether they will transfer the skills to their practice. The most effective way to promote assessment and case-planning skills is to build an opportunity for follow-up after the classroom training with reinforcement opportunities, such as the case consultation approach in the Louisville Training Evaluation Model.

The present study suggests that training can be used to effect organizational change. In this case, the Louisville Training Evaluation Model used the SBC model of child welfare practice, which had a significant impact on achieving federally mandated outcomes related to child safety and well-being. This type of organizational change (i.e., improvements in core child welfare outcomes) is the very intention of the ASFA and the CFSR process.

Practice Guidelines

Some final considerations are suggested with respect to organizational change. First, those interested in using training as a mechanism to change public child welfare organizations and outcomes should consider using the best training model. In the case of this study, training content centered on the SBC model of practice. This practice model has strong theoretical foundations and a growing body of evidence to support its effectiveness (e.g., Antle et al., 2008a; Antle, Barbee, Sullivan, & Christensen, 2008b). A training program should be based on an empirically supported intervention if the organization plans to use its training curriculum to promote change.

Second, one should consider the best training methods to promote organizational change. The Louisville Training Evaluation Model used a team-training approach with training reinforcement and assessment of training fidelity and trainer competence to assure an optimal intervention.

Third, in attempting to build the case for training as an organizational change strategy, researchers should collect the entire chain of evidence, including individual, team, and organizational characteristics, as well as training outcomes such as knowledge retention and transfer of skills, and then ultimately target outcomes that align with the organization's federal mandates and mission.

References

Adoption and Safe Families Act of 1997, Pub. Law No. 105–89, § 203(a).

Alliger, G. M., & Tannenbaum, S. I. (1997). A meta-analysis of the relations among training criteria. *Personnel Psychology, 50*(2), 341–359.

Alvarez, K., Salas, E, & Garofano, C. M. (2004). An integrated model of training evaluation and effectiveness. *Human Resource Development Review, 3*(4), 385–416.

Antle, B., Barbee, A., Christensen, D., & Martin, M. (2008a). Solution-based casework in child welfare: A paradigm shift to effective, strengths-based practice for child protection. *Journal of Public Child Welfare, 2*(2), 197–227.

Antle, B., Barbee, A. P., Sullivan, D. J., & Christensen, D. (2008b). *The effects of training reinforcement on training transfer in child welfare.* Manuscript submitted for publication.

Barbaranelli, C., Caprara, G. V., & Maslach, C. (1997). Individuation and the five factor model of personality traits. *European Journal of Psychological Assessment, 13*(2), 75–84.

Barbee, A. P., & Barber, G. (1995). *A multidisciplinary training approach to substance abuse as it relates to child abuse and neglect* (Final Evaluation Report for Grant #90-CP-0059 to National Center on Child Abuse and Neglect). Louisville, KY: University of Louisville, Kent School of Social Work.

Barbee, A. P., Bledsoe, L., Antle, B. F., & Yankeelov, P. A. (1999). *An evaluation of the virtual office pilot project for the Cabinet for Families and Children* (Final Evaluation Report for Child Welfare Training Assessment Grant). Louisville, KY: University of Louisville, Kent School of Social Work.

Burke, L. A. (1997). Improving positive transfer: A test of relapse prevention training on transfer outcomes. *Human Resource Development Quarterly, 8*(2), 115–128.

Caprara, G. V., Barbaranelli, C., Borgogni, L., & Perugini, M. (1993). The "Big Five Questionnaire": A new questionnaire to assess the five factor model. *Personality and Individual Differences, 15*(3), 281–288.

Cauble, A. E., & Thurston, L. P. (2000). Effects of interactive multimedia training on knowledge, attitudes, and self-efficacy of social work students. *Research on Social Work Practice, 10*(4), 428–437.

Christensen, D. N., Todahl, J., & Barrett, W. G. (1999). *Solution-based casework: An introduction to clinical and case management skills in casework practice.* New York: Aldine DeGruyter.

Coetsee, W. J. (1998). *An evaluation model for human resources interventions.* Unpublished doctoral dissertation, Rand Afrikaans University, Johannesburg, South Africa.

Curry, D. (2001). Evaluating transfer of learning in human services. *Journal of Child and Youth Care Work, 15–16*(1), 155–170.

Curry, D., Caplan, P., & Knuppel, J. (1994). Transfer of training and adult learning (TOTAL). *Journal of Continuing Social Work Education, 6*(1), 8–14.

Curry, D., McCarragher, T., & Dellmann-Jenkins, M. (2005). Training, transfer, and turnover: Exploring the relationships among transfer of learning factors and staff retention in child welfare. *Children and Youth Services Review, 27*(8), 931–948.

Delewski, C. H., & Pecora, P. J. (1986). Evaluating CPS training: The participant action plan approach. *Child Welfare, 65*(6), 579–591.

Fleishman, E. A. (1957). A leader behavior description for industry. In R. M. Stogdill & A. E. Coons (Eds.), *Leader behavior: Its description and measurement* (pp. 103–119). Columbus: Columbus Bureau of Business Research, Ohio State University.

Ford, J. K., Quinones, M. A., Sego, D. J., & Sorra, J. S. (1992). Factors affecting the opportunity to perform trained tasks on the job. *Personnel Psychology, 45*(3), 511–524.

Gendell, S. J. (2001). In search of permanency: A reflection on the first three years of ASFA implementation. *Family Court Review, 39*(1), 25–42.

Gleeson, J. P., & Philbin, C. M. (1996). Preparing caseworkers for practice in kinship foster care: The supervisor's dilemma. *Clinical Supervisor, 14*(1), 19–34.

Jones, M. L., & Biesecker, J. L. (1980). Training in permanency planning: Using what is known. *Child Welfare, 59*(8), 481–489.

Kaufman, R., & Keller, J. M. (1994). Levels of evaluation: Beyond Kirkpatrick. *Human Resources Development Quarterly, 5*(4), 371–381.

Kautz, J. R., Netting, F. E., Huber, R., Borders, K., & Davis, T. (1997). The Government Performance and Results Act of 1993: Implications for social work practice. *Social Work, 22*(2), 364–373.

Kirkpatrick, D. L. (1959). Techniques for evaluating programs. *Journal of the American Society of Training Directions, 13*(11), 3–9.

Leung, P., Cheung, K. M., & Stevenson, K. M. (1994). A strengths approach to ethnically sensitive practice for child protective service workers. *Child Welfare, 73*(6), 707.

McCowan, R. J., McGregor, E. N., & LoTempio, S. J. (1989). Competency-based evaluation of social services training. *Journal of Continuing Social Work Education, 2*(1), 11–31.

Miller, J., & Dore, M. M. (1991). Innovations in child protective services in-service training: Commitment to excellence. *Child Welfare, 70*(4), 437–450.

Moore, T. D., Rapp, C. A., & Roberts, B. (2000). Improving child welfare performance through supervisory use of client outcome data. *Child Welfare, 79*(5), 475–497.

Pecora, P. J., Delewski, C. H., Booth, C., Haapala, D. A., & Kinney, J. (1985). Comparing intensive family preservation services with other family-based service programs. In E. M. Tracy, D. A. Haapala, J. Kinney, & P. J. Pecora (Eds.), *Intensive family preservation services: An instructional sourcebook* (pp. 117–142). Cleveland, OH: Mandel School of Applied Social Sciences, Case Western Reserve University.

Phillips, J. J. (1996a). How much is the training worth? *Training and Development, 50*(4), 20–26.

Phillips, J. J. (1996b). *Handbook of training evaluation and measurement methods.* Houston, TX: Gulf.

Scale, P. C. (1997). The role of family support programs in building developmental assets among young adolescents: A national survey of services and staff training needs. *Child Welfare, 76*(5), 611–635.

Shelton, S., & Alliger, G. (1993). Who's afraid of level four evaluation? *Training and Development, 47*(6), 43–50.

Smith, T. E., Schinke, S. P., & Springer, D. W. (2000). Single-system evaluation of child protective services training. *Professional Development: The International Journal of Continuing Social Work Education, 3*(2), 33–39.

Sullivan, D. J., & van Zyl, M. A. (2008). The well-being of children in foster care in Kentucky: Exploring physical and emotional health needs. *Children and Youth Services Review, 30*(7), 774–786.

Szilagyi, A. D., & Sims, H. P. (1974). Cross-sample stability of the Supervisory Behavior Description Questionnaire. *Journal of Applied Psychology, 59*(6), 767–770.

Tracy, E. M., & Pine, B. A. (2000). Child welfare education and training: Future trends and influences. *Child Welfare, 79*(1), 93–113.

van Zyl, K., & van Zyl, M. A. (2000). *Re-conceptualizing learning readiness and standardizing the Learning Benefit Inventory.* Unpublished manuscript, University of Louisville, Kentucky.

Viswesvaran, C., & Oanes, D. S. (2000). Perspectives on models of job performance. *International Journal of Selection and Assessment, 8*(4), 216–226.

Yankeelov, P. A., Barbee, A. P., Barber, G., & Fox, S. (2000). Timing isn't everything, but it can be important. *Training and Development in Human Services, 1,* 67–81.

CHAPTER TWELVE

Participation in Congregation-Based Organizing

A Mixed-Method Study of Civic Engagement

Paul W. Speer, N. Andrew Peterson, Allison Zippay, and Brian Christens

Statement of the Problem

Empowerment refers to a social action process through which individuals, organizations, and communities gain greater control over issues of concern to them (Peterson & Zimmerman, 2004; Speer, 2000; Zippay, 1995). Community participation in activities such as community organizing has been identified as a critical route to empowerment (Cox, 1991; Gutierrez, GlenMaye, & DeLois, 1995; Speer & Hughey, 1995). Although there are numerous models and approaches to community organizing (Brager, Specht, & Torczyner, 1987; Rothman, 1996; Smock, 2004), the approach of congregation-based organizing emphasizes relationship building and joint action that improves a community's quality of life (Swarts, 2008). Whatever the approach, community organizing is an activity that involves a set of strategies that an organization undertakes to create individual, organizational, and community change.

This research was supported in part by a grant from the Raskob Foundation for Catholic Activities Inc. Contents of the chapter are solely the responsibility of the authors and do not necessarily represent the official views of the funding organization.

This chapter presents a study that applied a mixed-methods approach incorporating multiple designs (i.e., pretest-posttest comparison group design and case study methods) and levels of analysis (i.e., individual, organizational, and community levels of analysis) to evaluate factors including participation and civic engagement in a community organizing initiative affiliated with the Pacific Institute for Community Organizations (PICO) National Network (www.piconetwork.org). Most published studies of community organizing have been case studies (Fisher, Brooks, & Russell, 2007; Warren, 2004; Wood, 2002) or cross-sectional studies of organizing members (Speer, Hughey, Gensheimer, & Adams-Leavitt, 1995; Swarts, 2008). Few studies have evaluated organizing outcomes using mixed-methods designs incorporating experimental or quasi-experimental approaches. This study of a community organizing initiative is unique because it provides rich, long-term data about the process of this planned change effort. A key aim of the study is to measure the degree to which the PICO National Network organizing effort engaged and empowered citizens toward changing policies and practices of community institutions that shape the context for the development and maintenance of quality of life in one community organizing site.

Literature Review

The PICO National Network builds community organizations that are primarily based on organizing efforts through religious congregations, and to a lesser extent through schools and community centers (Keddy, 2001). The PICO organizing model brings people together on the basis of faith and values while embracing an American pragmatic philosophy of using the tools of democracy to improve communities (Boyte, 2003). From a values perspective, religion offers one of the most powerful alternatives to market-driven ideology. Across denominations and faiths, religion often presents an anchoring in the inherent dignity and worth of all individuals, regardless of race, class, sex, or other characteristics along which society is divided. Community organizing that draws on these common values has the potential to be a force for positive change in communities.

From a pragmatic perspective, religion is one of the strongest institutions in American society. Particularly in working-class and lower-income neighborhoods, disinvestment, deindustrialization, school busing, and similar processes have served to substantially weaken traditional community institutions (Pilisuk, McAllister, & Rothman, 1999). Despite the resultant weakening of established mechanisms of collective action and the social capital necessary for such action, religious institutions have remained relatively strong and uniquely viable in these communities.

Neighborhood organizing and faith-based community organizing have become leading forms of social action since the 1960s (Fisher, 2008; Warren, 2008). DeFilippis and Saegert (2008) note that concepts of social power and empowerment are critical in understanding traditional community organizing.

Empowerment can be considered a construct involving multiple levels of analysis (Gutierrez, Lewis, Nagda, Wernik, & Shore, 2005; Zimmerman, 2000). Theories of empowerment are relevant to community organizing especially when considered at the individual and organizational levels of analysis. At the individual level, participation in a community organization provides experience that challenges individual cognitions of social power and provides a collective context through which one can process or reflect on emotional reactions to that power. Freire (1970) described this action-reflection process as dynamic praxis. This principle comports with two concepts from empowerment theory: (1) empowerment as an intrapsychic phenomenon and (2) empowerment as a process cultivated by specific settings, that is, empowering organizations (Peterson & Speer, 2000; Zimmerman, 2000). For example, a feature of an empowerment setting would be "opportunity role structure" (Maton & Salem, 1995, p. 643), or the roles available in organizational settings that encourage individual participation (Speer & Hughey, 1995). These structures refer to the amount, accessibility, and arrangement of formal positions or roles in an organization that provide chances or opportunities for members to cooperate and build relationships and to strengthen their leadership skills and competencies.

At the organizational level, empowerment theory is relevant to community organizing because it involves the development of collective or organizational power that can change policies or practices of communities (Peterson & Zimmerman, 2004). Although theories of empowerment are crucial to community organizing, few systematic evaluation studies have been conducted to empirically demonstrate those linkages.

In their review of the literature related to community interventions, Ohmer and Korr (2006) noted that only a small number of studies using comparison group designs or statistical control have been conducted to evaluate community organizing initiatives. Although important to the knowledge base, the few studies conducted in this area of macro practice have consisted of cross-sectional studies or case studies of an organizing effort to demonstrate a particular approach to community organizing. For example, Slessarev-Jamir (2004) conducted interviews with fifteen pastors to explore the reasons their faith institutions became involved in community organizing. She found that pastors perceived organizing as a fit with the congregations' localized priorities and viewed organizing as leading to tangible community improvements, especially in poorer communities, which are often excluded from professionalized forms of civic engagement. Although faith-based organizing groups vary, they typically engage in a process that has its roots in the work of Saul Alinsky. However, none of the studies included in Ohmer and Korr's (2006) review focused specifically on faith-based community organizing.

Faith-based community organizing draws on religious congregations as its institutional base. In general, the initiatives reflect broad-based efforts to bring people together primarily through their religious organizations, although some of these organizing groups also include unions and other types of not-for-profit organizations. Two national faith-based community-organizing networks, the Industrial Areas Foundation (IAF) and the PICO National Network, have received substantial attention in the academic literature.

Speer and colleagues have contributed much of the empirical work on the faith-based organizing of the PICO National Network (e.g., Christens, Hanlin, & Speer, 2007; Peterson et al., 2008; Speer, 2008; Speer et al., 2003). However, like other areas of research on community organizing, much of that work has been cross-sectional, descriptive case studies, or the development of measures for use in organizing contexts. None of those studies used a mixed-methods evaluation design to assess the effectiveness of PICO on individual, organizational, and community outcomes. The present study applied a mixed-methods approach incorporating multiple designs (i.e., pretest-posttest comparison group design and case study methods) to gather data from several levels of analysis (i.e., individual, organizational, and community levels of analysis).

Methodology

The current study focused on a community organizing initiative that the PICO National Network launched in five communities across the country. Results presented here are from one site in northern Colorado: Congregations Building Community (CBC). Ten congregations in the CBC were actively involved over the course of this study, but another twenty-two less involved congregations participated in CBC activities during the period. Four factors were analyzed to document the impact of the CBC's efforts on community organizing:

1. Rates of participation in community organizing over time
2. Levels of civic engagement

3. Levels of empowerment
4. Community-level variables (e.g., city policies and availability of affordable housing) affecting the quality of life

STUDY POPULATION AND SAMPLING PROCEDURES

Five communities were selected for a larger study using a set of criteria defined by the funding organization rather than being selected by the research team. All five communities were part of the PICO National Network. However, data on only one of the communities are reported here.

To study organizing effects on individual participants, a pretest-post-test comparison group design was employed. The sampling frame was generated from the population of individuals who had signed attendance sheets at organizing events over a two-year period. To ensure a balance of participation levels, the sampling frame was divided into two groups: (1) individuals who had attended one, two, or three events over two years and (2) individuals who had attended four or more events. For each group, the sample was drawn at random for inclusion in this study. To develop a comparison group, random-digit dialing was targeted to the same geographic neighborhoods in which the CBC is located.

Both CBC participants and the comparison group of residents were contacted in year 3 and again in year 5 to complete a twenty-minute telephone survey on civic engagement, empowerment, and several other constructs, as well as a series of demographic questions. The survey response rate for CBC participants was 48 percent; for the comparison group, it was 20 percent.

The measures of civic engagement and psychological empowerment were consistent with those used in prior research. An abbreviated version of Speer and Peterson's (2000) Behavioral Scale was used to assess civic involvement and participatory behaviors in community-action activities. Six items asked respondents to indicate their frequency of participation in a variety of community meetings and events (e.g., wrote a letter to influence local policies, attended a public meeting to pressure for a policy change) over a three-month period. Respondents answered the items using a six-point scale ranging from "not at all" to "about weekly." In addition, an abbreviated version of the Sociopolitical Control Scale (SPCS) (Zimmerman & Zahniser, 1991) was used as the measure of empowerment. Respondents answered the eight SPCS items using a five-point, Likert-type scale ranging from "strongly disagree" to "strongly agree."

SOURCES FOR COLLECTING DATA

Sign-in sheets. Participation in community organizing activities is documented through sign-in sheets. At every organizing activity, staff persons have attendees sign an attendance form. These meetings vary from small planning committee meetings to large, public actions. Over the five years that the research team tracked attendance in the meetings at CBC, there were 724 meetings. The mean number of attendees at meetings was 9.39. Infrequent, large public actions involved up to 356 attendees. Data from the sign-in sheets were entered into a database that tracked individual participants over time. The number of individuals participating (N = 1,919) and the frequency (M = 3.54 meetings) of their attendance at meetings were tracked over the five years of this study.

Surveys. The impact of participation in CBC was examined through telephone surveys with a random sample of CBC participants, compared to a group of randomly selected residents from the same neighborhoods who were not participants in CBC. A total of 309 individuals completed wave 1 of the survey: 108 were participants in CBC and 201 were nonparticipating residents in the same communities. In contrast, a total of 106 individuals completed wave 2: forty-nine participants from CBC and fifty-seven nonparticipating residents completed the survey.

Archival data. In addition to individual-level data, archival data sources were collected to gather neighborhood and community characteristics. Archival sources included the U.S. Census and Home Mortgage Disclosure Act (HMDA) data.

Statistical procedures. Analyses employed in this study include descriptive and inferential statistics. Inferential statistical procedures include multivariate analysis of variance (MANOVA) and repeated-measures MANOVA.

Results

ANNUAL RATE OF PARTICIPATION

Analysis of sign-in sheets gathered from organizing activities showed a wide range of participation. Both the unique number of attendees and the total attendance were extracted from the sign-in sheets. By dividing the total attendance at organizing activities by the number of unique individuals participating in CBC, a rate (calculated annually) was generated. Figure 12.1 expresses these rates on a yearly basis. As Figure 12.1 shows, the average participant in CBC increased their level of participation from 2.1 meetings per year to 2.7 meetings per year. The number of

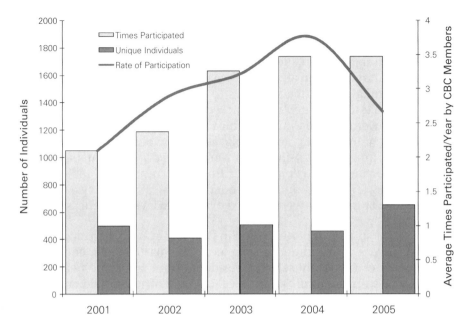

FIGURE 12.1.   *Participants, participation, and participation rates over time*

unique participants involved in CBC varied between four hundred and five hundred in each of the first four years studied, whereas the number of times people participate in organizing events increases in all five years. The rate of participation dipped in 2005 because, although the number of times people participated increases, the number of unique people attending had a greater proportional increase.

In addition, organizing events were analyzed to assess the interaction of CBC with other groups in the community. This assessment at the organizational level of analysis can be thought of as a bridging form of social capital (see Stolle & Rochon, 1998). The CBC connects with other organizations via meetings between organizational participants and representatives of other groups, agencies, and organizations. In 2001, CBC met with fifty-six organizations in the community, such as other faith groups, local governmental entities, banks, policy groups, and social service agencies. In 2002, the CBC met with sixty-four organizations, as compared to sixty-three in 2003 and seventy-six in 2004. In 2005, CBC met with only twenty-eight organizations.

INDIVIDUAL IMPACTS FROM TELEPHONE SURVEYS

In the third year of the study, the comparison group consisting of a random sample of residents was compared with CBC participants. To scrutinize the comparability of CBC participants relative to the random sample of residents, an analysis of variance was conducted to test for differences between the two groups on five demographic characteristics: age, gender, ethnicity (African American, white, and Latino were each tested separately), education, and income. The comparison group was comparable to the CBC group on all but two of the characteristics: age ($F = 12.4$ (1, 307), $p < .001$) and Latino ethnicity ($F = 8.68$ (1, 307), $p < .001$). Residents in the CBC group were older and had more Latino members.

One question examined in this study was the PICO organizing model's assertion that there were practical advantages from organizing through religious congregations. Levels of civic engagement were compared between CBC and the non-CBC community sample. Non-CBC community members were asked to identify the local organization or mediating structure in which they were most involved (e.g., church, synagogue, school group, block or neighborhood group, another group, no group).

The data suggested that working through churches for community change is effective because so many people are connected to a religious institution. Among those contacted through random-digit dialing, 50 percent were members of religious organizations, 9 percent were members of school groups, 8 percent were members of neighborhood groups, and 32 percent were not members of any of these organizations. (Two non-CBC respondents identified "other" local group as a group that they were most involved with, but because of their small sample size, they were dropped from analysis.)

An analysis of covariance was performed on the data to examine group differences with regard to civic engagement, adjusting for differences between groups based on age, gender, ethnicity, education, or income. In the multivariate analysis, only two demographic characteristics were significant: gender and education level. Members of school groups were more often female and more educated. As Table 12.1 reports, after holding demographics constant, there was a significant difference in civic engagement between these groups ($F = 10.1$ (4, 295), $p < .001$).

Individuals participating in CBC demonstrated the greatest degree of civic engagement. The CBC participants had significantly greater levels of civic engagement than participants who were members of churches or synagogues, groups, and those who identified as not being an active group member, and greater levels, but not significantly greater, than parent-teacher organizations and/or school groups or block and neighborhood groups. Because there were relatively few citizens engaged with schools or neighborhood groups, the variability of participation of those members fluctuated greatly, thereby limiting the confidence in

TABLE 12.1. Mean civic engagement scores for individuals by most active group membership category

Groups	Mean	Standard error
CBC (N = 108)	1.57	.079
Non-CBC		
Church/synagogue (N = 100)	1.07	.080
Parent-teacher organizing/school group (N = 18)	1.36	.194
Block/neighborhood group (N = 16)	1.30	.189
No active group (N = 65)	0.79	.102

Note: F = 10.1 (4, 295), p < .001.

statistical significance between CBC and participants of block and neighborhood groups. In addition, the difference between participants of CBC and those of non-CBC involved churches was great, undermining the idea that CBC simply capitalizes on the elevated levels of civic engagement among members of churches, synagogues, and other religious institutions.

To understand the differences between the organizing efforts in CBC and the comparison group, we explored two questions:

1. Does CBC (and other congregation-based organizations) simply recruit the most active individuals within religious congregations?
2. Does the organizing process itself add value to individuals in religious congregations?

A pretest-posttest design was constructed. In year 5, a second wave of the survey was conducted. A total of 106 individuals, 49 from CBC and 57 randomly selected residents, participated in the survey at two time periods. To explore for bias in the retention of research participants for each group (45 percent for CBC and 28 percent for the comparison group), an analysis was conducted to determine whether those participating at posttest were significantly different from those participating at pretest according to demographic characteristics. No demographic differences among the posttest respondents compared to the pretest respondents were found. A repeated-measures MANOVA was conducted to test for differences between the pretest and posttest scores on measures of civic engagement and empowerment between the community organizing and comparison groups. This analysis applied to the within-subjects design reduces error variance while allowing for a comparison of the vectors of mean differences across the two independent variables and the two measurement occasions.

Results of the repeated-measures MANOVA are noted in Table 12.2. (Covariates were not used, as there were no significant demographic effects.) A statistically significant interaction effect was found between the two groups (i.e., CBC versus the comparison group) for both civic engagement (Wilks's lambda = .82; $F_{(1,104)}$ = 22.36, $p < .001$) and empowerment (Wilks's lambda = .95; $F_{(1,104)}$ = 5.42, $p < .05$). Members of CBC showed increased civic engagement over time (wave 1 M = 1.68, wave 2 M = 1.88), though there was no change in civic engagement among individuals in the comparison group (wave 1 M = 1.00, wave 2 M = 1.01). Table 12.2 also suggests that members of CBC showed increased empowerment over time (wave 1 M = 3.62, wave 2 M = 3.82), whereas there was no significant change in the empowerment among individuals in the comparison group (wave 1 M = 3.74, wave 2 M = 3.65). Taken together, the data show that, although CBC members initially had higher rates of civic engagement than non-CBC members, participation in CBC organizing activities further differentiated the groups over time, with a significant increase in both civic engagement and empowerment for members of CBC.

COMMUNITY IMPACTS

Community impacts are difficult to assess because communities are dynamic, with complex, multilayered influences. Given that local initiative determines CBC organizing, and that strategies, goals, and targeted impacts evolve through the organizing process, standard research methods that measure baselines and change in dependent variables

TABLE 12.2. Pretest and posttest means and standard deviations for civic engagement and empowerment

Groups	Civic engagement (CE)		Empowerment (EMP)	
	Mean	Standard deviation	Mean	Standard deviation
Community organizing (CBC)				
Pretest (*N* = 49)	1.67	.89	3.62	.71
Posttest (*N* = 49)	1.88	1.01	3.82	.69
Comparison group				
Pretest (*N* = 57)	1.01	.76	3.74	.68
Posttest (*N* = 57)	1.00	.803	.65	.70

Note: CE = group × time interaction: Wilks's lambda = .82; $F_{(1,104)}$ = 22.36, $p < .001$. EMP = group × time interaction: Wilks's lambda = .95; $F_{(1,104)}$ = 5.42, $p < .05$.

over time are not available. Nevertheless, case studies can capture community impacts of organizing efforts.

An example of the community impacts generated by CBC's organizing is described here through the work of one congregation on the issue of affordable housing. Members of a particular congregation, who were primarily Latino and resided in a largely Latino area, identified housing affordability as a critical issue in their community.

In early 2003, the organizing group in the congregation began a research process to understand the issues around affordable housing and to learn about the causes and magnitude of the problem. This research was instigated by a team of leaders in the congregation who engaged their membership and communicated with others in the congregation. This research started with surveys of the congregation at worship services. Specifically, the survey was based on issues that surfaced in the one-on-one organizing process (see Speer et al., 1995) and inquired about issues of housing quality, landlords, rents, down payments, residency documentation, and credit. Next, the organizing group conducted fourteen research-related meetings and attended three meetings sponsored by other groups (the city council and a nonprofit housing provider) to learn about affordable housing. The group also gathered information about affordable housing by meeting with governmental housing agencies, nonprofit housing providers, nonprofit service providers, mortgage lenders, real estate developers, media, and local elected officials.

On the basis of this information, the organizing group in the congregation found that the city had no plan or coherent policy regarding affordable housing. This group then held an action meeting—conducted in both English and Spanish and attended by 214 people—with the mayor, a city council member, and the director of city planning. The group requested that city officials develop a task force to examine the affordable housing issues that had been raised as result of the group's research. The officials were committed to developing a task force to consider affordable housing. Members of the organizing group participated in the subsequent task force meetings, raised issues, presented research, and actively shaped how the task force deliberated during its decision-making processes.

In April 2004, the task force completed its report and made recommendations to the city council. The organizing group pushed the council to accept and implement a set of recommendations. The council approved the recommendations in May 2004. Four new policies that the city adopted included the following: (1) the creation of mixed-income housing developments, where at least 20 percent of housing would be developed for lower-income families (80 percent of median or below-poverty level); (2) expansion of a city program to help low-income home buyers with down-payment assistance via low-interest loans (from $4,000 to $10,000, with 70 percent of this financial support to come from Department of Housing and Urban Development or Community Development Block Grant monies, and 30 percent from the city); (3) the development of a program in two neglected neighborhoods that made $15,000 loans available to support renters who wanted to purchase their rental property and become homeowners; and (4) housing rehabilitation funding for low-income households needing maintenance and repairs (up to $30,000 in low-interest loans per household, and 50 percent of the loan could be held until the sale of the property).

In conjunction with these successful efforts to alter policies regarding affordable housing in the city, CBC also worked to increase access to home mortgages by residents in the largely Latino neighborhoods of the city. For example, very few mortgages were available in the neighborhood of the congregation and the surrounding neighborhoods. In response, through a series of meetings with several banks, the group discovered that local banks claimed that they could not make loans to families who did not have permanent resident alien status. In response, CBC conducted more research efforts that leveraged several organizational relationships. For example, through the PICO National Network, CBC contacted the National Training and Information Center, which directed the local congregation to a bank in Milwaukee that understood how loans could be made, legally and profitably, to those who did not have permanent resident alien status (i.e., families similar to the types of families in CBC's local community). During a conference call, organizing leaders from CBC asked the Milwaukee bank president to call a local bank president with whom CBC had been meeting. In the end, by leveraging the social capital embedded in organizational networks (Hughey & Speer, 2002), CBC was successful. The local bank developed a loan program for members of the congregation that included bilingual trainings by the bank (held at the church) about how to apply for a home loan, eligibility considerations for non–permanent resident aliens, acceptance of nontraditional credit sources, and down payments set at 3 percent.

In an effort to analyze the impacts of these policy changes, an analysis of Home Mortgage Disclosure Act (HMDA) data (www.ffiec.gov/hmda) examined whether increases in mortgage loans were made in targeted neighborhoods of the community where CBC was working to increase mortgage loans. To conduct this analysis, the census tract of the congregation and the five census tracts contiguous with the congregation's tract were identified and compared with the other census tracts in the county. The six tracts composing the target of this policy change in bank lending represented 9.2 percent of the county's population. The target area was 61 percent Latino and represented 24 percent of the county residents.

By analyzing HMDA data over time, annual rates of change in conventional loan dollar amounts invested in the target neighborhoods were compared with other areas in the county. Figure 12.2 depicts these changes over time and reveals substantial fluctuations. Overall, Figure 12.2 does not support evidence that congregation-based organizing had an impact on changing mortgage investment policies. Although a substantial percentage change was realized between 2005 and 2006 (when the program was implemented), it is still less than the change between 2002 and 2003, raising the question as to whether the change in the targeted time period can be attributed to CBC activity or simply to normal variation.

Implications for Decision Making

This study generated empirical evidence on changes in participation, civic engagement, and psychological empowerment among members of a PICO-affiliated community organizing initiative (i.e., CBC), as well as community-level policy changes. It used a longitudinal, mixed-methods research design including quasi-experimental and case study methods. The study found that average rates of participation among CBC

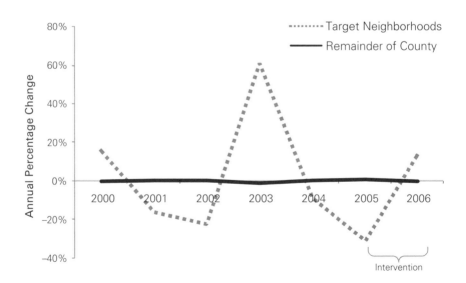

FIGURE 12.2. *Conventional loan amounts invested over time*

members increased from 2.1 to 2.7 meetings yearly over a five-year period, peaking at 3.7 meetings in year 4. Tracking interorganizational contacts, analyses found that the CBC leadership had a total of 287 formal organizational contacts, with a high of 76 contacts in year 4. In a pre- and posttest comparison, members of CBC were significantly more likely to be engaged in civic activities than were nonmembers affiliated with other organizations, including churches.

It is important to note that CBC members also had significantly greater rates of empowerment and civic engagement than did nonmembers over the five-year period. Case study material illustrates the ways that participation, civic engagement, and empowerment were realized. For example, members carried out an action in which a systematic research effort and a series of carefully planned meetings with town officials resulted in the design and implementation of municipal policies to enhance housing affordability. Similarly, by leveraging organizational networks, members were able to alter the lending policies of a private banking entity.

STRATEGIES

The findings of the present study suggest that congregation-based organizing involves a set of strategies that might be generalizable to other organizations in their efforts to facilitate relationship building and collaborative activities. These include development of an opportunity role structure for community-based groups, accessing the social networks of other organizations, and implementation of community actions.

Community organizers often strive to develop strong opportunity role structures among groups and initiatives (Speer et al., 1995; Speer et al., 2003). Previous empirical work suggests that opportunity role structure is an important organizational characteristic that can promote civic engagement and empowerment. One specific tactic to improve opportunity role structure may be role creation. By expanding the organizational roles available for individuals to fill, the development of opportunity role structures may facilitate civic engagement, empowerment, and change, as well as strengthen the capacity of an organization.

The second strategy involves efforts to access the social networks of other institutions in the community. This may be an important interorganizational process because it represents activity intended to establish links with other organizations in ways that can result in alliances to leverage policy change. In this way, accessing the social networks of other organizations may be crucial in the establishment of collaborative arrangements needed for organizations to influence their communities.

Another crucial strategy in which community-organizing efforts affect conditions is the implementation of community actions. A community action is a public meeting or event that an organization holds in an attempt to exercise social power. Community actions provide members opportunities to bring public attention to specific problems. Members can invite other community residents to the event, as well as the news media, and then provide testimony, present research, and publicly challenge community targets, such as elected officials, to change policies and resource allocations that might offer solutions to the problems plaguing their families and neighborhoods.

Conclusions

The findings indicate that the institutionally based community-organizing strategies used by the PICO National Network had the effect of increasing civic engagement and psychological empowerment among CBC members in a northern Colorado site. With initial facilitation from PICO organizers, members gained knowledge of a community change process. That information was then translated into action via issue identification; research; and strategic engagement with a wide network of fellow citizens, organizational leaders, and public officials. The process gave political voice to a wider range of community members and broadened democratic processes, thereby leading to initiatives for change, including those involving affordable housing.

As a contribution to theory, this study has showed, at an individual level, that participation in community organizing increased civic engagement and empowerment, although the direction of causality between civic engagement and empowerment itself was not specified and tested in this study. In general, most theorists would posit that civic engagement precedes the development of empowerment (Itzhaky & York, 2003; Zimmerman, 2000), although others have suggested that this link may be more reciprocal in nature (Speer & Hughey, 1995) or that civic engagement may actually be a manifestation of empowerment rather than a contribution to it for some individuals (Peterson & Speer, 2000). Future research should employ the use of cross-lagged panel analyses and other longitudinal techniques to more carefully articulate the direction of causality between these constructs and the principles that govern the relationship between civic engagement and empowerment.

The CBC also was successful in creating policy change in both public (municipality) and private (bank) domains. Many efforts at local policy change are unsuccessful (Saxe et al., 2006), so the CBC's accomplishments in policy changes are important. Despite impressive work to alter these policies, the increase in mortgage investment levels between 2005 and 2006 was consistent with but could not be clearly attributed to CBC's efforts to change policies. Therefore, it is critical to scrutinize whether policy changes produce the type of impacts they claim to affect (Speer, 2008). Future research should continue to examine the relationships between process and outcome in congregation-based organizing and delineate the specific structural and relational components that are positively associated with sustained civic engagement.

Practice Guidelines

On the basis of evidence from this study, we suggest a few practice guidelines for practitioners to use in their planned change efforts to enhance civic engagement and empowerment:

- Consider congregation-based organizational settings as viable contexts for planned change efforts. Organizing initiatives formed in religious venues can draw on values of faith and social justice to identify, implement, and evaluate solutions to deep-seated community problems. Congregations are strong community institutions, particularly in neighborhoods with less access to material resources, through which the mechanisms of collective action can be developed and exercised.
- Provide community participants with formal roles or opportunity structures through which to build relationships, leadership skills, and organizational competencies. Practitioners can configure roles in ways that are multifunctional and provide opportunities for organizing members to assume responsibility for a wide variety of tasks and decision making. Community members can also be encouraged to rotate through multiple roles so that the organization benefits from an expanded range of positions in which people can function successfully.
- Pursue interorganizational connections to build relational and material resources. Practitioners should facilitate links between the organizing initiative and other community institutions to gain the legitimacy and support needed to effectively challenge policies in communities. Interorganizational connections may be crucial for organizing groups to marshal resources, provide and receive information, and achieve desired outcomes.

References

Boyte, H. (2003). A different kind of politics: John Dewey and the meaning of citizenship in the 21st century. *Good Society, 12*(2), 1–15.

Brager, G., Specht, H., & Torczyner, J. L. (1987). *Community organizing* (2nd ed.). New York: Columbia University Press.

Christens, B. D., Hanlin, C. E., & Speer, P. W. (2007). Getting the social organism thinking: Strategy for systems change. *American Journal of Community Psychology, 39*(3–4), 229–238.

Cox, E. O. (1991). The critical role of social action in empowerment oriented groups. In A. Vinik & M. Levin (Eds.), *Social action in group work* (pp. 77–90). New York: Haworth.

DeFilippis, J., & Saegert, S. (2008). Communities develop: The question is how? In J. DeFilippis, & S. Saegert (Eds.), *The community development reader* (pp. 1–6). New York: Routledge.

Fisher, R. (2008). Neighborhood organizing: The importance of historical context. In J. DeFilippis, & S. Saegert (Eds.), *The community development reader* (pp. 204–213). New York: Routledge.

Fisher, R., Brooks, F., & Russell, D. (2007). Don't be a blockhead: ACORN, protest tactics and refund anticipation loans. *Urban Affairs Review, 42*(4), 553–582.

Freire, P. (1970). *Pedagogy of the oppressed.* New York: Continuum.

Gutierrez, L. M., GlenMaye, L., & DeLois, K. (1995). The organizational context of empowerment practice: Implications for social work administration. *Social Work, 40*(2), 249–258.

Gutierrez, L., Lewis, E. A., Nagda, B. A., Wernik, L., & Shore, N. (2005). Multicultural community strategies and intergroup empowerment. In M. Weil (Ed.), *The handbook of community practice* (pp. 341–359). Thousand Oaks, CA: Sage.

Hughey, J., & Speer, P. W. (2002). Community, sense of community, and networks. In A. Fisher, C. Sonn, & B. Bishop (Eds.), *Psychological sense of community: Research, applications and implications* (pp. 69–84). New York: Kluwer/ Plenum.

Itzhaky, H., & York, A. S. (2003). Leadership competence and political control: The influential factors. *Journal of Community Psychology, 31*(4), 371–381.

Keddy, J. (2001). Human dignity and grassroots leadership development. *Social Policy, 31*(4), 48–62.

Maton, K. I., & Salem, D. A. (1995). Organizational characteristics of empowering community settings: A multiple case study approach. *American Journal of Community Psychology, 23*(5), 631–656.

Ohmer, M. L., & Korr, W. S. (2006). The effectiveness of community practice interventions: A review of the literature. *Research on Social Work Practice, 16*(2), 132–145.

Peterson, N. A., & Speer, P. W. (2000). Linking organizational characteristics to psychological empowerment: Contextual issues in empowerment theory. *Administration in Social Work, 24*(4), 39–58.

Peterson, N. A., Speer, P. W., Hughey, J., Armstead, T. L., Schneider, J. E., & Sheffer, M. A. (2008). Community organizations and sense of community: Further development in theory and measurement. *Journal of Community Psychology, 36*(6), 1–16.

Peterson, N. A., & Zimmerman, M. A. (2004). Beyond the individual: Toward a nomological network of organizational empowerment. *American Journal of Community Psychology, 34*(1–2), 129–145.

Pilisuk, M., McAllister, J., & Rothman, J. (1999). Coming together for action: The challenge of contemporary grassroots community organizing. *Journal of Social Issues, 52*(1), 15–37.

Rothman, J. D. (1996). The interweaving of community intervention approaches. *Journal of Community Practice, 3*(3–4), 69–99.

Saxe, L., Kadushin, C., Tighe, E., Beverage, A. A., Livert, D., Brodsky, A., et al. (2006). Community-based prevention programs in the war on drugs: Findings from the "Fighting Back" demonstration. *Journal of Drug Issues, 36*(2), 263–293.

Slessarev-Jamir, H. (2004). Exploring the attraction of local congregations to community organizing. *Nonprofit and Voluntary Sector Quarterly, 33*(4), 585–605.

Smock, K. (2004). *Democracy in action: Community organizing and urban change.* New York: Columbia University Press.

Speer, P. W. (2000). Intrapersonal and interactional empowerment: Implications for theory. *Journal of Community Psychology, 28*(1), 51–61.

Speer, P. W. (2008). Social power and forms of change: Implications for psychopolitical validity. *Journal of Community Psychology, 36*(2), 199–213.

Speer, P. W., & Hughey, J. (1995). Community organizing: An ecological route to empowerment and power. *American Journal of Community Psychology, 23*(5), 729–748.

Speer, P. W., Hughey, J., Gensheimer, L. K., & Adams-Leavitt, W. (1995). Organizing for power: A comparative case study. *Journal of Community Psychology, 23*(1), 57–73.

Speer, P. W., Ontkush, M., Schmitt, B., Raman, P., Jackson, C., Rengert, K. M., et al. (2003). The intentional exercise of power: Community organizing in Camden, New Jersey. *Journal of Community and Applied Social Psychology, 13*(5), 399–408.

Speer, P. W., & Peterson, N. A. (2000). Psychometric properties of an empowerment scale: Testing cognitive, emotional and behavioral domains. *Social Work Research, 24*(2), 109–118.

Stolle, D., & Rochon, T. R. (1998). Are all associations alike? Member diversity, associational type, and the creation of social capital. *American Behavioral Scientist, 42*(1), 47–65.

Swarts, H. J. (2008). *Organizing urban America: Secular and faith-based progressive movements.* Minneapolis: University of Minnesota Press.

Warren, M. (2004). *Dry bones rattling: Community building to revitalize American democracy.* Princeton, NJ: Princeton University Press.

Warren, M. (2008). A theology of organizing: From Alinsky to the modern IAF. In J. DeFilippis & S. Saegert (Eds.), *The community development reader* (pp. 194–203). New York: Routledge.

Wood, R. L. (2002). *Faith in action: Religion, race and democratic organizing in America.* Chicago: University of Chicago Press.

Zimmerman, M. (2000). Empowerment theory: Psychological, organizational, and community levels of analysis. In J. Rappaport & E. Seidman (Eds.), *Handbook of community psychology* (pp. 43–63). New York: Plenum.

Zimmerman, M. A., & Zahniser, J. H. (1991). Refinements of sphere-specific measures of perceived control: Development of a sociopolitical control scale. *Journal of Community Psychology, 19*(2), 189–204.

Zippay, A. (1995). The politics of empowerment. *Social Work, 40*(2), 263–267.

CHAPTER THIRTEEN

Implementation of Multidimensional Treatment Foster Care in California

A Randomized Control Trial of an Evidence-Based Practice

*Patricia Chamberlain, Lisa Saldana, C. Hendricks Brown,
and Leslie D. Leve*

Statement of the Problem

An increasing number of rigorous randomized control trials have indicated that theoretically based, developmentally sensitive interventions can produce positive outcomes for children and adolescents with mental health and behavioral problems (National Institutes of Mental Health [NIMH], 2004). Multidimensional treatment foster care (MTFC) is an example of one such intervention. The MTFC model was developed as an alternative to placement in group or residential care for youths with severe delinquency or mental health problems (Chamberlain, 2003). As the number and variety of well-validated interventions similar to MTFC have increased, pressure from a wide range of government and privately funded entities has mounted to incorporate evidence-based practices into publicly funded child welfare, mental health, and juvenile justice systems. In recent years, federal scientific and practice institutes, state legislatures, policy groups, and public-interest legal challenges have all demonstrated interest in evidence-based programs.

However, despite the increasing availability and demand for well-validated interventions, it is estimated that 90 percent of public systems do not deliver treatments or services that are evidence based (Hoagwood & Olin, 2002). The purpose of this chapter is to describe how variations in implementation methods can help narrow this large gap. Given that only about 10 percent of child-serving public agencies are early adopters of evidence-based programs, the present study targets the non–early adopters to address questions that discern the contexts and circumstances that could be improved to increase a system's willingness and ability to adopt, implement, and sustain evidence-based practice models.

Although integrating evidence-based practices, such as MTFC, into existing systems promises to improve the quality of care for children and their families, several well-documented challenges preclude successful adoption and implementation. Often, the successful incorporation of such interventions requires pervasive changes in existing agency policies, procedures, and practices. Further, such changes necessitate leadership and buy-in from key individuals and groups at multiple levels, such as system and agency leaders, practitioners, and consumers. This multilevel approach to studying implementation has been characterized as ecological and contrasted with the more commonly used clinically focused approach, which is concerned primarily with how clinicians implement the practice (Raghavan, Bright, & Shadoin, 2008).

The experimental randomized control trial described in the present study uses a multilevel, ecological approach (along with a measurement model designed to capture the approach) to evaluate the implementation of MTFC under two different implementation conditions in forty California counties. In the experimental condition, community development teams (CDTs) (Sosna & Marsenich, 2006) promote peer-to-peer exchanges and support among key stakeholders in implementing counties. The CDT model is a theory-driven intervention designed to engage and support evidence-based programming for non–early adopters. This study contrasts CDT with the traditional model of transport that was previously used with early-adopting agencies implementing MTFC that included more than sixty sites. Ultimately, the trial design might help increase understanding of what it takes to engage and support non–early adopters to implement an evidence-based practice.

Literature Review

Patricia Chamberlain and colleagues established the MTFC model in 1983 (see TFC Consultants, n.d.). The MTFC model provides a community-based alternative to incarceration by placing youths in residential or group care. This intensive model provides twenty-four-hour support to foster parents who implement a well-validated behavioral program in their home under the direction of a clinical team. Throughout the program, the clinical team undergoes evaluation to assess the level of model adherence. TFC Consultants identifies the specific components of MTFC to include the following:

1. Behavioral parent training and support for MTFC foster parents,
2. Family therapy for biological parents (or other aftercare resources),
3. Skills training for youth,
4. Supportive therapy for youth,
5. School-based behavioral interventions and academic support, and
6. Psychiatric consultation and medication management, when needed. (n.p.)

Since their development, MTFC programs have been implemented via state and county contracts for youths referred from the mental health, child welfare, and juvenile justice systems. In partnership with these systems, a number of randomized control trials have been conducted to test the efficacy of MTFC (Chamberlain & Reid, 1998; Leve, Chamberlain, & Reid, 2005). Publication of these studies attracted national attention, leading to MTFC's designation as a cost-effective alternative to institutional and residential care (Aos, Phipps, Barnoski, & Leib, 1999). The MTFC model is among ten evidence-based National Model Programs rated by the Office of Juvenile Justice and Delinquency Prevention (OJJDP) (Elliott, 1998) and among nine National Exemplary Safe, Disciplined, and Drug-Free Schools Model Programs. Also, MTFC was highlighted in two U.S. Surgeon General's reports (U.S. Department of Health and Human Services, 2000a, 2000b) and selected by the Center for Substance Abuse Prevention and OJJDP as an Exemplary I program for Strengthening America's Families (Chamberlain, 1998). Results from these studies suggested the following:

- Children (between the ages of nine and eighteen) leaving Oregon's state mental hospital fared better in MTFC than in usual community services. They were placed more quickly, had lower rates of behavioral and emotional problems, and stayed out of the hospital for more days (Chamberlain & Reid, 1991).
- Boys (between the ages of twelve and eighteen) from the juvenile justice system with an average of fourteen criminal referrals fared better in MTFC than in group care. They had fewer official and self-reported follow-up offenses, spent more time in assigned placements, returned to their families more often, spent less time incarcerated and as runaways, and had fewer violent offenses (Chamberlain & Reid, 1998; Eddy, Whaley, & Chamberlain, 2004).

- Girls (between the ages of thirteen and seventeen) from the juvenile justice system with an average of eleven previous criminal referrals fared better in MTFC than in group care. They had fewer incarcerations and less delinquency at follow-up (Chamberlain, Leve, & DeGarmo, 2007).
- Providing state foster and kinship parents with elements of the MTFC model lowered rates of placement disruption, child problem behaviors, and foster parent dropout in the child welfare system (Chamberlain et al., 2008; Price et al., 2008).

KEY COMPONENTS OF THE MTFC MODEL

Mediational analyses were conducted to identify specific processes that drive positive outcomes. Four key factors were associated with positive youth outcomes at follow-up: (1) positive relationship with a mentoring adult, (2) close supervision, (3) fair and consistent discipline for rule violations and antisocial behavior, and (4) completion of homework assignments. In addition, the amount of unsupervised time youths spent associating with antisocial peers was a strong predictor of official and self-reported delinquent activities at follow-up (Eddy & Chamberlain, 2000). Compared with MTFC, in group care, caregivers used fewer contingencies, spent more time engaged in negative strategies (e.g., restraint, seclusion, long periods of restricted activities), spent less one-on-one time with youths, and allowed for greater involvement of peers (compared to adults) in deciding discipline (Chamberlain, Ray, & More, 1996). The key components of MTFC that drive positive outcomes are considered essential elements of model-adherent MTFC programs implemented in community sites. As described later, training to these model specifications is a standardized process of building a successful implementation plan.

OVERVIEW OF THEORIES THAT INFORMED THE CDT MODEL

Pioneering research on the diffusion of innovations emphasized the important role that social processes play in moving innovative methods from narrowly controlled settings to broader implementations (i.e., from the research laboratory to clinical practice). Rogers (1995) emphasized the role that context plays in an organization's ability to adopt and implement innovation. Organizations that succeed in adopting such innovations were characterized by greater flexibility, better interpersonal interconnections, more resources, members with a greater level of professionalism, and more experience with previous efforts at innovation (Rogers, 1995). Rogers conceptualized this set of circumstances as providing an explanation for the innovation-needs paradox in which the individuals or units who would benefit the most from a new idea are generally the last to adopt innovations.

The adoption of innovation requires a shift from conventional, traditional beliefs and practices; this shift is facilitated by factors that previous studies have identified. Research in the field of organizational development shows that successful implementation of new technology largely depends on the fit between the new technology and the social context (Glisson, 1992). For example, meta-analyses have shown that strategies aimed to improve work attitudes can positively affect work performance (Guzzo, Jette, & Katzell, 1985). In one meta-analysis, organizational intervention strategies targeting social factors (e.g., culture, climate) were shown to have positive effects (Robertson, Roberts, & Porras, 1993). However, those targeting multiple dimensions (e.g., social, technological, strategic factors) had more effective results. The findings are in accord with other recent work that emphasizes that targeting multiple levels, including the organization's external environment, the organization, and the service provider, are all needed in efforts to improve practice (Shortell, 2004).

Although targeting multiple levels is important, each level has unique (and sometimes conflicting) needs. Thus, progress at one level does not necessarily imply or directly lead to progress at other levels. This potential discontinuity speaks to the need for measurement models that have the potential to capture data from multiple informants and various stages of the implementation process (e.g., the initial engagement of key stakeholders, practitioners implementing the model, and consumers participating in the model).

Valente's (1996) social network thresholds model is based on identifying individuals who manage organizational agenda setting and change and matching these champions within peer networks. The joint focus on building networks with individual adopters and organizational change processes reflects the integration of multilevel models. Both the influence of trusted individuals in one's personal network and the access and exposure to external information are important influences on rates of new program adoption. In the social network thresholds model, Valente incorporated both influences of personal networks and exposure to external or cosmopolitan actions linking the individual to outside information. Across a series of studies, he found that individuals who were most innovative almost always had the highest exposure to external influences. Although external influence played a crucial role in bringing the innovation to individuals' awareness, it was usually the interpersonal persuasion of trusted others that ultimately convinced individuals to actually adopt the program. These theoretical underpinnings informed the development of the CDT model used in the current study. The model is designed to bring together groups of key stakeholders at multiple levels (e.g., leaders, practitioners) with local experts to facilitate information exchange and problem solving.

Methodology

The present study examined the efficacy of using peer-to-peer networks involving key personnel from multiple counties (CDT model) in a county-level randomized design. The primary research goal was to determine whether participation in the CDT model improved program adoption, implementation, and fidelity. In comparing the CDT to the standard individualized implementation, we examined four primary outcomes:

1. Proportion of counties that adopt MTFC and rate of adoption
2. Stage of MTFC implementation that counties attain
3. Fidelity of implementation, including model adherence and practitioner competence
4. Sustainability of the program over time

RESEARCH METHOD

Two methods of MTFC program implementation, CDT and individualized implementation (IND), are contrasted by employing a randomized control trial at the county level. The CDT condition used seven core processes to facilitate adoption, implementation, and sustainability: peer-to-peer networking, need-benefit analysis, planning, mentoring and support, fidelity focus, technical investigation and problem solving, and procedural skill development. The CDT activities occur during six face-to-face development team meetings and monthly conference calls involving multiple counties that are implementing the practice. Participation in the IND (control) condition involves delivery of the standard MTFC clinical training and consultation package to individual counties. This includes the county's participation in a readiness process through six planning-related contacts and an on-site stakeholder meeting before implementation. In both conditions, the county's MTFC program staff receives five days of clinical training and weekly supervision from an MTFC expert for one year.

STUDY POPULATION, SAMPLING, AND RANDOMIZATION

A three-step randomization process was used to assign counties to a time frame and condition. The forty eligible California counties were first matched on background variables (e.g., size, number of children in poverty, use of Medicaid, per capita group-home placement rate) to form three equivalent groupings. Next, the three matched groups were randomly assigned to three sequential cohorts with start-up times staggered at yearly intervals (2007, 2008, 2009). This three-step randomization process addressed capacity issues for implementation. Finally, in each of the yearly cohorts, counties were randomly assigned to the CDT or IND condition. The random assignments generated six replicate groups of counties, with three assigned to CDT and three assigned to IND, as depicted in Figure 13.1.

Cohorts 2 and 3 were wait-listed until their start times in 2008 and 2009, respectively, which allowed the research team to train only one-third of the counties at a time. Participating counties in both conditions receive all of the standard consulting and technical assistance typically

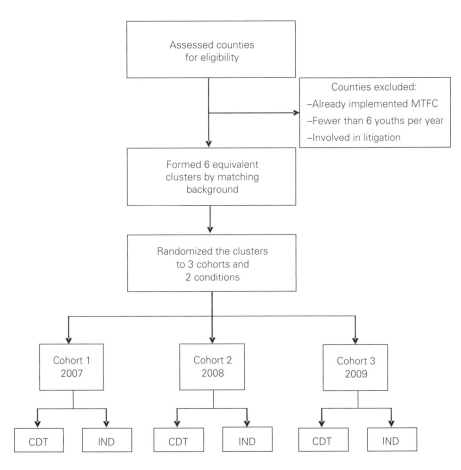

FIGURE 13.1. *Implementation trial evaluating multidimensional treatment foster care across counties in California*

offered to sites implementing MTFC. Half of the counties receive additional CDT intervention services, such as peer-to-peer networking and needs-benefit analysis.

DATA COLLECTION AND MEASURES

Before study design, the research team developed a scale to evaluate completion of the ten stages of implementation of MTFC for both the CDT and the IND conditions. Table 13.1 provides an overview of the stages of implementation completion (SIC). Each stage involves multiple activities or substages that tap information from several levels of participants (e.g., system leaders, practitioners, consumers of services). Now that the study is under way, assessment of the progress through each of the ten stages is coded from data entered into the Web-based study database, where all contacts with county participants are recorded. This database contains in-person, e-mail, and telephone contacts between research and intervention personnel, including contacts initiated by study team or by county personnel. Coding procedures are specified in a written protocol and are 100 percent double-entered to assess interrater reliability.

ASSESSING THE STAGES AND QUALITY OF IMPLEMENTATION

The SIC includes steps that have been identified as essential to the successful adoption, implementation, and sustainability of MTFC. As with most evidence-based practices, MTFC follows a manualized protocol that includes numerous organizational and planning tasks and areas of clinical skill development that occur in substages. This protocol is used to develop a model-adherent program and is aimed to achieve outcomes for youths and families comparable with those obtained in the randomized control trials. These steps are operationalized and sequential, ranging from (1) assessing the fit between the needs of the county and the goals of MTFC (i.e., feasibility); (2) procuring fiscal resources; (3) developing the time line, (4) analyzing the impact of staff recruitment on the implementing organization (i.e., readiness), and (5) focusing on the long-term sustainability of MTFC.

The time it takes for a county to complete each step within the ten stages of implementation is viewed as a measure of progress toward successful implementation and eventual sustainability. Because of the unique contexts within counties, the individual activities in each stage (i.e., substages) are not necessarily expected to occur in sequential order for each county (e.g., for County X, the date of the foster parent recruitment review [3c] might occur before completion of the time line and hire plan [3b]). The date of activity completion is tracked in each

TABLE 13.1. Stages of implementation completion

Stage	Description	Substages
1	Engagement	1a. Invited to participate; 1b. First consent
2	Consideration of feasibility	2a. Cohort letter sent; 2b. Launch preimp. planning; 2c. Preimp. planning contact; 2d. CDT 1/stakeholder scheduled; 2e. CDT 1/stakeholder mtg; 2f. Feasibility questionnaire; 2g. Feasibility call
3	Readiness planning	3a. Cost calculator/funding review; 3b. Staff timeline, hiring plan; 3c. FP recruitment review; 3d. Referral criteria review; 3e. Case management review; 3f. Communication plan; 3g. Timeline set; 3h. CDT 2
4	Implementation plan	4a. Readiness questionnaire/implementation plan; 4b. MTFC provider selected; 4c. Agency questionnaire
5	Clinical team hired and trained	5a. MTFC staff hired; 5b. Clinical training scheduled; 5c. Training; 5d. New staff training; 5e. Number of staff members trained
6	Other staff hired/ assessment training	6a. CDT 3/FP training scheduled; 6b. CDT 4/FP training; 6c. Assessment training scheduled; 6d. Training
7	Fidelity monitoring and support	7a1. Fidelity monitoring (A); 7a2. Fidelity monitoring (B); 7a3. Number of fidelity contacts; 7b1. Agency administration contact (A); 7b2. Agency administration contact (B); 7b3. Number of agency admin. contacts; 7c. Join cohort Listserv; 7d. Site consultant assigned
8	Youth and families served	8a. First youths served; 8b1. Consultation begins; 8b2. Consultation ends; 8b3. Number of consultant calls; 8c. Clinical mtg. video review; 8d. FP mtg. video review
9	Model fidelity, adherence, staff competence monitored	9a. CDT 5; 9b. Site visit 1; 9c. Site visit 2; 9d. Implementation review 1; 9e. Implementation review 2; 9f. Program review 1; 9g. Program review 2
10	Site certification as model adherent program	10a. CDT 6; 10b. Pre-certification review; 10c. Site certification application; 10d. Site certified

Notes: CDT = community development team; FP = foster parent.

stage; the stage is considered complete on final accomplishment of each substage activity in that stage.

The SIC defines and quantifies the movement toward successful implementation (or lack thereof) from participants at multiple levels. In each county, there are multiple levels of participants who provide data to the study even as counties are considering whether to adopt MTFC. This spans from the initial agreement to learn more about the model (e.g., system leaders in child welfare, mental health and juvenile justice at stage 1) to engaging in readiness-planning activities (e.g., agency directors and practitioners at stage 3) and receiving certification (e.g., practitioners and consumers at stage 10). This methodology incorporates the notion that to achieve and maintain widespread and sustainable implementation of evidence-based programs, a framework is needed to integrate implementation activities across multiple levels (e.g., political, policy, organizational, practitioner) within a wide ecological context rather than focusing solely on clinical competence of the practitioner in implementing a given evidence-based protocol.

Data Analysis Strategy

Currently, outcomes from this randomized control trial are limited to preliminary descriptive results. That is, counties participating in the trial have not yet completed the ten stages because enough time has not elapsed since recruitment. Consequently, the current section describes procedures that will be used when data become available.

STATISTICAL PROCEDURES

The primary research question examines whether CDT counties show greater and faster adoption of MTFC than IND counties. Several analyses are planned that examine engagement, degree of adoption, and the multilevel data structure. As one primary outcome of the trial, the time it takes for a county to place the first child in an MTFC home will be examined. This will involve survival analysis techniques, including Cox regression modeling, because the cohorts will vary in the amount of time that they have been involved in the study; the primary outcome is right censored. These survival analyses will use the entire time period available for each cohort (4.5 years for cohort 1; 2.5 years for cohort 2; and 1.5 years for cohort 3). By modeling how the hazard rate depends on intervention status and other covariates, a formal test can be conducted to assess the intervention impact. The semiparametric Cox, which gives a direct test on the impact of the intervention regarding the increased rate of adoption, can also be used to provide estimates of adoption more appropriate for policy makers. These findings will be converted into traditional rate comparisons by plotting the predicted proportion of counties that place foster children across time for each of the two intervention conditions.

An unusual feature in this study is that the outcomes for counties in the CDT groups could be correlated because they work together in a peer-to-peer setting. The IND group outcomes are expected to be independent. To account for how this clustering effect in the CDT group affects the standard error and testing of the intervention, the generalized estimating equation (GEE) sandwich-type variance estimator will be used to adjust for nonindependence in Cox regression modeling, with techniques similar to those employed previously in schizophrenia studies in which family factors caused clustering. These methods correct for nonindependence; test statistics are based on exact tests in which the distribution under the null is simulated and critical values thereby obtained.

In addition to these primary outcome analyses, additional analyses that further articulate levels of adoption, implementation, and sustainability will be conducted. The SIC presented in Table 13.1 depicts an ordinal measure of implementation that ranges from no contact with MTFC to achieving full credential status. This ordinal measure was designed to be directly and reliably measured for each county and used in the analyses to identify how CDT compares with IND across time. A major advantage of this ordinal scale is that it allows for greater power in testing for intervention impact with the primary outcome, time of first placement. The SIC will be used as an outcome in a random-effects probit regression model with intervention as a predictor.

NARRATIVE RESULTS

As Table 13.2 shows, a preliminary examination of the data collected to date on the SIC for the first cohort of counties suggests that, as predicted, activities during the initial stages were highly successful. All counties in cohort 1 ($n = 10$, 100 percent) that were invited to learn more about the MTFC model responded to engagement attempts (i.e., completed stage 1). Of these, all participated in some of the implementation feasibility activities in stage 2; however, four counties did not complete that stage. Three of the four counties that did not reach stage 3 expressed interest in the model but indicated systemic barriers (e.g., funding) to implementation at the current time. The fourth county determined that implementation was not feasible for it.

Of the six cohort 1 counties that completed stage 2, one county recently completed training of the clinical team (stage 5). Four counties have progressed through all of the activities in stages 3–5, and three of those have completed stage 8 and are progressing into stage 9. These latter counties have successfully hired and trained a clinical team; started the expert consultation process; engaged clients in treatment; and started to participate in the measurements of fidelity, adherence, and competence. Interestingly, of the three counties currently in stage 9, two have chosen to implement with multiple clinical teams at their

TABLE 13.2. Preliminary status at twelve months of first cohort of counties ($n = 10$) in the stages of implementation completion in an RCT of multidimensional treatment foster care in California

Stage of implementation	Number of counties active	Number of counties completed
1. Engagement	10	10
2. Consideration of feasibility	10	6
3. Readiness planning	6	4
4. Implementation plan	4	4
5. Clinical team hired/trained	4	4
6. Staff hired/trained, assessment training	3	3
7. Fidelity monitoring and support	3	3
8. Youths and families served	3	3
9. Fidelity, competence, adherence monitored	3	0
10. Site certified as model adherent[a]		

[a] Stage 10 is not yet applicable; not enough time has passed since recruitment.

sites. It is unclear at this time whether any of the counties that are slower to progress through the implementation stages will eventually accomplish sustainable implementations of MTFC. As noted previously, not enough time has passed for any of the counties to achieve stage 10.

Although the overall purpose of this randomized control trial is to compare the effectiveness of implementing MTFC with the support of CDT versus the control condition (IND), it is too early in the study to suggest whether there is a difference between these two conditions related to the progress on the SIC. This will continue to be a source of evaluation as the project completes implementation enrollment for cohorts 2 and 3.

Discussion

This chapter describes a randomized control trial focusing on two implementation strategies for the uptake of MTFC, which is an evidence-based practice designed as an alternative to group-home care for youths with serious clinical problems. Evidence-based practices, by nature, are manualized and highly structured, yet maintain a degree of flexibility to meet individual client needs. As a result, protocols involve program evaluation of adherence to the principle components of model execution, as well as fidelity to targeted treatment goals. Recently, the transport of evidence-based programs has received considerable attention in the clinical and public policy fields, as communities have moved toward adopting interventions that have demonstrated positive and cost-effective outcomes (Henggeler, Schoenwald, Borduin, Rowland, & Cunningham, 1998; Stoolmiller, Eddy, & Reid, 2000; Stuart, Treat, & Wade, 2000; Webster-Stratton, Reid, & Hammond, 2004). However, little attention has been devoted to what it takes to transport such structured and standardized models into real-world communities while maintaining program adherence and fidelity. The trial described in this chapter is one of the first to seek an understanding of the process that dictates successful implementation for communities that are non–early adopters of an evidence-based practice.

To evaluate the processes involved in a community's decision to adopt or not adopt, and then successfully implement an available evidence-based program, a quantifiable procedure for assessing the stages of implementation must first be developed. The SIC was designed to assess, in a structured way, the completion of implementing each stage of the MTFC implementation in non-early-adopting counties. These stages range from engaging with intervention developers to determining the feasibility of program implementation to achieving certification criteria. The ten stages directly apply to the implementation of MTFC and, though the activities in each of the substages are clearly specific to MTFC, the broader measure may be relevant to other evidence-based programs.

Non-early-adopting counties appear open to engagement efforts in receiving information about the MTFC model (stage 1). Many counties also appear to be willing to consider the feasibility of implementing such a program (stage 2), and to proceed into the readiness process (stage 3). Thus far, only 40 percent of the study counties have moved forward to achieve an implementation plan (stage 4). However, after reaching stage 4, the counties appear to have the capacity to move through the remaining stages that are necessary to begin implementation, engage in the monitoring process, and execute a clinical program (stages 5–9). Because it is early in the randomized control trial, it cannot yet be determined whether receiving support from CDT versus usual IND services affects the progression through the ten stages.

Implications for Decision Making

Although data from the current study are not yet available to evaluate whether the SIC can predict successful implementation of an evidence-based practice or the amount of time it takes to achieve each stage, the data suggest some implications for making decisions. First, it is noteworthy that all counties were open to the opportunity to learn about current evidence-based programs that might benefit their populations. Although speculative in nature, this finding suggests that communities that are non–early adopters might consider availing themselves of opportunities to gain knowledge regarding programs that are available and could meet their needs.

Second, moving through the stages on the SIC in a systematic way might provide information to a community that it might not be feasible to implement a program, thus preventing it from prematurely forging ahead to meet an implementation goal. This could potentially save resources that might have otherwise been needlessly spent. Conversely, moving through the stages also might allow a community that prematurely ruled out the possibility of implementing a model program because of its perceived complicated nature to reconsider the feasibility of program adoption.

Third, the pacing of the implementation process outlined by the SIC has demonstrated success for at least some non-early-adopting counties to execute the program. In addition, the sequential nature of implementation activities is embedded in this element of pacing. Although flexible within stages, the sequence is structured purposefully across stages to maximize the opportunity for program success. As more data are collected using the SIC, a greater understanding will be attained to elucidate the stages that present the greatest barriers to non-early-adopting communities. Future research efforts can emerge from the identification of these obstacles.

Summary

The present study is a large-scale experiment that compares the efficacy of two methods of implementing an evidence-based treatment model (MTFC) in up to forty California counties. One primary outcome of the experiment measures how far counties progress through a series of implementation stages. To track this progress, the research team designed the SIC. The stages allow for the inclusion of data from multiple levels of county participants at various stages of the implementation process. The stages also allow for some flexibility in the way that specific implementation tasks are ordered to reflect contextual differences in the counties. In this study, non–early adopters of MTFC were engaged. This differentiates the study participants from typical consumers of research-based interventions, who tend to initiate contact with program developers, are highly motivated, and are often well resourced. Implementation efforts that focus only on early adopters of an evidence-based practice could result in the neglect of working with practice settings where the intervention is needed most. Future research studies will continue to inform the conceptualization of the number of implementation stages, as well as the sequencing of these stages.

References

Aos, S., Phipps, P., Barnoski, R., & Leib, R. (1999). *The comparative costs and benefits of programs to reduce crime: A review of national research findings with implications for Washington state.* Olympia: Washington State Institute for Public Policy.

Chamberlain, P. (1998). *Treatment foster care. Family strengthening series* (OJJDP Bulletin NCJ No. 173421). Washington, DC: U.S. Department of Justice.

Chamberlain, P. (2003). *Treating chronic juvenile offenders: Advances made through the Oregon multidimensional treatment foster care model.* Washington, DC: American Psychological Association.

Chamberlain, P., Leve, L. D., & DeGarmo, D. S. (2007). Multidimensional treatment foster care for girls in the juvenile justice system: 2-year follow-up of a randomized clinical trial. *Journal of Consulting and Clinical Psychology, 75*(1), 187–193.

Chamberlain, P., Price, J., Leve, L. D., Laurent, H., Landsverk, J. A., & Reid, J. B. (2008). Prevention of behavior problems for children in foster care: Outcomes and mediation effects. *Prevention Science, 9*(1), 17–27.

Chamberlain, P., Ray, J., & Moore, K. J. (1996). Characteristics of residential care for adolescent offenders: A comparison of assumptions and practices in two models. *Journal of Child and Family Studies, 5*(3), 259–271.

Chamberlain, P., & Reid, J. B. (1991). Using a specialized foster care treatment model for children and adolescents leaving the state mental hospital. *Journal of Community Psychology, 19*(3), 266–276.

Chamberlain, P., & Reid, J. (1998). Comparison of two community alternatives to incarceration for chronic juvenile offenders. *Journal of Consulting and Clinical Psychology, 6*(4), 624–633.

Eddy, J. M., & Chamberlain, P. (2000). Family management and deviant peer association as mediators of the impact of treatment condition on youth antisocial behavior. *Journal of Consulting and Clinical Psychology, 68*(5), 857–863.

Eddy, M. J., Whaley, R. B., & Chamberlain, P. (2004). The prevention of violent behavior by chronic and serious male juvenile offenders: A 2-year follow-up of a randomized clinical trial. *Journal of Family Psychology, 12*(1), 2–8.

Elliott, D. S. (Ed.). (1998). *Blueprints for violence prevention.* Boulder: Institute of Behavioral Science, Regents of the University of Colorado.

Glisson, C. (1992). Structure and technology in human service organizations. In Y. Hasenfeld (Ed.), *Human services as complex organizations* (pp. 184–202). Beverly Hills, CA: Sage.

Guzzo, R. A., Jette, R. D., & Katzell, R. A. (1985). The effects of psychologically based intervention programs on worker productivity: A meta-analysis. *Personnel Psychology, 38*(2), 275–291.

Henggeler, S. W., Schoenwald, S. K., Borduin, C. M., Rowland, M. D., & Cunningham, P. B. (1998). *Multisystemic treatment of antisocial behavior in children and adolescents.* New York: Guilford Press.

Hoagwood, K., & Olin, S. (2002). The NIMH blueprint for change report: Research priorities in child and adolescent mental health. *Journal of American Academy of Child and Adolescent Psychiatry, 41*(7), 760–767.

Leve, L. D., Chamberlain, P., & Reid, J. B. (2005). Intervention outcomes for girls referred from juvenile justice: Effects on delinquency. *Journal of Consulting and Clinical Psychology, 73*(6), 1181–1185.

National Institutes of Mental Health. (2004). *Treatment research in mental illness: Improving the nation's public mental health care through NIMH funded interventions research.* Washington, DC: Author, National Advisory Mental Health Council's Workgroup on Clinical Trials.

Price, J. M., Chamberlain, P., Landsverk, J., Reid, J., Leve, L., & Laurent, H. (2008). Effects of a foster parent training intervention on placement changes of children in foster care. *Child Maltreatment, 13*(1), 64–75.

Raghavan, R., Bright, C. L., & Shadoin, A. L. (2008). Toward a policy ecology of implementation of evidence-based practices in public mental health settings. *Implementation Science, 26*(3). Retrieved October 1, 2008, from http://www.implementationscience.com/contents/3/1/26.

Robertson, P. J., Roberts, D. R., & Porras, J. I. (1993). Dynamics of planned organizational change: Assessing empirical support for a theoretical model. *Academy of Management Journal, 36*(3), 619–634.

Rogers, E. M. (1995). *Diffusion of innovation* (4th ed.). New York: Free Press.

Shortell, S. M. (2004). Increasing value: A research agenda for addressing the managerial and organizational challenges facing health care delivery in the United States. *Medical Care Research and Review, 61*(3), 12S–30S.

Sosna, T., & Marsenich, L. (2006). *Community development team model: Supporting the model adherent implementation of programs and practices.* Sacramento: California Institute for Mental Health.

Stoolmiller, M., Eddy, J. M., & Reid, J. B. (2000). Detecting and describing preventive intervention effects in a universally school-based randomized trial targeting delinquent and violent behavior. *Journal of Consulting and Clinical Psychology, 68*(2), 296–306.

Stuart, G. L., Treat, T. A., & Wade, W. A. (2000). Effectiveness of an empirically based treatment for panic disorder delivered in a service clinic setting: 1-year follow-up. *Journal of Consulting and Clinical Psychology, 68*(3), 506–512.

TFC Consultants. (n.d.) *Implementation of evidence-based programs: Multidimensional treatment foster care.* Retrieved October 21, 2008, from http://www.mtfc.com/overview.html.

U.S. Department of Health and Human Services. (2000a). Children and mental health. In *Mental health: A report of the Surgeon General* (DHHS Publication No. DSL 2000–0134-P). Washington, DC: U.S. Government Printing Office.

U.S. Department of Health and Human Services. (2000b). Prevention of violence. In *Mental health: A report of the Surgeon General* (DHHS Publication No. DSL 2000–0134-P). Washington, DC: U.S. Government Printing Office.

Valente, T. W. (1996). Social network thresholds in the diffusion of innovations. *Social Networks, 18*(1), 69–89.

Webster-Stratton, C., Reid, M. J., & Hammond, M. (2004). Treating children with early-onset conduct problems: Intervention outcomes for parent, child, and teacher training. *Journal of Clinical Child and Adolescent Psychology, 33*(1), 105–124.

Conclusion

Sondra J. Fogel and Maria Roberts-DeGennaro

The chapters in this edited book offer examples of how community and organizational practice interventions can be strengthened through the use of evidence. This book is intended to contribute to the development of evidence-informed practice in promoting planned change efforts in these settings. A systematic investigation of what happens in these practice areas can contribute to learning how to improve program outcomes and how to achieve desired client outcomes. This is critically important because changing the activities of human service providers to incorporate new practices into service delivery can be quite difficult (Bhattacharryya, Reeves, & Zwarenstien, 2009). Yet knowing how to do this so that the best evidence is implemented in and diffused through the context in which the practice is taking place is necessary, even if it remains a challenge (Dearing, 2009; Kerner & Hall, 2009; Simpson, 2009).

The fundamentals of community and organizational practice do not change (Tropman, Erlich, & Rothman, 2001). Attention to the core values of the profession—creating human organizations and a socially and economically just society for all—continues to inspire students and seasoned professionals alike to engage in activities that promote change. What is undeniable, however, is that the social work professional of the twenty-first century will need diverse skills and knowledge to demonstrate outcomes in his or her practice in community and organization settings (Weil & Gamble, 2005). The chapters here offer real-world examples of how community and organization practitioners use critical-thinking processes and evidence to inform decision making in the planned change process. They also help demonstrate how social work research and practice are engaged in timely activities to build our knowledge of evidence-informed practice and to use this to meet our professional mission.

References

Bhattacharyya, O., Reeves, S., & Zwarenstien, M. (2009). What is implementation research? Rationale, concepts, and practices. *Research on Social Work Practice*, 19(5), 491–502.

Dearing, J. W. (2009). Applying diffusion of innovation theory to intervention development. *Research on Social Work Practice*, 19(5), 503–518.

Kerner, J. F., & Hall, K. L. (2009). Research dissemination and diffusion: Translation within science and society. *Research on Social Work Practice*, 19(5), 519–530.

Simpson, D. D. (2009). Organizational readiness for stage-based dynamics of innovation implementation. *Research on Social Work Practice*, 19(5), 541–551.

Tropman, J. E., Erlich, J. L., Rothman, J. (2001). *Tactics & techniques of community intervention* (4th ed.). Itasca, IL: Peacock.

Weil, M., & Gamble, D. N. (2005). Evolution, models, and the changing context of community practice. In M. Weil (Ed.), *Handbook of community practice* (pp. 117–149). Thousand Oaks. CA: Sage.

Index

Note: Page numbers followed by "f" or "t" refer to figures or tables respectively.